R Data Analysis Projects

Build end to end analytics systems to get deeper insights from your data

Gopi Subramanian

BIRMINGHAM - MUMBAI

R Data Analysis Projects

First published: November 2017

Production reference: 1151117

Published by Packt Publishing Ltd.
Livery Place
35 Livery Street
Birmingham
B3 2PB, UK.
ISBN 978-1-78862-187-8

www.packtpub.com

Credits

Author
Gopi Subramanian

Copy Editors
Safis Editing

Reviewer
Mark Hodnett

Project Coordinator
Manthan Patel

Commissioning Editor
Amey Varangaonkar

Proofreader
Safis Editing

Acquisition Editor
Tushar Gupta

Indexer
Tejal Daruwale Soni

Content Development Editor
Aaryaman Singh

Graphics
Tania Dutta

Technical Editor
Dharmendra Yadav

Production Coordinator
Arvindkumar Gupta

About the Author

Gopi Subramanian is a scientist and author with over 18 years of experience in the fields of data mining and machine learning. During the past decade, he has worked extensively in data mining and machine learning, solving a variety of business problems.

He has 16 patent applications with the US and Indian patent offices and several publications to his credit. He is the author of *Python Data Science Cookbook* by Packt Publishing.

I would like to thank my parents Vijaya and Mani and sister Geetha for being a great source of inspiration. My family Anita and Rishi for their support.

About the Reviewer

Mark Hodnett is a data scientist with over 20 years of industry experience. He has worked in a variety of industries, ranging from website development, retail loyalty, and industrial systems to accountancy software. He holds a master's in data science and an MBA.

His current role is with AltViz as a senior data scientist. Altviz applies machine learning, optimization, and intelligent evaluation to companies in many sectors, including retail and insurance.

I would like to thank the author, Gopi, for giving me the opportunity to collaborate on this project. I would also like to thank Sharon and Conor for their patience while I worked on this project.

www.PacktPub.com

For support files and downloads related to your book, please visit www.PacktPub.com. Did you know that Packt offers eBook versions of every book published, with PDF and ePub files available? You can upgrade to the eBook version at www.PacktPub.com and as a print book customer, you are entitled to a discount on the eBook copy. Get in touch with us at service@packtpub.com for more details. At www.PacktPub.com, you can also read a collection of free technical articles, sign up for a range of free newsletters and receive exclusive discounts and offers on Packt books and eBooks.

https://www.packtpub.com/mapt

Get the most in-demand software skills with Mapt. Mapt gives you full access to all Packt books and video courses, as well as industry-leading tools to help you plan your personal development and advance your career.

Why subscribe?

- Fully searchable across every book published by Packt
- Copy and paste, print, and bookmark content
- On demand and accessible via a web browser

Customer Feedback

Thanks for purchasing this Packt book. At Packt, quality is at the heart of our editorial process. To help us improve, please leave us an honest review on this book's Amazon page at https://www.amazon.com/dp/1788621875.

If you'd like to join our team of regular reviewers, you can email us at customerreviews@packtpub.com. We award our regular reviewers with free eBooks and videos in exchange for their valuable feedback. Help us be relentless in improving our products!

Table of Contents

Preface

This book is for readers who want to leverage the R platform for their data analysis projects/problems. We introduce readers to different R packages for various data analysis purposes and help them use the right package for the right task. A complete project built from scratch in each chapter will help readers better understand building end-to-end predictive analytics solutions. This book covers a variety of topics, including building deep learning networks in R, graph mining, streaming data analysis, sentiment classification, and recommender systems.

What this book covers

Chapter 1, *Association Rule Mining*, builds recommender systems with transaction data. We identify cross-sell and upsell opportunities.

Chapter 2, *Fuzzy Logic Induced Content-Based Recommendation*, addresses the cold start problem in the recommender system. We handle the ranking problem with multi-similarity metrics using a fuzzy sets approach.

Chapter 3, *Collaborative Filtering*, introduces different approaches to collaborative filtering for recommender systems.

Chapter 4, *Taming Time Series Data Using Deep Neural Networks*, introduces MXNet R, a package for deep learning in R. We leverage MXNet to build a deep connected network to predict stock closing prices.

Chapter 5, *Twitter Text Sentiment Classification Using Kernel Density Estimates*, shows ability to process Twitter data in R. We introduce delta-tfidf, a new metric for sentiment classification. We leverage the kernel density estimate based Naïve Bayes algorithm to classify sentiments.

Chapter 6, *Record Linkage - Stochastic and Machine Learning Approaches*, covers the problem of master data management and how to solve it in R using the recordLinkage package.

Chapter 7, *Streaming Data Clustering Analysis in R,* introduces a package stream for handling streaming data in R, and the clustering of streaming data, as well as the online/offline clustering model.

Chapter 8, *Analyzing and Understanding Networks Using R,* covers the igraph package for performing graph analysis in R. We solve product network analysis problems with graph algorithms.

What you need for this book

Base R must be installed. The code in this book was written using R version 3.4.1 (2017-06-30), single candle, on a Mac OS darwin15.6.0. They should be compatible with Linux and Windows operating systems. RStudio Version 0.99.491 was used as an editor to write and compile R code.

Who this book is for

If you are looking for a book that takes you all the way through the practical applications of advanced and effective analytics methodologies in R, then this is the book for you. A fundamental understanding of R and the basic concepts of data analysis are all you need to get started with this book.

Conventions

In this book, you will find a number of text styles that distinguish between different kinds of information. Here are some examples of these styles and an explanation of their meaning.

Code words in text, database table names, folder names, filenames, file extensions, pathnames, dummy URLs, user input, and Twitter handles are shown as follows: "We can include other contexts through the use of the `include` directive."

Any command-line input or output is written as follows:

```
zero.matrix.gup <- mx.nd.zeros(c(3,3), mx.gpu(0))
```

New terms and **important words** are shown in bold.

Words that you see on the screen, for example, in menus or dialog boxes, appear in the text like this: "Clicking the **Next** button moves you to the next screen."

Warnings or important notes appear like this.

Tips and tricks appear like this.

Reader feedback

Feedback from our readers is always welcome. Let us know what you think about this book-what you liked or disliked. Reader feedback is important for us as it helps us develop titles that you will really get the most out of.

To send us general feedback, simply email feedback@packtpub.com, and mention the book's title in the subject of your message.

If there is a topic that you have expertise in and you are interested in either writing or contributing to a book, see our author guide at www.packtpub.com/authors.

Customer support

Now that you are the proud owner of a Packt book, we have a number of things to help you to get the most from your purchase.

Downloading the example code

You can download the example code files for this book from your account at
`http://www.packtpub.com`. If you purchased this book elsewhere, you can visit
`http://www.packtpub.com/support` and register to have the files emailed directly to you.
You can download the code files by following these steps:

1. Log in or register to our website using your email address and password.
2. Hover the mouse pointer on the **SUPPORT** tab at the top.
3. Click on **Code Downloads & Errata**.
4. Enter the name of the book in the **Search** box.
5. Select the book for which you're looking to download the code files.
6. Choose from the drop-down menu where you purchased this book from.
7. Click on **Code Download**.

Once the file is downloaded, please make sure that you unzip or extract the folder using the
latest version of:

- WinRAR / 7-Zip for Windows
- Zipeg / iZip / UnRarX for Mac
- 7-Zip / PeaZip for Linux

The code bundle for the book is also hosted on GitHub at
`https://github.com/PacktPublishing/R-Data-Analysis-Projects`. We also have other
code bundles from our rich catalog of books and videos available at
`https://github.com/PacktPublishing/`. Check them out!

Errata

Although we have taken every care to ensure the accuracy of our content, mistakes do
happen. If you find a mistake in one of our books-maybe a mistake in the text or the code-
we would be grateful if you could report this to us. By doing so, you can save other readers
from frustration and help us improve subsequent versions of this book. If you find any
errata, please report them by visiting `http://www.packtpub.com/submit-errata`, selecting
your book, clicking on the **Errata Submission Form** link, and entering the details of your
errata. Once your errata are verified, your submission will be accepted and the errata will
be uploaded to our website or added to any list of existing errata under the Errata section of
that title. To view the previously submitted errata, go to
`https://www.packtpub.com/books/content/support` and enter the name of the book in the
search field. The required information will appear under the **Errata** section.

Piracy

Piracy of copyrighted material on the internet is an ongoing problem across all media. At Packt, we take the protection of our copyright and licenses very seriously. If you come across any illegal copies of our works in any form on the internet, please provide us with the location address or website name immediately so that we can pursue a remedy. Please contact us at copyright@packtpub.com with a link to the suspected pirated material. We appreciate your help in protecting our authors and our ability to bring you valuable content.

Questions

If you have a problem with any aspect of this book, you can contact us at questions@packtpub.com, and we will do our best to address the problem.

1
Association Rule Mining

This chapter is ordered in ascending complexity. We will start with our use case, designing a cross-sell campaign for an imaginative retailer. We will define the goals for this campaign and the success criteria for these goals. Having defined our problem, we will proceed to our first recommendation algorithm, association rule mining. **Association rule mining**, also called market basket analysis, is a method used to analyze transaction data to extract product associations.

The subsequent sections are devoted to unveiling the plain vanilla version of association rule mining and introducing some of the interest measures. We will then proceed to find ways to establish the minimum support and confidence thresholds, the major two interest measures, and also the parameters of the association rule mining algorithm. We will explore more interest measures toward the end, such as lift and conviction, and look at how we can use them to generate recommendations for our retailer's cross-selling campaign.

We will introduce a variation of the association rule mining algorithm, called the **weighted association rule mining** algorithm, which can incorporate some of the retailer input in the form of weighted transactions. The profitability of a transaction is treated as a weight. In addition to the products in a transaction, the profitability of the transaction is also recorded. Now we have a smarter algorithm that can produce the most profitable product associations.

We will then introduce the (HITS) algorithm. In places where a retailer's weight input is not available, namely, when there is no explicit information about the importance of the transactions, HITS provides us with a way to generate weights (importance) for the transactions.

Next, we will introduce a variation of association rule mining called **negative association rule mining**, which is an efficient algorithm used to find anti-patterns in the transaction database. In cases where we need to exclude certain items from our analysis (owing to low stock or other constraints), negative association rule mining is the best method. Finally, we will wrap up this chapter by introducing package `arulesViz`: an R package with some cool charts and graphics to visualize the association rules, and a small web application designed to report our analysis using the `RShiny` R package.

The topics to be covered in this chapter are as follows:

- Understanding the recommender systems
- Retailer use case and data
- Association rule mining
- The cross-selling campaign
- Weighted association rule mining
- Hyperlink-induced topic search (HITS)
- Negative association rules
- Rules visualization
- Wrapping up
- Further reading

Understanding the recommender systems

Recommender systems or recommendation engines are a popular class of machine learning algorithms widely used today by online retail companies. With historical data about users and product interactions, a recommender system can make profitable/useful recommendations about users and their product preferences.

In the last decade, recommender systems have achieved great success with both online retailers and brick and mortar stores. They have allowed retailers to move away from group campaigns, where a group of people receive a single offer. Recommender systems technology has revolutionized marketing campaigns. Today, retailers offer a customized recommendation to each of their customers. Such recommendations can dramatically increase customer stickiness.

Retailers design and run sales campaigns to promote up-selling and cross-selling. Up-selling is a technique by which retailers try to push high-value products to their customers. Cross-selling is the practice of selling additional products to customers. Recommender systems provide an empirical method to generate recommendations for retailers up-selling and cross-selling campaigns.

Retailers can now make quantitative decisions based on solid statistics and math to improve their businesses. There are a growing number of conferences and journals dedicated to recommender systems technology, which plays a vital role today at top successful companies such as Amazon.com, YouTube, Netflix, LinkedIn, Facebook, TripAdvisor, and IMDb.

Based on the type and volume of available data, recommender systems of varying complexity and increased accuracy can be built. In the previous paragraph, we defined historical data as a user and his product interactions. Let's use this definition to illustrate the different types of data in the context of recommender systems.

Transactions

Transactions are purchases made by a customer on a single visit to a retail store. Typically, transaction data can include the products purchased, quantity purchased, the price, discount if applied, and a timestamp. A single transaction can include multiple products. It may register information about the user who made the transaction in some cases, where the customer allows the retailer to store his information by joining a rewards program.

A simplified view of the transaction data is a binary matrix. The rows of this matrix correspond to a unique identifier for a transaction; let's call it transaction ID. The columns correspond to the unique identifier for a product; let's call it product ID. The cell values are zero or one, if that product is either excluded or included in the transaction.

A binary matrix with n transactions and m products is given as follows:

Txn/Product	P1	P2	P3	....	Pm
T1	0	1	1	...	0
T2	1	1	1	....	1
...	...	...	...	...	...
Tn	o	1	1	...	1

Weighted transactions

This is additional information added to the transaction to denote its importance, such as the profitability of the transaction as a whole or the profitability of the individual products in the transaction. In the case of the preceding binary matrix, a column called weight is added to store the importance of the transaction.

In this chapter, we will show you how to use transaction data to support cross-selling campaigns. We will see how the derived user product preferences, or recommendations from the user's product interactions (transactions/weighted transactions), can fuel successful cross-selling campaigns. We will implement and understand the algorithms that can leverage this data in R. We will work on a superficial use case in which we need to generate recommendations to support a cross-selling campaign for an imaginative retailer.

Our web application

Our goal, by the the end of this chapter, is to understand the concepts of association rule mining and related topics, and solve the given cross-selling campaign problem using association rule mining. We will understand how different aspects of the cross-selling campaign problem can be solved using the family of association rule mining algorithms, how to implement them in R, and finally build the web application to display our analysis and results.

We will be following a code-first approach in this book. The style followed throughout this book is to introduce a real-world problem, following which we will briefly introduce the algorithm/technique that can be used to solve this problem. We will keep the algorithm description brief. We will proceed to introduce the R package that implements the algorithm and subsequently start writing the R code to prepare the data in a way that the algorithm expects. As we invoke the actual algorithm in R and explore the results, we will get into the nitty-gritty of the algorithm. Finally, we will provide further references for curious readers.

Retailer use case and data

A retailer has approached us with a problem. In the coming months, he wants to boost his sales. He is planning a marketing campaign on a large scale to promote sales. One aspect of his campaign is the cross-selling strategy. Cross-selling is the practice of selling additional products to customers. In order to do that, he wants to know what items/products tend to go together. Equipped with this information, he can now design his cross-selling strategy. He expects us to provide him with a recommendation of top N product associations so that he can pick and choose among them for inclusion in his campaign.

He has provided us with his historical transaction data. The data includes his past transactions, where each transaction is uniquely identified by an `order_id` integer, and the list of products present in the transaction called `product_id`. Remember the binary matrix representation of transactions we described in the introduction section? The dataset provided by our retailer is in exactly the same format.

Let's start by reading the data provided by the retailer. The code for this chapter was written in **RStudio Version 0.99.491**. It uses **R version 3.3.1**. As we work through our example, we will introduce the `arules` R package that we will be using. In our description, we will be using the terms order/transaction, user/customer, and item/product interchangeably. We will not be describing the installation of R packages used through the code. It's assumed that the reader is well aware of the method for installing an R package and has installed those packages before using it.

This data can be downloaded from:

```
data.path = '../../data/data.csv'
 data = read.csv(data.path)
 head(data)
order_id product_id
 1 837080 Unsweetened Almondmilk
 2 837080 Fat Free Milk dairy
 3 837080 Turkey
 4 837080 Caramel Corn Rice Cakes
 5 837080 Guacamole Singles
 6 837080 HUMMUS 10OZ WHITE BEAN EAT WELL
```

The given data is in a tabular format. Every row is a tuple of `order_id`, representing the transaction, `product_id`, the item included in that transaction, and the `department_id`, that is the department to which the item belongs to. This is our binary data representation, which is absolutely tenable for the classical association rule mining algorithm. This algorithm is also called **market basket analysis**, as we are analyzing the customer's basket—the transactions. Given a large database of customer transactions where each transaction consists of items purchased by a customer during a visit, the association rule mining algorithm generates all significant association rules between the items in the database.

What is an association rule? An example from a grocery transaction would be that the association rule is a recommendation of the form `{peanut butter, jelly} => { bread }`. It says that, based on the transactions, it's expected that `bread` will most likely be present in a transaction that contains `peanut butter` and `jelly`. It's a recommendation to the retailer that there is enough evidence in the database to say that customers who buy peanut butter and jelly will most likely buy bread.

Let's quickly explore our data. We can count the number of unique transactions and the number of unique products:

```
library(dplyr)
data %>%
 group_by('order_id') %>%
 summarize(order.count = n_distinct(order_id))

 data %>%
 group_by('product_id') %>%
 summarize(product.count = n_distinct(product_id))
# A tibble: 1 <U+00D7> 2
 `"order_id"` order.count
 <chr> <int>
 1 order_id 6988
# A tibble: 1 <U+00D7> 2
 `"product_id"` product.count
 <chr> <int>
 1 product_id 16793
```

We have `6988` transactions and `16793` individual products. There is no information about the quantity of products purchased in a transaction. We have used the `dplyr` library to perform these aggregate calculations, which is a library used to perform efficient data wrangling on data frames.

dplyr is part of `tidyverse`, a collection of R packages designed around a common philosophy. `dplyr` is a grammar of data manipulation, and provides a consistent set of methods to help solve the most common data manipulation challenges. To learn more about `dplyr`, refer to the following links:
`http://tidyverse.org/`
`http://dplyr.tidyverse.org/`

In the next section, we will introduce the association rule mining algorithm. We will explain how this method can be leveraged to generate the top *N* product recommendations requested by the retailer for his cross-selling campaign.

Association rule mining

There are several algorithmic implementations for association rule mining. Key among them is the `apriori` algorithm by Rakesh Agrawal and Ramakrishnan Srikanth, introduced in their paper, *Fast Algorithms for Mining Association Rules*. Going forward, we will use both the `apriori` algorithm and the association rule mining algorithm interchangeably.

`Apriori` is a parametric algorithm. It requires two parameters named **support** and **confidence** from the user. Support is needed to generate the frequent itemsets and the confidence parameter is required to filter the induced rules from the frequent itemsets. Support and confidence are broadly called interest measures. There are a lot of other interest measures in addition to support and confidence.

We will explain the association rule mining algorithm and the effect of the interest measures on the algorithm as we write our R code. We will halt our code writing in the required places to get a deeper understanding of how the algorithm works, the algorithm terminology such as itemsets, and how to leverage the interest measures to our benefit to support the cross-selling campaign.

We will use the `arules` package, **version 1.5-0**, to help us perform association mining on this dataset.

Type `SessionInfo()` into your R terminal to get information about the packages, including the version of the packages loaded in the current R session.

```
library(arules)
transactions.obj <- read.transactions(file = data.path, format = "single",
  sep = ",",
  cols = c("order_id", "product_id"),
  rm.duplicates = FALSE,
  quote = "", skip = 0,
  encoding = "unknown")
```

We begin with reading our transactions stored in the text file and create an `arules` data structure called `transactions`. Let's look at the parameters of `read.transactions`, the function used to create the transactions object. For the first parameter, `file`, we pass our text file where we have the transactions from the retailer. The second parameter, `format`, can take any of two values, `single` or `basket`, depending on how the input data is organized. In our case, we have a tabular format with two columns--one column representing the unique identifier for our transaction and the other column for a unique identifier representing the product present in our transaction. This format is named `single` by `arules`. Refer to the `arules` documentation for a detailed description of all the parameters.

On inspecting the newly created transactions object `transaction.obj`:

```
transactions.obj
transactions in sparse format with
 6988 transactions (rows) and
 16793 items (columns)
```

We can see that there are `6988` transactions and `16793` products. They match the previous count values from the `dplyr` output.

Let's explore this transaction object a little bit more. Can we see the most frequent items, that is, the items that are present in most of the transactions and vice versa—the least frequent items and the items present in many fewer transactions?

The `itemFrequency` function in the `arules` package comes to our rescue. This function takes a transaction object as input and produces the frequency count (the number of transactions containing this product) of the individual products:

```
data.frame(head(sort(itemFrequency(transactions.obj, type = "absolute")
 , decreasing = TRUE), 10)) # Most frequent
Banana 1456
  Bag of Organic Bananas 1135
  Organic Strawberries 908
  Organic Baby Spinach 808
  Organic Hass Avocado 729
  Organic Avocado 599
  Large Lemon 534
  Limes 524
  Organic Raspberries 475
  Organic Garlic 432
head(sort(itemFrequency(transactions.obj, type = "absolute")
 , decreasing = FALSE), 10) # Least frequent
0% Fat Black Cherry Greek Yogurt y 1
  0% Fat Blueberry Greek Yogurt 1
```

```
0% Fat Peach Greek Yogurt 1
0% Fat Strawberry Greek Yogurt 1
1 % Lowfat Milk 1
1 Mg Melatonin Sublingual Orange Tablets 1
Razor Handle and 2 Freesia Scented Razor Refills Premium BladeRazor System
1
1 to 1 Gluten Free Baking Flour 1
1% Low Fat Cottage Cheese 1
1% Lowfat Chocolate Milk 1
```

In the preceding code, we print the most and the least frequent items in our database using the `itemFrequency` function. The `itemFrequency` function produces all the items with their corresponding frequency, and the number of transactions in which they appear. We wrap the `sort` function over `itemFrequency` to sort this output; the sorting order is decided by the `decreasing` parameter. When set to `TRUE`, it sorts the items in descending order based on their transaction frequency. We finally wrap the `sort` function using the `head` function to get the top 10 most/least frequent items.

The `Banana` product is the most frequently occurring across 1,456 transactions. The `itemFrequency` method can also return the percentage of transactions rather than an absolute number if we set the `type` parameter to `relative` instead of `absolute`.

Another convenient way to inspect the frequency distribution of the items is to plot them visually as a histogram. The `arules` package provides the `itemFrequencyPlot` function to visualize the item frequency:

```
itemFrequencyPlot(transactions.obj,topN = 25)
```

In the preceding code, we plot the top 25 items by their relative frequency, as shown in the following diagram:

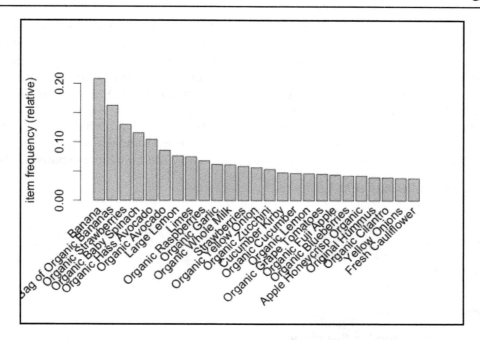

As per the figure, **Banana** is the most frequent item, present in 20 percent of the transactions. This chart can give us a clue about defining the support value for our algorithm, a concept we will quickly delve into in the subsequent paragraphs.

Now that we have successfully created the transaction object, let's proceed to apply the `apriori` algorithm to this transaction object.

The `apriori` algorithm works in two phases. Finding the frequent itemsets is the first phase of the association rule mining algorithm. A group of product IDs is called an **itemset**. The algorithm makes multiple passes into the database; in the first pass, it finds out the transaction frequency of all the individual items. These are itemsets of `order 1`. Let's introduce the first interest measure, `Support`, here:

- `Support`: As said previously, support is a parameter that we pass to this algorithm—a value between zero and one. Let's say we set the value to 0.1. We now say an itemset is considered frequent, and it should be used in the subsequent phases if—and only if—it appears in at least 10 percent of the transactions.

Now, in the first pass, the algorithm calculates the transaction frequency for each product. At this stage, we have `order 1` itemsets. We will discard all those itemsets that fall below our support threshold. The assumption here is that items with a high transaction frequency are more interesting than the ones with a very low frequency. Items with very low support are not going to make for interesting rules further down the pipeline. Using the most frequent items, we can construct the itemsets as having two products and find their transaction frequency, that is, the number of transactions in which both the items are present. Once again, we discard all the two product itemsets (itemsets of `order 2`) that are below the given support threshold. We continue this way until we have exhausted them.

Let's see a quick illustration:

Pass 1 :

```
Support = 0.1
Product, transaction frequency
{item5}, 0.4
{item6}, 0.3
{item9}, 0.2
{item11}, 0.1
```

`item11` will be discarded in this phase, as its transaction frequency is below the support threshold.

Pass 2:

```
{item5, item6}
{item5, item9}
{item6, item9}
```

As you can see, we have constructed itemsets of `order 2` using the filtered items from pass 1. We proceed to find their transaction frequency, discard the itemsets falling below our minimum support threshold, and step on to pass 3, where once again we create itemsets of order 3, calculate the transaction frequency, and perform filtering and move on to pass 4. In one of the subsequent passes, we reach a stage where we cannot create higher order itemsets. That is when we stop:

```
# Interest Measures
  support <- 0.01
# Frequent item sets
  parameters = list(
  support = support,
  minlen = 2, # Minimal number of items per item set
  maxlen = 10, # Maximal number of items per item set
  target = "frequent itemsets")
  freq.items <- apriori(transactions.obj, parameter = parameters)
```

The `apriori` method is used in `arules` to get the most frequent items. This method takes two parameters, the `transaction.obj` and the second parameter, which is a named list. We create a named list called `parameters`. Inside the named list, we have an entry for our support threshold. We have set our support threshold to 0.01, namely, one percent of the transaction. We settled at this value by looking at the histogram we plotted earlier. By setting the value of the `target` parameter to `frequent itemsets`, we specify that we expect the method to return the final frequent itemsets. `Minlen` and `maxlen` set lower and upper cut off on how many items we expect in our itemsets. By setting our `minlen` to 2, we say we don't want itemsets of `order 1`. While explaining the `apriori` in phase 1, we said that the algorithm can do many passes into the database, and each subsequent pass creates itemsets that are of `order 1`, greater than the previous pass. We also said `apriori` ends when no higher order itemsets can be found. We don't want our method to run till the end, hence by using `maxlen`, we say that if we reach itemsets of `order 10`, we stop. The `apriori` function returns an object of type `itemsets`.

It's good practice to examine the created object, `itemset` in this case. A closer look at the `itemset` object should shed light on how we ended up using its properties to create our data frame of itemsets:

```
str(freq.items)
Formal class 'itemsets' [package "arules"] with 4 slots
  ..@ items :Formal class 'itemMatrix' [package "arules"] with 3 slots
  .. .. ..@ data :Formal class 'ngCMatrix' [package "Matrix"] with 5 slots
  .. .. .. .. ..@ i : int [1:141] 1018 4107 4767 11508 4767 6543 4767 11187
4767 10322 ...
  .. .. .. .. ..@ p : int [1:71] 0 2 4 6 8 10 12 14 16 18 ...
  .. .. .. .. ..@ Dim : int [1:2] 14286 70
  .. .. .. .. ..@ Dimnames:List of 2
  .. .. .. .. .. ..$ : NULL
  .. .. .. .. .. ..$ : NULL
  .. .. .. .. ..@ factors : list()
  .. .. ..@ itemInfo :'data.frame': 14286 obs. of 1 variable:
  .. .. .. ..$ labels: chr [1:14286] "10" "1000" "10006" "10008" ...
  .. .. ..@ itemsetInfo:'data.frame': 0 obs. of 0 variables
  ..@ tidLists: NULL
  ..@ quality :'data.frame': 70 obs. of 1 variable:
  .. ..$ support: num [1:70] 0.0108 0.0124 0.0124 0.0154 0.0122 ...
  ..@ info :List of 4
  .. ..$ data : symbol transactions.obj
  .. ..$ ntransactions: int 4997
  .. ..$ support : num 0.01
  .. ..$ confidence : num 1
```

To create our `freq.items.df` data frame, we used the third slot of the `quality freq.items` object. It contains the support value for all the itemsets generated, 70 in this case. By calling the function `label` and passing the `freq.items` object, we retrieve the item names:

```
# Let us examine our freq item sites
 freq.items.df <- data.frame(item_set = labels(freq.items)
 , support = freq.items@quality)
head(freq.items.df)

item_set support
1 {Banana,Red Vine Tomato} 0.01030338
2 {Bag of Organic Bananas,Organic D'Anjou Pears} 0.01001717
3 {Bag of Organic Bananas,Organic Kiwi} 0.01016027
4 {Banana,Organic Gala Apples} 0.01073268
5 {Banana,Yellow Onions} 0.01302232

tail(freq.items.df)

item_set support
79 {Organic Baby Spinach,Organic Strawberries} 0.02575844
80 {Bag of Organic Bananas,Organic Baby Spinach} 0.02690326
81 {Banana,Organic Baby Spinach} 0.03048082
82 {Bag of Organic Bananas,Organic Strawberries} 0.03577562
83 {Banana,Organic Strawberries} 0.03305667
```

We create our data frame using these two lists of values. Finally, we use the `head` and `tail` functions to quickly look at the itemsets present at the top and bottom of our data frame.

Before we move on to phase two of the association mining algorithm, let's stop for a moment to investigate a quick feature present in the `apriori` method. If you had noticed, our itemsets consist mostly of the high frequency itemsets. However, we can ask the `apriori` method to ignore some of the items:

```
exclusion.items <- c('Banana','Bag of Organic Bananas')freq.items <-
apriori(transactions.obj, parameter = parameters,
 appearance = list(none = exclusion.items,
 default = "both"))

freq.items.df <- data.frame(item_set = labels(freq.items)
 , support = freq.items@quality)
```

We can create a vector of items to be excluded, and pass it as an `appearance` parameter to the `apriori` method. This will ensure that the items in our list are excluded from the generated itemsets:

```
head(freq.items.df,10)
item_set support.support support.confidence
 1 {Organic Large Extra Fancy Fuji Apple} => {Organic Strawberries}
0.01030338 0.2727273
 2 {Organic Cilantro} => {Limes} 0.01187750 0.2985612
 3 {Organic Blueberries} => {Organic Strawberries} 0.01302232 0.3063973
 4 {Cucumber Kirby} => {Organic Baby Spinach} 0.01001717 0.2089552
 5 {Organic Grape Tomatoes} => {Organic Baby Spinach} 0.01016027 0.2232704
 6 {Organic Grape Tomatoes} => {Organic Strawberries} 0.01144820 0.2515723
 7 {Organic Lemon} => {Organic Hass Avocado} 0.01016027 0.2184615
 8 {Organic Cucumber} => {Organic Hass Avocado} 0.01244991 0.2660550
 9 {Organic Cucumber} => {Organic Baby Spinach} 0.01144820 0.2446483
10 {Organic Cucumber} => {Organic Strawberries} 0.01073268 0.2293578
```

As you can see, we have excluded `Banana` and `Bag of Organic Bananas` from our itemsets.

Congratulations, you have successfully finished implementing the first phase of the `apriori` algorithm in R!

Let's move on to phase two, where we will induce rules from these itemsets. It's time to introduce our second interest measure, confidence. Let's take an itemset from the list given to us from phase one of the algorithm, {Banana, Red Vine Tomato}.

We have two possible rules here:

- `Banana => Red Vine Tomato`: The presence of `Banana` in a transaction strongly suggests that `Red Vine Tomato` will also be there in the same transaction.
- `Red Vine Tomato => Banana`: The presence of `Red Vine Tomato` in a transaction strongly suggests that `Banana` will also be there in the same transaction.

How often are these two rules found to be true in our database? The confidence score, our next interest measure, will help us measure this:

- Confidence: For the rule Banana => Red Vine Tomato, the confidence is measured as the ratio of support for the itemset {Banana, Red Vine Tomato} and the support for the itemset {Banana}. Let's decipher this formula. Let's say that item Banana has occurred in 20 percent of the transactions, and it has occurred in 10 percent of transactions along with Red Vine Tomato, so the support for the rule is 50 percent, 0.1/0.2.

Similar to support, the confidence threshold is also provided by the user. Only those rules whose confidence is greater than or equal to the user-provided confidence will be included by the algorithm.

Let's say we have a rule, A => B, induced from itemset <A, B>. The support for the itemset <A, B> is the number of transactions where A and B occur divided by the total number of the transactions. Alternatively, it's the probability that a transaction contains <A, B>.
Now, confidence for A => B is P (B | A); which is the conditional probability that a transaction containing B also has A? P(B | A) = P (A U B) / P (A) = Support (A U B) / Support (A).
Remember from probability theory that when two events are independent of each other, the joint probability is calculated by multiplying the individual probability. We will use this shortly in our next interest measure lift.

With this knowledge, let's go ahead and implement phase two of our apriori algorithm in R:

```
> confidence <- 0.4 # Interest Measure

parameters = list(
support = support,
confidence = confidence,
minlen = 2, # Minimal number of items per item set
maxlen = 10, # Maximal number of items per item set
target = "rules"
)
rules <- apriori(transactions.obj, parameter = parameters)
rules.df <- data.frame(rules = labels(rules)
, rules@quality)
```

Once again, we use the `apriori` method; however, we set the `target` parameter in our `parameters` named list to `rules`. Additionally, we also provide the confidence threshold. After calling the method `apriori` using the returned object `rules`, we finally build our data frame, `rules.df`, to explore/view our rules conveniently. Let's look at our output data frame, `rules.df`. For the given confidence threshold, we can see the set of rules thrown out by the algorithm:

```
head(rules.df)
rules support confidence lift
  1 {Red Vine Tomato} => {Banana} 0.01030338 0.4067797 1.952319
  2 {Honeycrisp Apple} => {Banana} 0.01617058 0.4248120 2.038864
  3 {Organic Fuji Apple} => {Banana} 0.01817401 0.4110032 1.972590
```

The last column titled `lift` is yet another interest measure.

- `Lift`: Often, we may have rules with high support and confidence but that are, as yet, of no use. This occurs when the item at the right-hand side of the rule has more probability of being selected alone than with the associated item. Let's go back to a grocery example. Say there are 1,000 transactions. 900 of those transactions contain milk. 700 of them contain strawberries. 300 of them have both strawberries and milk. A typical rule that can come out of such a scenario is `strawberry => milk`, with a confidence of 66 percent. The `support (strawberry, milk) / support ( strawberry)`. This is not accurate and it's not going to help the retailer at all, as the probability of people buying milk is 90 percent, much higher than the 66 percent given by this rule.

This is where `lift` comes to our rescue. For two products, A and B, lift measures how many times A and B occur together, more often than expected if they were statistically independent. Let's calculate the lift value for this hypothetical example:

```
lift ( strawberry => milk ) = support ( strawberry, milk) / support(
strawberry) * support (milk)
= 0.3 / (0.9)(0.7)
= 0.47
```

`Lift` provides an increased probability of the presence of milk in a transaction containing strawberry. Rules with lift values greater than one are considered to be more effective. In this case, we have a lift value of less than one, indicating that the presence of a strawberry is not going to guarantee the presence of milk in the transaction. Rather, it's the opposite—people who buy strawberries will rarely buy milk in the same transaction.

There are tons of other interest measures available in `arules`. They can be obtained by calling the `interestMeasure` function. We show how we can quickly populate these measures into our rules data frame:

```
interestMeasure(rules, transactions = transactions.obj)
rules.df <- cbind(rules.df, data.frame(interestMeasure(rules,
transactions = transactions.obj)))
We will not go through all of them here. There is a ton of literature
available to discuss these measures and their use in filtering most useful
rules.
```

Alright, we have successfully implemented our association rule mining algorithm; we went under the hood to understand how the algorithm works in two phases to generate rules. We have examined three interest measures: support, confidence, and lift. Finally, we know that lift can be leveraged to make cross-selling recommendations to our retail customers. Before we proceed further, let's look at some more functions in the `arules` package that will allow us to do some sanity checks on the rules. Let us start with redundant rules:

```
is.redundant(rules) # Any redundant rules ?
```

To illustrate redundant rules, let's take an example:

```
Rule 1: {Red Vine Tomato, Ginger} => {Banana}, confidence score 0.32
Rule 2: {Red Vine Tomato} => {Banana}, confidence score 0.45
```

Rules 1 and Rule 2 share the same right-hand side, Banana. The left-hand side of Rule 2 has a subset of items from Rule 1. The confidence score of Rule 2 is higher than Rule 1. In this case, Rule 2 is considered a more general rule than Rule 1 and hence Rule 2 will be considered as a redundant rule and removed. Another sanity check is to find duplicated rules:

```
duplicated(rules) # Any duplicate rules ?
```

To remove rules with the same left- and right-hand side, the duplicated function comes in handy. Let's say we create two rules objects, using two sets of support and confidence thresholds. If we combine these two rules objects, we may have a lot of duplicate rules. The duplicated function can be used to filter these duplicate rules. Let us now look at the significance of a rule:

```
is.significant(rules, transactions.obj, method = "fisher")
```

Given the rule `A => B`, we explained that lift calculates how many times A and B occur together more often than expected. There are other ways of testing this independence, like a chi-square test or a Fisher's test. The `arules` package provides the `is.significant` method to do a Fisher or a chi-square test of independence. The parameter method can either take the value of `fisher` or `chisq` depending on the test we wish to perform. Refer to the `arules` documentation for more details. Finally let us see the list of transactions where these rules are supported:

```
>as(supportingTransactions(rules, transactions.obj), "list")
```

Here is the complete R script we have used up until now to demonstrate how to leverage `arules` to extract frequent itemsets, induce rules from those itemsets, and filter the rules based on interest measures.

Here is the following code:

```
##############################################################################
#
# R Data Analysis Projects
#
# Chapter 1
#
# Building Recommender System
# A step step approach to build Association Rule Mining
#
# Script:
#
# RScript to explain how to use arules package
# to mine Association rules
#
# Gopi Subramanian
##############################################################################
data.path = '../../data/data.csv' ## Path to data file
data = read.csv(data.path) ## Read the data file
 head(data)
library(dplyr)
 data %>% group_by('order_id') %>% summarize(order.count =
n_distinct(order_id))
 data %>% group_by('product_id') %>% summarize(product.count =
n_distinct(product_id)
library(arules)
 transactions.obj <- read.transactions(file = data.path, format = "single",
 sep = ",",
 cols = c("order_id", "product_id"),
 rm.duplicates = FALSE,
 quote = "", skip = 0,
 encoding = "unknown")
```

```r
transactions.obj
# Item frequency
head(sort(itemFrequency(transactions.obj, type = "absolute")
, decreasing = TRUE), 10) # Most frequent
head(sort(itemFrequency(transactions.obj, type = "absolute")
, decreasing = FALSE), 10) # Least frequent
itemFrequencyPlot(transactions.obj,topN = 25)
# Interest Measures
support <- 0.01
# Frequent item sets
parameters = list(
support = support,
minlen = 2, # Minimal number of items per item set
maxlen = 10, # Maximal number of items per item set
target = "frequent itemsets"
)
freq.items <- apriori(transactions.obj, parameter = parameters)
# Let us examine our freq item sites
freq.items.df <- data.frame(item_set = labels(freq.items)
, support = freq.items@quality)
head(freq.items.df, 5)
tail(freq.items.df, 5)
# Let us now examine the rules
confidence <- 0.4 # Interest Measure
parameters = list(
support = support,
confidence = confidence,
minlen = 2, # Minimal number of items per item set
maxlen = 10, # Maximal number of items per item set
target = "rules"
)
rules <- apriori(transactions.obj, parameter = parameters)
rules.df <- data.frame(rules = labels(rules)
,rules@quality)
interestMeasure(rules, transactions = transactions.obj)

rules.df <- cbind(rules.df, data.frame(interestMeasure(rules, transactions
= transactions.obj)))
rules.df$coverage <- as(coverage(rules,
transactions = transactions.obj), "list")
## Some sanity checks
duplicated(rules) # Any duplicate rules ?
is.significant(rules, transactions.obj)
## Transactions which support the rule.
as(supportingTransactions(rules, transactions.obj), "list")
```

Support and confidence thresholds

It should be clear now that, for our association rule mining algorithm, we need to provide the minimum support and confidence threshold values. Are there are any set guidelines? No, it all depends on the dataset. It would be worthwhile to run a quick experiment to check how many rules are generated for different values of support and confidence. This experiment should give us an idea of what our minimum support/confidence threshold value should be, for the given dataset.

Here is the code for the same:

```
################################################################################
#
# R Data Analysis Projects
#
# Chapter 1
#
# Building Recommender System
# A step step approach to build Association Rule Mining
#
# Script:
# A simple experiment to find support and confidence values
#
#
# Gopi Subramanian
################################################################################
library(ggplot2)
library(arules)

get.txn <- function(data.path, columns){
# Get transaction object for a given data file
#
# Args:
# data.path: data file name location
# columns: transaction id and item id columns.
#
# Returns:
# transaction object
transactions.obj <- read.transactions(file = data.path, format = "single",
sep = ",",
cols = columns,
rm.duplicates = FALSE,
quote = "", skip = 0,
encoding = "unknown")
return(transactions.obj)
}
```

```r
get.rules <- function(support, confidence, transactions){
# Get Apriori rules for given support and confidence values
#
# Args:
# support: support parameter
# confidence: confidence parameter
#
# Reurns:
# rules object
parameters = list(
support = support,
confidence = confidence,
minlen = 2, # Minimal number of items per item set
maxlen = 10, # Maximal number of items per item set
target = "rules")

rules <- apriori(transactions, parameter = parameters)
return(rules)
}

explore.parameters <- function(transactions){
# Explore support and confidence space for the given transactions
#
# Args:
# transactions: Transaction object, list of transactions
#
# Returns:
# A data frame with no of rules generated for a given
# support confidence pair.

support.values <- seq(from = 0.001, to = 0.1, by = 0.001)
confidence.values <- seq(from = 0.05, to = 0.1, by = 0.01)
support.confidence <- expand.grid(support = support.values,
confidence = confidence.values)

# Get rules for various combinations of support and confidence
rules.grid <- apply(support.confidence[,c('support','confidence')], 1,
function(x) get.rules(x['support'], x['confidence'], transactions))

no.rules <- sapply(seq_along(rules.grid),
function(i) length(labels(rules.grid[[i]])))

no.rules.df <- data.frame(support.confidence, no.rules)
return(no.rules.df)

}

get.plots <- function(no.rules.df){
```

```
# Plot the number of rules generated for
# different support and confidence thresholds
#
# Args:
# no.rules.df : data frame of number of rules
# for different support and confidence
# values
#
# Returns:
# None

exp.plot <- function(confidence.value){
print(ggplot(no.rules.df[no.rules.df$confidence == confidence.value,],
aes(support, no.rules), environment = environment()) + geom_line()
+ ggtitle(paste("confidence = ", confidence.value)))
}
confidence.values <- c(0.07,0.08,0.09,0.1)
mapply(exp.plot, confidence.value = confidence.values)
}

columns <- c("order_id", "product_id") ## columns of interest in data file
 data.path = '../../data/data.csv' ## Path to data file

transactions.obj <- get.txn(data.path, columns) ## create txn object
 no.rules.df <- explore.parameters(transactions.obj) ## explore number of
rules

head(no.rules.df) ##

get.plots(no.rules.df) ## Plot no of rules vs support
```

In the preceding code, we show how we can wrap what we have discussed so far into some functions to explore the support and confidence values. The get.rules function conveniently wraps the rule generation functionality. For a given support, confidence, and threshold, this function will return the rules induced by the association rule mining algorithm. The explore.parameters function creates a grid of support and confidence values. You can see that support values are in the range of 0.001 to 0.1, that is, we are exploring the space where items are present in 0.1 percent of the transactions up to 10 percent of the transactions. Finally, the function evaluates the number of rules generated for each support confidence pair in the grid. The function nicely wraps the results in a data frame. For very low support values, we see an extremely large number of rules being generated. Most of them would be spurious rules:

```
support confidence no.rules
1 0.001 0.05 23024
2 0.002 0.05 4788
3 0.003 0.05 2040
```

```
4  0.004  0.05  1107
5  0.005  0.05  712
6  0.006  0.05  512
```

Analysts can take a look at this data frame, or alternatively plot it to decide the right minimum support/confidence threshold. Our `get.plots` function plots a number of graphs for different values of confidence. Here is the line plot of the number of rules generated for various support values, keeping the confidence fixed at 0.1:

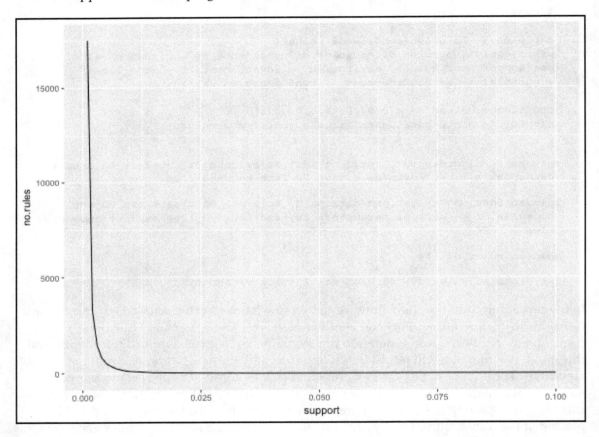

The preceding plot can be a good guideline for selecting the support value. We generated the preceding plot by fixing the confidence at 10 percent. You can experiment with different values of confidence. Alternatively, use the `get.plots` function.

The paper, *Mining the Most Interesting Rules*, by Roberto J. Bayardo Jr. and Rakesh Agrawal demonstrates that the most interesting rules are found on the support/confidence border when we plot the rules with support and confidence on the *x* and *y* axes respectively. They call these rules SC-Optimal rules.

The cross-selling campaign

Let's get back to our retailer. Let's use what we have built so far to provide recommendations to our retailer for his cross-selling strategy.

This can be implemented using the following code:

```
################################################################################
#
# R Data Analysis Projects
#
# Chapter 1
#
# Building Recommender System
# A step step approach to build Association Rule Mining
#
#
# Script:
# Generating rules for cross sell campaign.
#
#
# Gopi Subramanian
################################################################################
library(arules)
library(igraph)

get.txn <- function(data.path, columns){
  # Get transaction object for a given data file
  #
  # Args:
  # data.path: data file name location
  # columns: transaction id and item id columns.
  #
  # Returns:
  # transaction object
  transactions.obj <- read.transactions(file = data.path, format = "single",
  sep = ",",
  cols = columns,
```

```
  rm.duplicates = FALSE,
  quote = "", skip = 0,
  encoding = "unknown")
  return(transactions.obj)
  }

get.rules <- function(support, confidence, transactions){
  # Get Apriori rules for given support and confidence values
  #
  # Args:
  # support: support parameter
  # confidence: confidence parameter
  #
  # Returns:
  # rules object
  parameters = list(
  support = support,
  confidence = confidence,
  minlen = 2, # Minimal number of items per item set
  maxlen = 10, # Maximal number of items per item set
  target = "rules"

  )

  rules <- apriori(transactions, parameter = parameters)
  return(rules)
  }

find.rules <- function(transactions, support, confidence, topN = 10){
  # Generate and prune the rules for given support confidence value
  #
  # Args:
  # transactions: Transaction object, list of transactions
  # support: Minimum support threshold
  # confidence: Minimum confidence threshold
  # Returns:
  # A data frame with the best set of rules and their support and confidence
values


  # Get rules for given combination of support and confidence
  all.rules <- get.rules(support, confidence, transactions)

  rules.df <-data.frame(rules = labels(all.rules)
  , all.rules@quality)

  other.im <- interestMeasure(all.rules, transactions = transactions)
```

```
rules.df <- cbind(rules.df, other.im[,c('conviction','leverage')])


# Keep the best rule based on the interest measure
best.rules.df <- head(rules.df[order(-rules.df$leverage),],topN)

return(best.rules.df)
}

plot.graph <- function(cross.sell.rules){
# Plot the associated items as graph
#
# Args:
# cross.sell.rules: Set of final rules recommended
# Returns:
# None
edges <- unlist(lapply(cross.sell.rules['rules'], strsplit, split='=>'))

g <- graph(edges = edges)
plot(g)


}

support <- 0.01
confidence <- 0.2

columns <- c("order_id", "product_id") ## columns of interest in data file
 data.path = '../../data/data.csv' ## Path to data file

transactions.obj <- get.txn(data.path, columns) ## create txn object

cross.sell.rules <- find.rules( transactions.obj, support, confidence )
 cross.sell.rules$rules <- as.character(cross.sell.rules$rules)

plot.graph(cross.sell.rules)
```

After exploring the dataset for support and confidence values, we set the support and confidence values as 0.001 and 0.2 respectively.

We have written a function called `find.rules`. It internally calls `get.rules`. This function returns the list of top *N* rules given the transaction and support/confidence thresholds. We are interested in the top 10 rules. As discussed, we are going to use lift values for our recommendation. The following are our top 10 rules:

```
   rules support confidence lift conviction leverage
 59 {Organic Hass Avocado} => {Bag of Organic Bananas} 0.03219805 0.3086420
1.900256 1.211498 0.01525399
 63 {Organic Strawberries} => {Bag of Organic Bananas} 0.03577562 0.2753304
```

```
1.695162 1.155808 0.01467107
 64 {Bag of Organic Bananas} => {Organic Strawberries} 0.03577562 0.2202643
1.695162 1.115843 0.01467107
 52 {Limes} => {Large Lemon} 0.01846022 0.2461832 3.221588 1.225209
0.01273006
 53 {Large Lemon} => {Limes} 0.01846022 0.2415730 3.221588 1.219648
0.01273006
 51 {Organic Raspberries} => {Bag of Organic Bananas} 0.02318260 0.3410526
2.099802 1.271086 0.01214223
 50 {Organic Raspberries} => {Organic Strawberries} 0.02003434 0.2947368
2.268305 1.233671 0.01120205
 40 {Organic Yellow Onion} => {Organic Garlic} 0.01431025 0.2525253
4.084830 1.255132 0.01080698
 41 {Organic Garlic} => {Organic Yellow Onion} 0.01431025 0.2314815
4.084830 1.227467 0.01080698
 58 {Organic Hass Avocado} => {Organic Strawberries} 0.02432742 0.2331962
1.794686 1.134662 0.01077217
```

The first entry has a lift value of 1.9, indicating that the products are not independent. This rule has a support of 3 percent and the system has 30 percent confidence for this rule. We recommend that the retailer uses these two products in his cross-selling campaign as, given the lift value, there is a high probability of the customer picking up a {Bag of Organic Bananas} if he picks up an {Organic Hass Avocado}.

Curiously, we have also included two other interest measures—conviction and leverage.

Leverage

How many more units of A and B are expected to be sold together than expected from individual sales? With lift, we said that there is a high association between the {Bag of Organic Bananas} and {Organic Hass Avocado} products. With leverage, we are able to quantify in terms of sales how profitable these two products would be if sold together. The retailer can expect 1.5 more unit sales by selling the {Bag of Organic Bananas} and the {Organic Hass Avocado} together rather than selling them individually. For a given rule A => B:

Leverage(A => B) = Support(A => B) - Support(A)*Support(B)

Leverage measures the difference between A and B appearing together in the dataset and what would be expected if A and B were statistically dependent.

Conviction

Conviction is a measure to ascertain the direction of the rule. Unlike lift, conviction is sensitive to the rule direction. Conviction (A => B) is not the same as conviction (B => A).

For a rule A => B:

```
conviction ( A => B) = 1 - support(B) / 1 - confidence( A => B)
```

Conviction, with the sense of its direction, gives us a hint that targeting the customers of **Organic Hass Avocado** to cross-sell will yield more sales of **Bag of Organic Bananas** rather than the other way round.

Thus, using lift, leverage, and conviction, we have provided all the empirical details to our retailer to design his cross-selling campaign. In our case, we have recommended the top 10 rules to the retailer based on leverage. To provide the results more intuitively and to indicate what items could go together in a cross-selling campaign, a graph visualization of the rules can be very appropriate.

The plot.graph function is used to visualize the rules that we have shortlisted based on their leverage values. It internally uses a package called igraph to create a graph representation of the rules:

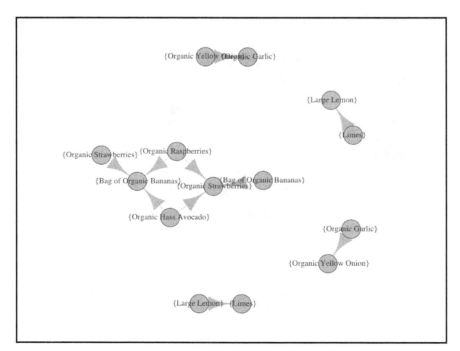

Our suggestion to the retailer can be the largest subgraph on the left. Items in that graph can be leveraged for his cross-selling campaign. Depending on the profit margin and other factors, the retailer can now design his cross-selling campaign using the preceding output.

Weighted association rule mining

You were able to provide recommendations to the retailer to design his cross-selling campaign. As you discuss these results with the retailer, you are faced with the following question:

> *Our output up until now has been great. How can I add some additional lists of products to my campaign?*

You are shocked; the data scientist in you wants to do everything empirically. Now the retailer is asking for a hard list of products to be added to the campaign. How do you fit them in?

> *The analysis output does not include these products. None of our top rules recommend these products. They are not very frequently sold items. Hence, they are not bubbling up in accordance with the rules.*

The retailer is insistent: "The products I want to add to the campaign are high margin items. Having them in the campaign will boost my yields."

Voila! The retailer is interested in high-margin items. Let's pull another trick of the trade—weighted association rule mining.

Jubilant, you reply, "Of course I can accommodate these items. Not just them, but also your other high-valued items. I see that you are interested in your margins; can you give me the margin of all your transactions? I can redo the analysis with this additional information and provide you with the new results. Shouldn't take much time."

The retailer is happy. "Of course; here is my margin for the transactions."

Let's introduce weighted association rule mining with an example from the seminal paper, *Weighted Association Rules: Models and Algorithms* by G.D.Ramkumar et al.

Caviar is an expensive and hence a low support item in any supermarket basket. Vodka, on the other hand, is a high to medium support item. The association, caviar => vodka is of very high confidence but will never be derived by the existing methods as the {caviar, vodka} itemset is of low support and will not be included.

The preceding paragraph echoes our retailer's concern. With the additional information about the margin for our transactions, we can now use weighted association rule mining to arrive at our new set of recommendations:

```
"transactionID","weight"
 "1001861",0.59502283788534
 "1003729",0.658379205926458
 "1003831",0.635451491097042
 "1003851",0.596453384749423
 "1004513",0.558612727312164
 "1004767",0.557096300448959
 "1004795",0.693775098285732
 "1004797",0.519395513963845
 "1004917",0.581376662057422
```

The code for the same is as follows:

```
##########################################################################
#
# R Data Analysis Projects
#
# Chapter 1
#
# Building Recommender System
# A step step approach to build Association Rule Mining
#
# Script:
#
# RScript to explain weighted Association rule mining
#
# Gopi Subramanian
##########################################################################

library(arules)
 library(igraph)

get.txn <- function(data.path, columns){
  # Get transaction object for a given data file
  #
  # Args:
  # data.path: data file name location
  # columns: transaction id and item id columns.
```

```
#
# Returns:
# transaction object
transactions.obj <- read.transactions(file = data.path, format = "single",
sep = ",",
cols = columns,
rm.duplicates = FALSE,
quote = "", skip = 0,
encoding = "unknown")
return(transactions.obj)
}

plot.graph <- function(cross.sell.rules){
# Plot the associated items as graph
#
# Args:
# cross.sell.rules: Set of final rules recommended
# Returns:
# None
edges <- unlist(lapply(cross.sell.rules['rules'], strsplit, split='=>'))

g <- graph(edges = edges)
plot(g)


}

columns <- c("order_id", "product_id") ## columns of interest in data file
data.path = '../../data/data.csv' ## Path to data file
transactions.obj <- get.txn(data.path, columns) ## create txn object

# Update the transaction objects
# with transaction weights
transactions.obj@itemsetInfo$weight <- NULL
# Read the weights file
weights <- read.csv('../../data/weights.csv')
transactions.obj@itemsetInfo <- weights

# Frequent item set generation
support <- 0.01

parameters = list(
support = support,
minlen = 2, # Minimal number of items per item set
maxlen = 10, # Maximal number of items per item set
target = "frequent itemsets"

)
weclat.itemsets <- weclat(transactions.obj, parameter = parameters)
```

```
weclat.itemsets.df <-data.frame(weclat.itemsets = labels(weclat.itemsets)
 , weclat.itemsets@quality)

head(weclat.itemsets.df)
 tail(weclat.itemsets.df)

# Rule induction
 weclat.rules <- ruleInduction(weclat.itemsets, transactions.obj,
confidence = 0.3)
 weclat.rules.df <-data.frame(rules = labels(weclat.rules)
 , weclat.rules@quality)
 head(weclat.rules.df)

weclat.rules.df$rules <- as.character(weclat.rules.df$rules)
 plot.graph(weclat.rules.df)
```

In the `arules` package, the `weclat` method allows us to use weighted transactions to generate frequent itemsets based on these weights. We introduce the weights through the `itemsetinfo` data frame in the `str(transactions.obj)` transactions object:

```
Formal class 'transactions' [package "arules"] with 3 slots
 ..@ data :Formal class 'ngCMatrix' [package "Matrix"] with 5 slots
 .. .. ..@ i : int [1:110657] 143 167 1340 2194 2250 3082 3323 3378 3630
4109 ...
 .. .. ..@ p : int [1:6989] 0 29 38 52 65 82 102 125 141 158 ...
 .. .. ..@ Dim : int [1:2] 16793 6988
 .. .. ..@ Dimnames:List of 2
 .. .. .. ..$ : NULL
 .. .. .. ..$ : NULL
 .. .. ..@ factors : list()
 ..@ itemInfo :'data.frame': 16793 obs. of 1 variable:
 .. ..$ labels: chr [1:16793] "#2 Coffee Filters" "0% Fat Black Cherry
Greek Yogurt y" "0% Fat Blueberry Greek Yogurt" "0% Fat Free Organic Milk"
...
 ..@ itemsetInfo:'data.frame': 6988 obs. of 1 variable:
 .. ..$ transactionID: chr [1:6988] "1001861" "1003729" "1003831" "1003851"
...
```

The third slot in the transaction object is a data frame with one column, `transactionID`. We create a new column called `weight` in that data frame and push our transaction weights:

```
weights <- read.csv("../../data/weights.csv")
 transactions.obj@itemsetInfo <- weights
 str(transactions.obj)
```

In the preceding case, we have replaced the whole data frame. You can either do that or only add the weight column.

Let's now look at the transactions object in the terminal:

```
Formal class 'transactions' [package "arules"] with 3 slots
  ..@ data :Formal class 'ngCMatrix' [package "Matrix"] with 5 slots
  .. .. ..@ i : int [1:110657] 143 167 1340 2194 2250 3082 3323 3378 3630
4109 ...
  .. .. ..@ p : int [1:6989] 0 29 38 52 65 82 102 125 141 158 ...
  .. .. ..@ Dim : int [1:2] 16793 6988
  .. .. ..@ Dimnames:List of 2
  .. .. .. ..$ : NULL
  .. .. .. ..$ : NULL
  .. .. ..@ factors : list()
  ..@ itemInfo :'data.frame': 16793 obs. of 1 variable:
  .. ..$ labels: chr [1:16793] "#2 Coffee Filters" "0% Fat Black Cherry
Greek Yogurt y" "0% Fat Blueberry Greek Yogurt" "0% Fat Free Organic Milk"
...
  ..@ itemsetInfo:'data.frame': 6988 obs. of 2 variables:
  .. ..$ transactionID: int [1:6988] 1001861 1003729 1003831 1003851 1004513
1004767 1004795 1004797 1004917 1004995 ...
  .. ..$ weight : num [1:6988] 0.595 0.658 0.635 0.596 0.559 ...
```

We have the `transactionID` and the weight in the `itemsetInfo` data frame now. Let's run the weighted itemset generation using these transaction weights:

```
support <- 0.01

parameters = list(
 support = support,
 minlen = 2, # Minimal number of items per item set
 maxlen = 10, # Maximal number of items per item set
 target = "frequent itemsets"
 )

weclat.itemsets <- weclat(transactions.obj, parameter = parameters)

weclat.itemsets.df <-data.frame(weclat.itemsets = labels(weclat.itemsets)
 , weclat.itemsets@quality
```

Once again, we invoke the `weclat` function with the parameter list and the transactions object. As the `itemInfo` data frame has the `weight` column, the function calculates the support using the weights provided. The new definition of support is as follows:

For a given item A:

```
Weighted support ( A ) = Sum of weights of the transactions containing A /
Sum of all weights.
```

The weighted support of an itemset is the sum of the weights of the transactions that contain the itemset. An itemset is frequent if its weighted support is equal to or greater than the threshold specified by support (assuming that the weights, sum is equal to one).

With this new definition, you can see now that low support times established by the old definition of support, if present in high value transactions, will be included. We have automatically taken care of our retailer's request to include high margin items while inducing the rules. Once again, for better reading, we create a data frame where each row is the frequent itemset generated, and a column to indicate the head(weclat.itemsets.df) support value:

```
   weclat.itemsets support
1 {Bag of Organic Bananas,Organic Kiwi} 0.01041131
2 {Bag of Organic Bananas,Organic D'Anjou Pears} 0.01042194
3 {Bag of Organic Bananas,Organic Whole String Cheese} 0.01034432
4 {Organic Baby Spinach,Organic Small Bunch Celery} 0.01039107
5 {Bag of Organic Bananas,Organic Small Bunch Celery} 0.01109455
6 {Banana,Seedless Red Grapes} 0.01274448

tail(weclat.itemsets.df)

    weclat.itemsets support
77 {Banana,Organic Hass Avocado} 0.02008700
78 {Organic Baby Spinach,Organic Strawberries} 0.02478094
79 {Bag of Organic Bananas,Organic Baby Spinach} 0.02743582
80 {Banana,Organic Baby Spinach} 0.02967578
81 {Bag of Organic Bananas,Organic Strawberries} 0.03626149
82 {Banana,Organic Strawberries} 0.03065132
```

In the case of `apriori`, we used the same function to generate/induce the rules. However, in the case of weighted association rule mining, we need to call the `ruleInduction` function to generate rules. We pass the frequent `itemsets` from the previous step, the transactions object, and finally the confidence threshold. Once again, for our convenience, we create a data frame with the list of all the rules that are induced and their interest measures:

```
weclat.rules <- ruleInduction(weclat.itemsets, transactions.obj, confidence
= 0.3)
weclat.rules.df <-data.frame(weclat.rules = labels(weclat.rules)
, weclat.rules@quality)

head(weclat.rules.df)
```

```
   rules support confidence lift itemset
1 {Organic Kiwi} => {Bag of Organic Bananas} 0.01016027 0.3879781 2.388715
1
3 {Organic D'Anjou Pears} => {Bag of Organic Bananas} 0.01001717 0.3846154
2.368011 2
5 {Organic Whole String Cheese} => {Bag of Organic Bananas} 0.00930166
0.3250000 2.000969 3
11 {Seedless Red Grapes} => {Banana} 0.01302232 0.3513514 1.686293 6
13 {Organic Large Extra Fancy Fuji Apple} => {Bag of Organic Bananas}
0.01445335 0.3825758 2.355453 7
15 {Honeycrisp Apple} => {Banana} 0.01617058 0.4248120 2.038864 8
```

Finally, let's use the `plot.graph` function to view the new set of interesting item associations:

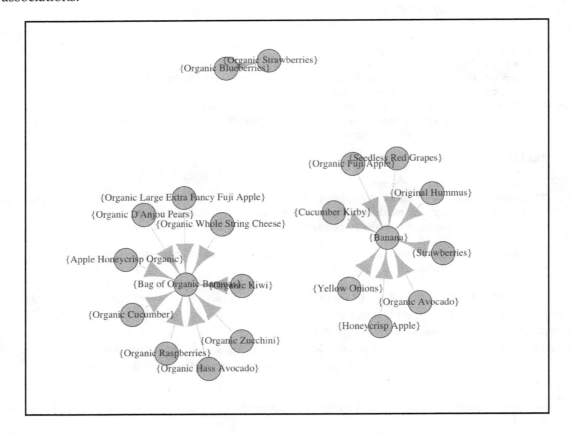

Our new recommendation now includes some of the rare items. It is also sensitive to the profit margin of individual transactions. With these recommendations, the retailer is geared toward increasing his profitability through the cross-selling campaign.

Hyperlink-induced topic search (HITS)

In the previous section, we saw that weighted association rule mining leads to recommendations that can increase the profitability of the retailer. Intuitively, weighted association rule mining is superior to vanilla association rule mining as the generated rules are sensitive to transactions, weights. Instead of running the plain version of the algorithm, can we run the weighted association algorithm? We were lucky enough to get transaction weights. What if the retailer did not provide us with the transaction weights? Can we infer weights from transactions? When our transaction data does not come with preassigned weights, we need some way to assign importance to those transactions. For instance, we can say that a transaction with a lot of items should be considered more important than a transaction with a single item.

The `arules` package provides a method called **HITS** to help us do the exact same thing—infer transaction weights. **HITS** stands for **Hyperlink-induced Topic Search**—a link analysis algorithm used to rate web pages developed by John Kleinberg. According to HITS, hubs are pages with large numbers of out degrees and authority are pages with large numbers of in degrees.

According to graph theory, a graph is formed by a set of vertices and edges. Edges connect the vertices. Graphs with directed edges are called directed graphs. The in degree is the number of inward directed edges from a given vertex in a directed graph. Similarly, the out degree is the number of outward directed edges from a given vertex in a directed graph.

The rationale is that if a lot of pages link to a particular page, then that page is considered an authority. If a page has links to a lot of other pages, it is considered a hub.

The paper, *Mining Weighted Association Rules without Preassigned Weights* by Ke Sun and Fengshan Bai, details the adaptation of the HITS algorithm for transaction databases.

The basic idea behind using the HITS algorithm for association rule mining is that frequent items may not be as important as they seem. The paper presents an algorithm that applies the HITS methodology to bipartite graphs.

 In the mathematical field of graph theory, a bipartite graph (or bigraph) is a graph whose vertices can be divided into two disjoint and independent sets U and V such that every edge connects a vertex in U to one in V. Vertex sets are usually called the parts of the graph. - Wikipedia (`https://en.wikipedia.org/wiki/Bipartite_graph`)

According to the HITS modified for the transactions database, the transactions and products are treated as a bipartite graph, with an arc going from the transaction to the product if the product is present in the transaction. The following diagram is reproduced from the paper, *Mining Weighted Association Rules without Preassigned Weights* by Ke Sun and Fengshan Bai, to illustrate how transactions in a database are converted to a bipartite graph:

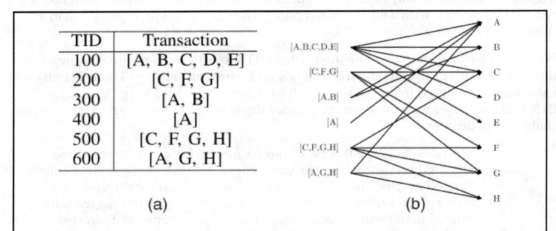

Fig. 1. The bipartite graph representation of a database. (a) Database. (b) Bipartite graph.

In this representation, the transactions can be ranked using the HITS algorithm. In this kind of representation, the support of an item is proportional to its degree. Consider item **A**. Its absolute support is 4; in the graph, the in degree of **A** is four. As you can see, considering only the support, we totally ignore transaction importance, unless the importance of the transactions is explicitly provided. How do we get the transaction weights in this scenario? Again, a way to get the weights intuitively is from a good transaction, which should be highly weighted and should contain many good items. A good item should be contained by many good transactions. By treating transactions as hubs and the products as authorities, the algorithm invokes HITS on this bipartite graph.

The `arules` package provides the method (HITS), which implements the algorithm that we described earlier:

```
weights.vector <- hits( transactions.obj, type = "relative")
weights.df <- data.frame(transactionID = labels(weights.vector), weight =
weights.vector)
```

We invoke the algorithm using the HITS method. We have described the intuition behind using the HITS algorithm in transaction databases to give weights to our transactions. We will briefly describe how the HITS algorithm functions. Curious readers can refer to *Authoritative Sources in a Hyperlinked Environment, J.M. Kleinberg, J. ACM, vol. 46, no. 5, pp. 604-632, 1999*, for a better understanding of the HITS algorithm.

The HITS algorithm, to begin with, initializes the weight of all nodes to one; in our case, the items and the transactions are set to one. That is, we maintain two arrays, one for hub weights and the other one for authority weights.

It proceeds to do the following three steps in an iterative manner, that is, until our hub and authority arrays stabilize or don't change with subsequent updates:

1. **Authority node score update**: Modify the authority score of each node to the sum of the hub scores of each node that points to it.
2. **Hub node score update**: Change the hub score of each node to the sum of the authority scores of each node that it points to.
3. **Unit normalize the hub and authority scores**: Continue with the authority node score update until the hub and authority value stabilizes.

At the end of the algorithm, every item has an authority score, which is the sum of the hub scores of all the transactions that contain this item. Every transaction has a hub score that is the sum of the authority score of all the items in that transaction. Using the weights created using the HITS algorithm, we create a `weights.df` data frame:

```
head(weights.df)

                transactionID weight
1000431 1000431 1.893931e-04
100082 100082 1.409053e-04
1000928 1000928 2.608214e-05
1001517 1001517 1.735461e-04
1001650 1001650 1.184581e-04
1001934 1001934 2.310465e-04
```

Pass weights.df our transactions object. We can now generate the weighted association rules:

```
transactions.obj@itemsetInfo <- weights.df

support <- 0.01
 parameters = list(
 support = support,
 minlen = 2, # Minimal number of items per item set
 maxlen = 10, # Maximal number of items per item set
 target = "frequent itemsets"

 )
 weclat.itemsets <- weclat(transactions.obj, parameter = parameters)
 weclat.itemsets.df <-data.frame(weclat.itemsets = labels(weclat.itemsets)
 , weclat.itemsets@quality)

weclat.rules <- ruleInduction(weclat.itemsets, transactions.obj, confidence
= 0.1)
 weclat.rules.df <-data.frame(weclat.rules = labels(weclat.rules)
 , weclat.rules@quality)
```

We can look into the output data frames created for frequent itemsets and rules:

```
head(weclat.itemsets.df)

  weclat.itemsets support
1 {Banana,Russet Potato} 0.01074109
2 {Banana,Total 0% Nonfat Greek Yogurt} 0.01198206
3 {100% Raw Coconut Water,Bag of Organic Bananas} 0.01024201
4 {Organic Roasted Turkey Breast,Organic Strawberries} 0.01124278
5 {Banana,Roma Tomato} 0.01089124
6 {Banana,Bartlett Pears} 0.01345293
```

```
tail(weclat.itemsets.df)

  weclat.itemsets support
540 {Bag of Organic Bananas,Organic Baby Spinach,Organic Strawberries}
0.02142840
541 {Banana,Organic Baby Spinach,Organic Strawberries} 0.02446832
542 {Bag of Organic Bananas,Organic Baby Spinach} 0.06536606
543 {Banana,Organic Baby Spinach} 0.07685530
544 {Bag of Organic Bananas,Organic Strawberries} 0.08640422
545 {Banana,Organic Strawberries} 0.08226264

head(weclat.rules.df)

weclat.rules support confidence lift itemset
weclat.rules support confidence lift itemset
1 {Russet Potato} => {Banana} 0.005580996 0.3714286 1.782653 1
3 {Total 0% Nonfat Greek Yogurt} => {Banana} 0.005580996 0.4148936 1.991261
2
6 {100% Raw Coconut Water} => {Bag of Organic Bananas} 0.004865484
0.3238095 1.993640 3
8 {Organic Roasted Turkey Breast} => {Organic Strawberries} 0.004579279
0.3440860 2.648098 4
9 {Roma Tomato} => {Banana} 0.006010303 0.3181818 1.527098 5
11 {Bartlett Pears} => {Banana} 0.007870635 0.4545455 2.181568 6
```

Based on the weights generated using the HITS algorithm, we can now order the items by their authority score. This is an alternate way of ranking the items in addition to ranking them by their frequency. We can leverage the itemFrequency function to generate the item scores:

```
freq.weights <- head(sort(itemFrequency(transactions.obj, weighted =
TRUE),decreasing = TRUE),20)
freq.nweights <- head(sort(itemFrequency(transactions.obj, weighted =
FALSE),decreasing = TRUE),20)

compare.df <- data.frame("items" = names(freq.weights),
"score" = freq.weights,
"items.nw" = names(freq.nweights),
"score.nw" = freq.nweights)
row.names(compare.df) <- NULL
```

Let's look at the `compare.df` data frame:

items	score	items.nw	score.nw
Banana	0.35465116	Banana	0.20835718
Bag of Organic Bananas	0.27215027	Bag of Organic Bananas	0.16242129
Organic Strawberries	0.25847376	Organic Strawberries	0.12993703
Organic Baby Spinach	0.22885376	Organic Baby Spinach	0.11562679
Organic Hass Avocado	0.19555103	Organic Hass Avocado	0.10432169
Organic Avocado	0.14426638	Organic Avocado	0.08571837
Limes	0.13660838	Large Lemon	0.07641671
Large Lemon	0.13349121	Limes	0.07498569
Organic Raspberries	0.11888793	Organic Raspberries	0.06797367
Organic Garlic	0.11691332	Organic Garlic	0.06182026
Organic Yellow Onion	0.10582600	Organic Whole Milk	0.06139096
Organic Whole Milk	0.10316587	Strawberries	0.05867201
Organic Zucchini	0.10287022	Organic Yellow Onion	0.05666857
Organic Cucumber	0.08936422	Organic Zucchini	0.05380653
Organic Grape Tomatoes	0.08272227	Cucumber Kirby	0.04793932
Organic Lemon	0.07780401	Organic Cucumber	0.04679450
Cucumber Kirby	0.07646078	Organic Lemon	0.04650830
Organic Small Bunch Celery	0.07339331	Organic Grape Tomatoes	0.04550658
Apple Honeycrisp Organic	0.07255845	Organic Fuji Apple	0.04421866
Strawberries	0.07153850	Organic Blueberries	0.04250143

The column score gives the relative transaction frequency. The **score.new** column is the authority score from the hits algorithm. You can see that **Limes** and **Large Lemon** have interchanged places. **Strawberries** has gone further up the order compared to the original transaction frequency score.

The code is as follows:

```
###########################################################################
####
 #
 # R Data Analysis Projects
 #
 # Chapter 1
 #
 # Building Recommender System
 # A step step approach to build Association Rule Mining
 #
 # Script:
 #
 # RScript to explain application of hits to
 # transaction database.
 #
 # Gopi Subramanian
###########################################################################
####

library(arules)

get.txn <- function(data.path, columns){
 # Get transaction object for a given data file
 #
 # Args:
 # data.path: data file name location
 # columns: transaction id and item id columns.
 #
 # Returns:
 # transaction object
 transactions.obj <- read.transactions(file = data.path, format = "single",
 sep = ",",
 cols = columns,
 rm.duplicates = FALSE,
 quote = "", skip = 0,
 encoding = "unknown")
 return(transactions.obj)
 }

## Create txn object
 columns <- c("order_id", "product_id") ## columns of interest in data file
 data.path = '../../data/data.csv' ## Path to data file
 transactions.obj <- get.txn(data.path, columns) ## create txn object

## Generate weight vector using hits
 weights.vector <- hits( transactions.obj, type = "relative")
 weights.df <- data.frame(transactionID = labels(weights.vector), weight =
```

```
weights.vector)

head(weights.df)

transactions.obj@itemsetInfo <- weights.df

## Frequent item sets generation
 support <- 0.01
 parameters = list(
 support = support,
 minlen = 2, # Minimal number of items per item set
 maxlen = 10, # Maximal number of items per item set
 target = "frequent itemsets"

 )
 weclat.itemsets <- weclat(transactions.obj, parameter = parameters)
 weclat.itemsets.df <-data.frame(weclat.itemsets = labels(weclat.itemsets)
 , weclat.itemsets@quality)

head(weclat.itemsets.df)
 tail(weclat.itemsets.df)

## Rule induction
 weclat.rules <- ruleInduction(weclat.itemsets, transactions.obj,
confidence = 0.3)
 weclat.rules.df <-data.frame(weclat.rules = labels(weclat.rules)
 , weclat.rules@quality)

head(weclat.rules.df)

freq.weights <- head(sort(itemFrequency(transactions.obj, weighted =
TRUE),decreasing = TRUE),20)
 freq.nweights <- head(sort(itemFrequency(transactions.obj, weighted =
FALSE),decreasing = TRUE),20)

compare.df <- data.frame("items" = names(freq.weights),
 "score" = freq.weights,
 "items.nw" = names(freq.nweights),
 "score.nw" = freq.nweights)
 row.names(compare.df) <- NULL
```

Negative association rules

Throughout, we have been focusing on inducing rules indicating the chance of an item being added to the basket, given that there are other items present in the basket. However, knowing the relationship between the absence of an item and the presence of another in the basket can be very important in some applications. These rules are called negative association rules. The association *bread implies milk* indicates the purchasing behavior of buying milk and bread together. What about the following associations: customers who buy tea do not buy coffee, or customers who buy juice do not buy bottled water? Associations that include negative items (that is, items absent from the transaction) can be as valuable as positive associations in many scenarios, such as when devising marketing strategies for promotions.

There are several algorithms proposed to induce negative association rules from a transaction database. `Apriori` is not a well-suited algorithm for negative association rule mining. In order to use `apriori`, every transaction needs to be updated with all the items—those that are present in the transaction and those that are absent. This will heavily inflate the database. In our case, every transaction will have 16,000 items. We can cheat; we can leverage the use of `apriori` for negative association rule mining only for a selected list of items. In transactions that do not contain the item, we can create an entry for that item to indicate that the item is not present in the transaction. The `arules` package's function, `addComplement`, allows us to do exactly that.

Let's say that our transaction consists of the following:

```
Banana, Strawberries
Onions, ginger, garlic
Milk, Banana
```

When we pass this transaction to `addComplement` and say that we want non-Banana entries to be added to the transaction, the resulting transaction from `addComplement` will be as follows:

```
Banana, Strawberries
Onions, ginger, garlic, !Banana
Milk, Banana
```

An exclamation mark is the standard way to indicate the absence; however, you can choose your own prefix:

```
get.neg.rules <- function(transactions, itemList, support, confidence){
  # Generate negative association rules for given support confidence value
  #
  # Args:
```

```
# transactions: Transaction object, list of transactions
# itemList : list of items to be negated in the transactions
# support: Minimum support threshold
# confidence: Minimum confidence threshold
# Returns:
# A data frame with the best set negative rules and their support and
confidence values

neg.transactions <- addComplement( transactions.obj, labels = itemList)
rules <- find.rules(neg.transactions, support, confidence)
return(rules)
}
```

In the preceding code, we have created a `get.neg.rules` function. Inside this method, we have leveraged the `addComplement` function to introduce the absence entry of the given items in `itemList` into the transactions. We generate the rules with the newly formed transactions, `neg.transactions`:

```
itemList <- c("Organic Whole Milk","Cucumber Kirby")
neg.rules <- get.neg.rules(transactions.obj,itemList, .05,.6)

neg.rules.nr <- neg.rules[!is.redundant(neg.rules)]
labels(neg.rules.nr)
```

Once we have the negative rules, we pass those through `is.redundant` to remove any redundant rules and finally print the rules:

```
[1]  "{Strawberries} => {!Organic Whole Milk}"
[2]  "{Strawberries} => {!Cucumber Kirby}"
[3]  "{Organic Whole Milk} => {!Cucumber Kirby}"
[4]  "{Organic Zucchini} => {!Cucumber Kirby}"
[5]  "{Organic Yellow Onion} => {!Organic Whole Milk}"
[6]  "{Organic Yellow Onion} => {!Cucumber Kirby}"
[7]  "{Organic Garlic} => {!Organic Whole Milk}"
[8]  "{Organic Garlic} => {!Cucumber Kirby}"
[9]  "{Organic Raspberries} => {!Organic Whole Milk}"
[10] "{Organic Raspberries} => {!Cucumber Kirby}"
```

The code is as follows:

```
################################################################################
#
# R Data Analysis Projects
#
# Chapter 1
#
# Building Recommender System
# A step step approach to build Association Rule Mining
```

```
#
# Script:
#
# RScript to explain negative associative rule mining
#
# Gopi Subramanian
################################################################################

library(arules)
library(igraph)

get.txn <- function(data.path, columns){
# Get transaction object for a given data file
#
# Args:
# data.path: data file name location
# columns: transaction id and item id columns.
#
# Returns:
# transaction object
transactions.obj <- read.transactions(file = data.path, format = "single",
sep = ",",
cols = columns,
rm.duplicates = FALSE,
quote = "", skip = 0,
encoding = "unknown")
return(transactions.obj)
}

get.rules <- function(support, confidence, transactions){
# Get Apriori rules for given support and confidence values
#
# Args:
# support: support parameter
# confidence: confidence parameter
#
# Returns:
# rules object
parameters = list(
support = support,
confidence = confidence,
minlen = 2, # Minimal number of items per item set
maxlen = 10, # Maximal number of items per item set
target = "rules"

)

rules <- apriori(transactions, parameter = parameters)
return(rules)
```

```
  }
  get.neg.rules <- function(transactions, itemList, support, confidence){
  # Generate negative association rules for given support confidence value
  #
  # Args:
  # transactions: Transaction object, list of transactions
  # itemList : list of items to be negated in the transactions
  # support: Minimum support threshold
  # confidence: Minimum confidence threshold
  # Returns:
  # A data frame with the best set negative rules and their support and
confidence values
  neg.transactions <- addComplement( transactions, labels = itemList)
  rules <- get.rules(support, confidence, neg.transactions)
  return(rules)
  }

columns <- c("order_id", "product_id") ## columns of interest in data file
  data.path = '../../data/data.csv' ## Path to data file

transactions.obj <- get.txn(data.path, columns) ## create txn object

itemList <- c("Organic Whole Milk","Cucumber Kirby")

neg.rules <- get.neg.rules(transactions.obj,itemList, support = .05,
  confidence = .6)

neg.rules.nr <- neg.rules[!is.redundant(neg.rules)]

labels(neg.rules.nr)
```

Rules visualization

In the previous sections, we leveraged plotting capability from the `arules` and `igraph` packages to plot induced rules. In this section, we introduce `arulesViz`, a package dedicated to plot association rules, generated by the `arules` package. The `arulesViz` package integrates seamlessly with the `arules` packages in terms of sharing data structures.

The following code is quite self-explanatory. A multitude of graphs, including interactive/non-interactive scatter plots, graph plots, matrix plots, and group plots can be generated from the rules data structure; it's a great visual way to explore the rules induced:

```
###################################################################
#
# R Data Analysis Projects
#
# Chapter 1
#
# Building Recommender System
# A step step approach to build Association Rule Mining
#
# Script:
#
# RScript to explore arulesViz package
# for Association rules visualization
#
# Gopi Subramanian
###################################################################
library(arules)
library(arulesViz)

get.txn <- function(data.path, columns){
  # Get transaction object for a given data file
  #
  # Args:
  # data.path: data file name location
  # columns: transaction id and item id columns.
  #
  # Returns:
  # transaction object
  transactions.obj <- read.transactions(file = data.path, format = "single",
  sep = ",",
  cols = columns,
  rm.duplicates = FALSE,
  quote = "", skip = 0,
  encoding = "unknown")
  return(transactions.obj)
  }

get.rules <- function(support, confidence, transactions){
  # Get Apriori rules for given support and confidence values
  #
  # Args:
  # support: support parameter
  # confidence: confidence parameter
```

```
#
# Returns:
# rules object
parameters = list(
support = support,
confidence = confidence,
minlen = 2, # Minimal number of items per item set
maxlen = 10, # Maximal number of items per item set
target = "rules"

)

rules <- apriori(transactions, parameter = parameters)
return(rules)

support <- 0.01
confidence <- 0.2

# Create transactions object
columns <- c("order_id", "product_id") ## columns of interest in data file
data.path = '../../data/data.csv' ## Path to data file
transactions.obj <- get.txn(data.path, columns) ## create txn object

# Induce Rules
all.rules <- get.rules(support, confidence, transactions.obj)

# Scatter plot of rules
plotly_arules(all.rules, method = "scatterplot", measure =
c("support","lift"), shading = "order")

# Interactive scatter plots
plot(all.rules, method = NULL, measure = "support", shading = "lift",
interactive = TRUE)

# Get top rules by lift
sub.rules <- head(sort(all.rules, by="lift"), 15

# Group plot of rules
plot(sub.rules, method="grouped")

# Graph plot of rule
plot(sub.rules, method="graph", measure = "lift")
```

The following diagram is the scatter plot of rules induced:

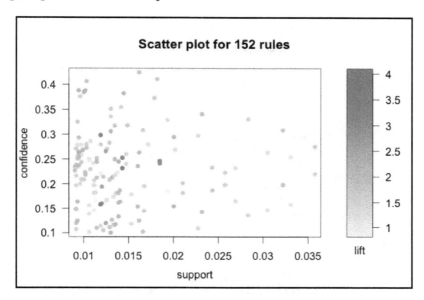

The following diagram is the grouped plot of rules induced:

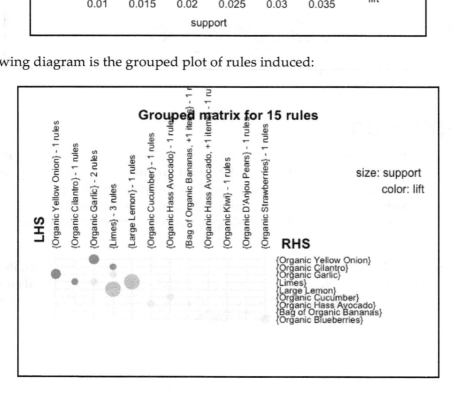

The following diagram is the graph plot of rules induced:

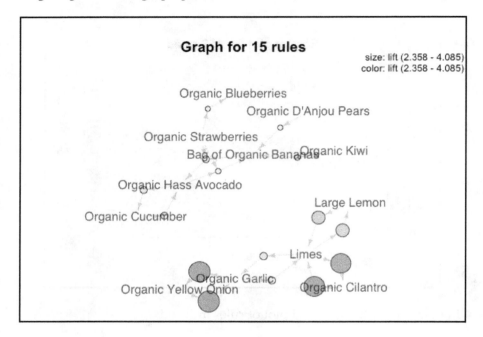

Wrapping up

The final step in any data analysis project is documentation—either generating a report of the findings or documenting the scripts and data used. In our case, we are going to wrap up with a small application. We will use `RShiny`, an R web application framework. `RShiny` is a powerful framework for developing interactive web applications using R. We will leverage the code that we have written to generate a simple, yet powerful, user interface for our retail customers.

To keep things simple, we have a set of three screens. The first screen, as shown in the following screenshot, allows the user to vary support and confidence thresholds and view the rules generated. It also has additional interest measures, lift, conviction, and leverage. The user can sort the rule by any of these interest measures:

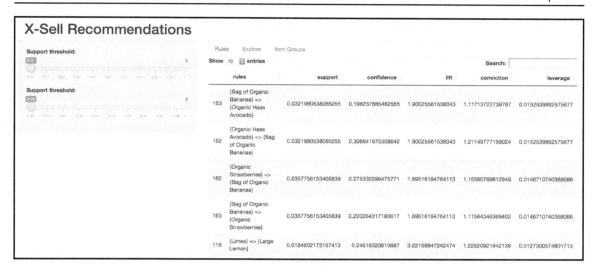

Another screen is a scatter plot representation of the rules:

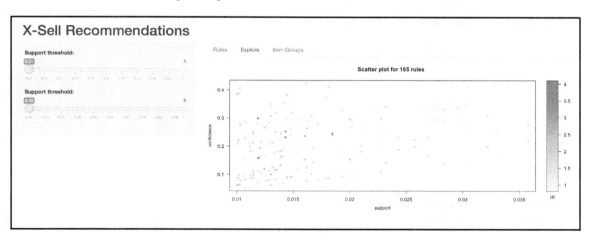

Finally, a graph representation to view the product grouping for the easy selection of products for the cross-selling campaign is as follows:

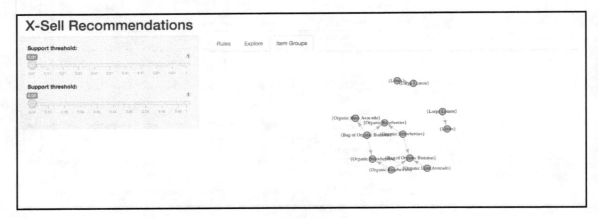

The complete source code is available in <../App.R>:

```
#####################################################################
#
# R Data Analysis Projects
#
# Chapter 1
#
# Building Recommender System
# A step step approach to build Association Rule Mining
#
# Script:
#
# Rshiny app
#
# Gopi Subramanian
#####################################################################
library(shiny)
library(plotly)
library(arules)
library(igraph)
library(arulesViz)

get.txn <- function(data.path, columns){
  # Get transaction object for a given data file
  #
  # Args:
  # data.path: data file name location
  # columns: transaction id and item id columns.
```

```
#
# Returns:
# transaction object
transactions.obj <- read.transactions(file = data.path, format = "single",
sep = ",",
cols = columns,
rm.duplicates = FALSE,
quote = "", skip = 0,
encoding = "unknown")
return(transactions.obj)
}

get.rules <- function(support, confidence, transactions){
# Get Apriori rules for given support and confidence values
#
# Args:
# support: support parameter
# confidence: confidence parameter
#
# Returns:
# rules object
parameters = list(
support = support,
confidence = confidence,
minlen = 2, # Minimal number of items per item set
maxlen = 10, # Maximal number of items per item set
target = "rules"

)

rules <- apriori(transactions, parameter = parameters)
return(rules)
}

find.rules <- function(transactions, support, confidence, topN = 10){
# Generate and prune the rules for given support confidence value
#
# Args:
# transactions: Transaction object, list of transactions
# support: Minimum support threshold
# confidence: Minimum confidence threshold
# Returns:
# A data frame with the best set of rules and their support and confidence
values


# Get rules for given combination of support and confidence
all.rules <- get.rules(support, confidence, transactions)
```

```
    rules.df <-data.frame(rules = labels(all.rules)
    , all.rules@quality)

    other.im <- interestMeasure(all.rules, transactions = transactions)

    rules.df <- cbind(rules.df, other.im[,c('conviction','leverage')])


    # Keep the best rule based on the interest measure
    best.rules.df <- head(rules.df[order(-rules.df$leverage),],topN)

    return(best.rules.df)
    }
plot.graph <- function(cross.sell.rules){
    # Plot the associated items as graph
    #
    # Args:
    # cross.sell.rules: Set of final rules recommended
    # Returns:
    # None
    edges <- unlist(lapply(cross.sell.rules['rules'], strsplit, split='=>'))
    g <- graph(edges = edges)
    return(g)

    }

columns <- c("order_id", "product_id") ## columns of interest in data file
    data.path = '../../data/data.csv' ## Path to data file
    transactions.obj <- get.txn(data.path, columns) ## create txn object

server <- function(input, output) {

cross.sell.rules <- reactive({
    support <- input$Support
    confidence <- input$Confidence
    cross.sell.rules <- find.rules( transactions.obj, support, confidence )
    cross.sell.rules$rules <- as.character(cross.sell.rules$rules)
    return(cross.sell.rules)

})

    gen.rules <- reactive({
    support <- input$Support
    confidence <- input$Confidence
    gen.rules <- get.rules( support, confidence ,transactions.obj)
    return(gen.rules)

})
```

```
output$rulesTable <- DT::renderDataTable({
cross.sell.rules()
})

output$graphPlot <- renderPlot({
g <-plot.graph(cross.sell.rules())
plot(g)
})

output$explorePlot <- renderPlot({
plot(x = gen.rules(), method = NULL,
measure = "support",
shading = "lift", interactive = FALSE)
})


}
ui <- fluidPage(
 headerPanel(title = "X-Sell Recommendations"),
 sidebarLayout(
 sidebarPanel(
 sliderInput("Support", "Support threshold:", min = 0.01, max = 1.0, value
= 0.01),
 sliderInput("Confidence", "Support threshold:", min = 0.05, max = 1.0,
value = 0.05)

 ),
 mainPanel(
 tabsetPanel(
 id = 'xsell',
 tabPanel('Rules', DT::dataTableOutput('rulesTable')),
 tabPanel('Explore', plotOutput('explorePlot')),
 tabPanel('Item Groups', plotOutput('graphPlot'))
 )
 )
 )
 )

shinyApp(ui = ui, server = server)
```

We have described the get.txn, get.rules, and find.rules functions in the previous section. We will not go through them again here. The preceding code is a single page RShiny app code; both the server and the UI component reside in the same file.

The UI component is as follows:

```
ui <- fluidPage(
headerPanel(title = "X-Sell Recommendations"),
sidebarLayout(
sidebarPanel(
sliderInput("Support", "Support threshold:", min = 0.01, max = 1.0, value
= 0.01),
sliderInput("Confidence", "Support threshold:", min = 0.05, max = 1.0,
value = 0.05)

),
mainPanel(
tabsetPanel(
id = 'xsell',
tabPanel('Rules', DT::dataTableOutput('rulesTable')),
tabPanel('Explore', plotOutput('explorePlot')),
tabPanel('Item Groups', plotOutput('graphPlot'))
)
)
)
)
```

We define the screen layout in this section. This section can also be kept in a separate file called UI.R. The page is defined by two sections, a panel in the left, defined by sidebarPanel, and a main section defined under mainPanel. Inside the side bar, we have defined two slider controls for the support and confidence thresholds respectively. The main panel contains a tab-separated window, defined by tabPanel.

The main panel has three tabs; each tab has a slot defined for the final set of rules, with their interest measures, a scatter plot for the rules, and finally the graph plot of the rules.

The server component is as follows:

```
server <- function(input, output) {

cross.sell.rules <- reactive({
 support <- input$Support
 confidence <- input$Confidence
 cross.sell.rules <- find.rules( transactions.obj, support, confidence )
 cross.sell.rules$rules <- as.character(cross.sell.rules$rules)
 return(cross.sell.rules)

})
```

The `cross.sell.rules` data frame is defined as a reactive component. When the values of the support and confidence thresholds change in the UI, `cross.sell.rules` data frame will be recomputed. This frame will be served to the first page, where we have defined a slot for this table, called `rulesTable`:

```
gen.rules <- reactive({
support <- input$Support
confidence <- input$Confidence
gen.rules <- get.rules( support, confidence ,transactions.obj)
return(gen.rules)
})
```

This reactive component retrieves the calculations and returns the rules object every time the support or/and confidence threshold is changed by the user in the UI:

```
output$rulesTable <- DT::renderDataTable({
cross.sell.rules()
})
```

The preceding code renders the data frame back to the UI:

```
output$graphPlot <- renderPlot({
g <-plot.graph(cross.sell.rules())
plot(g)
})

output$explorePlot <- renderPlot({
plot(x = gen.rules(), method = NULL,
measure = "support",
shading = "lift", interactive = FALSE)
})


}
```

The preceding two pieces of code render the plot back to the UI.

Summary

We started the chapter with an overview of recommender systems. We introduced our retail case and the association rule mining algorithm. Then we applied association rule mining to design a cross-selling campaign. We went on to understand weighted association rule mining and its applications. Following that, we introduced the HITS algorithm and its use in transaction data. Next, we studied the negative association rules discovery process and its use. We showed you different ways to visualize association rules. Finally, we created a small web application using R Shiny to demonstrate some of the concepts we learned.

In the next chapter, we will look at another recommendation system algorithm called content based filtering. We will see how this method can help address the famous cold start problem in recommendation systems. Furthermore, we will introduce the concept of fuzzy ranking to order the final recommendations.

2

Fuzzy Logic Induced Content-Based Recommendation

When a friend comes to you for a movie recommendation, you don't arbitrarily start shooting movie names. You try to suggest movies while keeping in mind your friend's tastes. Content-based recommendation systems try to mimic the exact same process. Consider a scenario in which a user is browsing through a list of products. Given a set of products and the associated product properties, when a person views a particular product, content-based recommendation systems can generate a subset of products with similar properties to the one currently being viewed by the user. Typical content-based recommendation systems tend to also include the user profile. In this chapter, however, we will not be including the user profiles. We will be working solely with the item/product profiles. Content-based recommendation systems are also called content-based filtering methods.

During winter, cars tend to have problems starting. But once the engine reaches the optimal temperature it starts to run smoothly. Recommender systems tend to have the same cold start problem. When deployed for the first time, the recommender system is unaware of the user preferences. It's in the dark when it comes to recommendations. Other recommender systems that use user preferences, such as collaborative filtering, which we covered in the previous chapter, need user preferences to make recommendations. In the absence of user preferences, these methods become ineffective.

Content-based recommendation is the best method to address the cold start problem. Since content-based methods rely on the product properties to create recommendations, they can ignore the user preferences, to begin with. While the content-based method dishes out the needed recommendation, the user profile can be built in the background. With a sufficient user profile, content-based methods can be further improved or can move on to using collaborative filtering methods.

Typically, the content-based filtering method provides a list of top N recommendations based on some similarity scores. In this chapter, we introduce a fuzzy-logic-based system to further rank these recommendations using multiple similarity scores. Fuzzy logic is based on the fuzzy sets theory. In the Standard Set theory, the boundaries between the sets are well defined. In fuzzy sets, the boundaries are not well defined and they may overlap. Another concept in fuzzy logic is fuzzy rules. They provide a mechanism for dealing with fuzzy consequents and fuzzy antecedents. Now, consider the ranking problem while serving recommendations. The ranking is crisp, based on the strict sorting of one or more similarity scores. We will replace this strict sorting system with a fuzzy-rule-based system.

A news aggregator collects syndicated web content such as new articles, blogs, video, and similar items at a centralized location for easy viewing. We will use an imaginary news aggregator website as an example to explain and build a content-based recommendation system. Our use case is as follows. When a person is reading a particular news article, we want to recommend to him other news article which might interest him. This will help us understand how the cold-start problem in recommender systems is addressed using content-based methods. Furthermore, our fuzzy logic rule system will shed light on how a fuzzy system can be leveraged for ranking.

In this chapter we will cover the following:

- An introduction to the content-based filtering method
- News aggregator use cases and data
- Designing our content-based filtering method
- Fuzzy recommendation ranking

The code for this chapter was written in RStudio version 0.99.491. It uses R version 3.3.1. As we work through our examples, we will introduce the R packages that we will be using. During our code description, we will be using some of the output printed in the console. We have included what will be printed in the console immediately following the statement which prints the information to the console, so as to not disturb the flow of the code.

Introducing content-based recommendation

To understand the inner workings of a content-based recommendation system, let's look at a simple example. We will use the wine dataset from https://archive.ics.uci.edu/ml/datasets/wine.

This dataset is the result of the chemical analysis of wine grown in the same region in Italy. We have data from three different cultivars (*From an assemblage of plants selected for desirable characters*, Wikipedia: https://en.wikipedia.org/wiki/Cultivar).

Let's extract the data from UCI machine learning repository:

```
> library(data.table)
> wine.data <-
fread('https://archive.ics.uci.edu/ml/machine-learning-databases/wine/wine.
data')
  % Total    % Received % Xferd  Average Speed   Time    Time     Time
Current
                                 Dload  Upload   Total   Spent    Left
Speed
  0      0    0     0    0     0      0       0 --:--:-- --:--:-- --:--:--
0100 10782  100 10782    0     0  22336       0 --:--:-- --:--:-- --:--:--
22369

> head(wine.data)
   V1    V2   V3   V4   V5  V6   V7   V8   V9  V10   V11  V12  V13  V14
1:  1 14.23 1.71 2.43 15.6 127 2.80 3.06 0.28 2.29 5.64 1.04 3.92 1065
2:  1 13.20 1.78 2.14 11.2 100 2.65 2.76 0.26 1.28 4.38 1.05 3.40 1050
3:  1 13.16 2.36 2.67 18.6 101 2.80 3.24 0.30 2.81 5.68 1.03 3.17 1185
4:  1 14.37 1.95 2.50 16.8 113 3.85 3.49 0.24 2.18 7.80 0.86 3.45 1480
5:  1 13.24 2.59 2.87 21.0 118 2.80 2.69 0.39 1.82 4.32 1.04 2.93  735
6:  1 14.20 1.76 2.45 15.2 112 3.27 3.39 0.34 1.97 6.75 1.05 2.85 1450
```

We have a total of 14 columns.

The column number 1, named V1 represents the cultivar:

```
> table(wine.data$V1)

 1  2  3
59 71 48
>
```

We see the distribution of the V1 column.

Let's remove the cultivar and only retain the chemical properties of the wine:

```
> wine.type <- wine.data[,1]
> wine.features <- wine.data[,-1]
```

`wine.features` has all the properties and without the cultivar column.

Let's scale this `wine.features` and create a matrix:

```
wine.features.scaled <- data.frame(scale(wine.features))
wine.mat <- data.matrix(wine.features.scaled)
```

We have converted our data frame to a matrix.

Let's add the row names and give an integer number for each wine:

```
> rownames(wine.mat) <- seq(1:dim(wine.features.scaled)[1])
> wine.mat[1:2,]
          V2          V3          V4          V5          V6          V7          V8
V9          V10         V11
1 1.5143408 -0.5606682  0.2313998 -1.166303 1.90852151 0.8067217 1.0319081
-0.6577078  1.2214385  0.2510088
2 0.2455968 -0.4980086 -0.8256672 -2.483841 0.01809398 0.5670481 0.7315653
-0.8184106 -0.5431887 -0.2924962
          V12         V13         V14
1 0.3611585 1.842721 1.0101594
2 0.4049085 1.110317 0.9625263
>
```

With our matrix ready, let's find the similarity between the wines.

We have numbered our rows representing the wine. The columns represent the properties of the wine.

We are going to use the pearson coefficient to find the similarities.

The **pearson coefficient** measures the correlation between two variables:

$$P_{x,y} = \frac{cov(x,y)}{\sigma_x \sigma_y}$$

`cov()` is the covariance, and it's divided by the standard deviation of x and standard deviation of y.

In our case, we want to find the pearson coefficient between the rows. We want the similarity between two wines. Hence we will transpose our matrix before invoking `cor` function.

Let's find the similarity matrix:

```
> wine.mat <- t(wine.mat)

> cor.matrix <- cor(wine.mat, use = "pairwise.complete.obs", method =
"Pearson")

> dim(cor.matrix)
[1] 178 178

> cor.matrix[1:5,1:5]
          1          2         3            4            5
1 1.0000000  0.7494842 0.5066551  0.7244043066  0.1850897291
2 0.7494842  1.0000000 0.4041662  0.6896539740 -0.1066822182
3 0.5066551  0.4041662 1.0000000  0.5985843958  0.1520360593
4 0.7244043  0.6896540 0.5985844  1.0000000000 -0.0003942683
5 0.1850897 -0.1066822 0.1520361 -0.0003942683  1.0000000000
```

We transpose the `wine.mat` matrix and pass it to the `cor` function. In the transposed matrix, our output will be the similarity between the different wines.

The `cor.matrix` matrix is the similarity matrix, which shows how closely related items are. The values range from -1 for perfect negative correlation, when two items have attributes that move in opposite directions, and +1 for perfect positive correlation, when attributes for the two items move in the same direction. For example, in row 1, wine 1 is more similar to wine 2 than wine 3. The diagonal values will be +1, as we are comparing a wine to itself.

Let's do a small recommendation test:

```
> user.view <- wine.features.scaled[3,]

> user.view
           V2          V3        V4         V5         V6        V7        V8
V9      V10        V11
3 0.1963252 0.02117152 1.106214 -0.2679823 0.08810981 0.8067217 1.212114
-0.497005 2.129959 0.2682629
          V12        V13       V14
3 0.3174085 0.7863692 1.391224
```

Let's a say a particular user is either tasting or looking at the properties of wine 3. We want to recommend him wines similar to wine 3.

Let's do the recommendation:

```
> sim.items <- cor.matrix[3,]

> sim.items
         1            2            3            4            5            6
 7            8            9
 0.50665507   0.40416617   1.00000000   0.59858440   0.15203606   0.54025182
0.57579895   0.18210803   0.42398729
        10           11           12           13           14           15
16           17           18
 0.55472235   0.66895949   0.40555308   0.61365843   0.57899194   0.73254986
0.36166695   0.44423273   0.28583467
        19           20           21           22           23           24
25           26           27
 0.49034236   0.44071794   0.37793495   0.45685238   0.48065399   0.52503055
0.41103595   0.04497370   0.56095748
        28           29           30           31           32           33
34           35           36
 0.38265553   0.36399501   0.53896624   0.70081585   0.61082768   0.37118102
-0.08388356   0.41537403   0.57819928
        37           38           39           40           41           42
43           44           45
 0.33457904   0.50516170   0.34839907   0.34398394   0.52878458   0.17497055
0.63598084   0.10647749   0.54740222
        46           47           48           49           50           51
52           53           54
-0.02744663   0.48876356   0.59627672   0.68698418   0.48261764   0.76062564
0.77192733   0.50767052   0.41555689.....
```

We look at the third row in our similarity matrix. We know that the similarity matrix has stored all the item similarities. So the third row gives us the similarity score between wine 3 and all the other wines. The preceding results are truncated.

We want to find the closest match:

```
> sim.items.sorted <- sort(sim.items, decreasing = TRUE)

> sim.items.sorted[1:5]
        3          52          51          85          15
1.0000000   0.7719273   0.7606256   0.7475886   0.7325499
>
```

First, we sort row 3 in decreasing order, so we have all the items close to wine 3 popping to the front. Then we pull out the top five matches. Great--we want to recommend wines 52, 51, 85, and 15 to this user. We ignore the first recommendation as it will be the same item we are searching for. In this case, the first element will be wine 3 with a similarity score of 1.0.

Let's look at the properties of wine 3 and the top five matches to confirm our recommendation:

```
> rbind(wine.data[3,]
+ ,wine.data[52,]
+ ,wine.data[51,]
+ ,wine.data[85,]
+ ,wine.data[15,]
+ )
     V1    V2   V3   V4   V5   V6   V7   V8   V9  V10  V11  V12  V13  V14
1:    1 13.16 2.36 2.67 18.6 101 2.80 3.24 0.30 2.81 5.68 1.03 3.17 1185
2:    1 13.83 1.65 2.60 17.2  94 2.45 2.99 0.22 2.29 5.60 1.24 3.37 1265
3:    1 13.05 1.73 2.04 12.4  92 2.72 3.27 0.17 2.91 7.20 1.12 2.91 1150
4:    2 11.84 0.89 2.58 18.0  94 2.20 2.21 0.22 2.35 3.05 0.79 3.08  520
5:    1 14.38 1.87 2.38 12.0 102 3.30 3.64 0.29 2.96 7.50 1.20 3.00 1547
>
```

Great—you can see that the wine properties in our recommendation are close to the properties of wine 3.

Hopefully, this explains the concept of content-based recommendation. Without any information about the user, based on the product he was browsing, we were able to make recommendations.

News aggregator use case and data

We have 1,000 news articles from different publishers. Each article belongs to a different category: technical, entertainment, and others. Our case is to alleviate the cold start problem faced by our customers. Simply put, what do we recommend to a customer when we don't have any information about his preferences? We are either looking at the customer for the first time or we don't have any mechanism set up yet to capture customer interaction with our products/items.

This data is a subset of the news aggregator dataset from https://archive.ics.uci.edu/ml/datasets/News+Aggregator.

A subset of the data is stored in a `csv` file.

Let's quickly look at the data provided:

```
> library(tidyverse)
> library(tidytext)
> library(tm)
> library(slam)
>
>
> cnames <- c('ID' , 'TITLE' , 'URL' ,
+             'PUBLISHER' , 'CATEGORY' ,
+             'STORY' , 'HOSTNAME' ,'TIMESTAMP')
>
> data <- read_tsv('newsCorpus.csv',
+                   col_names = cnames,
+                   col_types = cols(
+                   ID = col_integer(),
+                   TITLE = col_character(),
+                   URL = col_character(),
+                   PUBLISHER = col_character(),
+                   CATEGORY = col_character(),
+                   STORY = col_character(),
+                   HOSTNAME = col_character(),
+                   TIMESTAMP = col_double()
+                   )
+                   )
>
>
> head(data)
# A tibble: 6 x 8
      ID                                                     TITLE
   <int>                                                     <chr>
1 273675        More iWatch release hints, HealthKit lays groundwork
2 356956      Burger King debuts Proud Whopper to support LGBT rights
3 143853        A-Sides and B-Sides: Record Store Day Lives On
4 376630                       Smallpox virus found on NIH campus
5 160274 iPhone 6 Specs Leak: Curved Glass Display; Q3 Release Date
6 273554                    New Valve VR headset crops up in testing
# ... with 6 more variables: URL <chr>, PUBLISHER <chr>, CATEGORY <chr>,
STORY <chr>, HOSTNAME <chr>,
#    TIMESTAMP <dbl>
```

Every article has the following columns:

- ID: A unique identifier
- TITLE: The title of the article (free text)
- URL: The article's URL
- PUBLISHER: Publisher of the article
- CATEGORY: Some categorization under which the articles are grouped
- STORY: An ID for the group of stories the article belongs to
- HOSTNAME: Hostname of the URL
- TIMESTAMP: Timestamp published

We use the cnames vector to define these headings as we read the file using the read_tsv function. Further inside read_tsv, while defining the column types, we also specify the variable type for each of these columns.

The following are some distinct publishers and categories:

```
> data %>% group_by(PUBLISHER) %>% summarise()

# A tibble: 2,991 x 1
                     PUBLISHER
                         <chr>
 1               1011now
 2                10News
 3                  10TV
 4           123Jump.com
 5        12NewsNow.Com
 6            13WHAM-TV
 7      13abc Action News
 8  14 News WFIE Evansville
 9         "24\\/7 Wall St."
10       "2DayFM \\(blog\\)"
# ... with 2,981 more rows

> data %>% group_by(CATEGORY) %>% summarise()
# A tibble: 4 x 1
  CATEGORY
     <chr>
 1       b
 2       e
 3       m
 4       t
>
```

There are four categories and around 2,900 publishers.

Let's look a little closer at our publishers:

```
> publisher.count <- data.frame(data %>% group_by(PUBLISHER) %>%
summarise(ct =n()))

> head(publisher.count)
      PUBLISHER ct
1        1011now  1
2         10News  4
3           10TV  2
4    123Jump.com  1
5 12NewsNow.Com   3
6       13WHAM-TV  3

> dim(publisher.count)
[1] 2991     2

> dim(publisher.count[publisher.count$ct <= 10,])
[1] 2820     2
```

We first find the number of articles under each publisher. Looks like a lot of publishers have very few articles. Let's validate it to see the number of publishers with less than 10 articles. We can see 2,820 publishers, out of 2,991, have less than ten articles.

Let's get the top 100 publishers by looking at the number of articles they have published:

```
> publisher.top <- head(publisher.count[order(-publisher.count$ct),],100)

> head(publisher.top)
               PUBLISHER ct
1937              Reuters 90
309           Businessweek 58
1548               NASDAQ 49
495    Contactmusic.com 48
540          Daily Mail 47
882          GlobalPost 47
>
```

We can see that Reuters tops the list. We have retained only the articles from the top 100 publishers list for our exercise. Data frame publisher.top has the top 100 publishers.

For our top 100 publishers, let's now get their articles and other information:

```
> data.subset <- inner_join(publisher.top, data)
Joining, by = "PUBLISHER"

> head(data.subset)
  PUBLISHER ct      ID
TITLE
1   Reuters 90   38081           PRECIOUS-Gold ticks lower, US dollar holds
near peak
2   Reuters 90  306465              UKs FTSE rallies as Rolls-Royce races
higher
3   Reuters 90  371436 US economic growth to continue at modest pace - Feds
Lacker
4   Reuters 90  410152              Traders pare bets on earlier 2015 Fed
rate hike
5   Reuters 90  180407           FOREX-Dollar slides broadly, bullish data
helps euro
6   Reuters 90  311113 Fitch Publishes Sector Credit Factors for Japanese
Insurers
URL
1
http://in.reuters.com/article/2014/03/24/markets-precious-idINL4N0ML03U2014
0324
2
http://www.reuters.com/article/2014/06/19/markets-britain-stocks-idUSL6N0P0
1DM20140619
3
http://in.reuters.com/article/2014/07/08/usa-fed-idINW1N0OF00M20140708
4
http://www.reuters.com/article/2014/08/01/us-usa-fed-futures-idUSKBN0G144U2
0140801
5
http://in.reuters.com/article/2014/05/06/markets-forex-idINL6N0NS25P2014050
6
6
http://in.reuters.com/article/2014/06/24/fitch-publishes-sector-credit-fact
ors-fo-idINFit69752320140624
  CATEGORY                  STORY             HOSTNAME      TIMESTAMP
1        b df099bV_5_nKjKMqxhiVh1yCmHe3M  in.reuters.com 1.395753e+12
2        b dShvKW1yRq_Z3pM1C1lhuwYEY5MvM www.reuters.com 1.403197e+12
3        b dNJB5f4GzH0jT1MeEyWcKVpMod5UM  in.reuters.com 1.404897e+12
4        b dunL-T5pNDVbTpMZnZ-3oAUK1KybM www.reuters.com 1.406926e+12
5        b d8DabtT1hPalvyMKxQ7tSGkTnN_9M  in.reuters.com 1.399369e+12
6        b d3tIMfB2mg-9MZM4G_jGTEiRV13jM  in.reuters.com 1.403634e+12
> dim(data.subset)
[1] 2638    9
>
```

We join our top 100 publishers data frame `publisher.top` with data, get all the details for our top 100 publishers. Our `data.subset` has a total of 2,638 articles.

Having looked at our data, let's now move on to design our recommendation engine.

Designing the content-based recommendation engine

To rewrite our customer requirements in plain English: When a customer browses a particular article, what other articles should we suggest to him?

Let's quickly recap how a content-based recommendation engine works. When a user is browsing a product or item, we need to provide recommendations to the user in the form of other products or items from our catalog. We can use the properties of the items to come up with the recommendations. Let's translate this to our use case.

Items in our case, are news articles.

The properties of a news article are as follows:

- Its content, stored in a text column
- The publisher--who published the article
- The category to which the article belongs

So when a user is browsing a particular news article, we need to give him other news articles as recommendations, based on:

- The text content of the article he is currently reading
- The publisher of this document
- The category to which this document belongs

We are going to introduce another feature. It is a calculated feature from the text field:

- **Polarity** of the document. Subjective text tends to have an opinion about a topic. The opinion can be positive, negative, or neutral. A polarity score is a real number which captures these opinions. Polarity identification algorithms use text mining to get the document opinion. We are going to use one such algorithm to get the polarity of our texts.

For the `wine` example in the last section, we used the pearson coefficient as a similarity measure. Unlike the `wine` example, we need multiple similarity measures for this use case:

- **Cosine distance**/similarity for comparing words in two documents
- For the polarity, a **Manhattan distance** measure
- For the publisher and category, **Jaccard's distance**

We will explain these distance measures as we program them in R. Hopefully this gave you a good overview of our problem statement. Let's move on to the design of our content-based recommendation engine.

We are going to design our content-based recommendation engine in three steps, as shown in the following diagram:

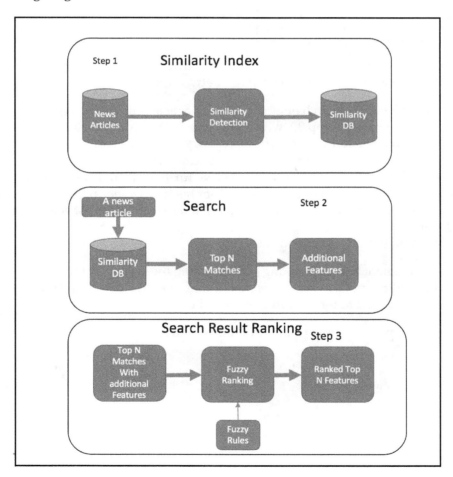

In step 1, we will create a similarity index. Think of this index as a matrix, with rows and columns as the articles and the cell value storing the similarity between the articles. The diagonal values of this matrix will be one. The similarity score is a value between zero and one. A cell value of 1.0 indicates that the two articles are an exact replica of each other.

Let's look at an example matrix:

Article ID / Article ID	1	2	3	...	N
1	1	0.2	0	...	0.8
2	0.4	1	0	...	0
3	0.1	0	1	...	0.1
....	...	...	...	...	...
N	...	...	...	...	...

Look at the first row; article 1 is closer to article N when compared to article 2. In our use case, the cell value will be the cosine similarity between two documents.

In step 2, we have a simple search engine. Given an article, this engine will first retrieve the top N articles, in our case the top 30, which are close to the given article, based on the similarity matrix developed in the previous step. Say we are searching for article number 2, then row 2 of this matrix will be accessed. After sorting the content of the row, the top 30 will be given as the match. For those 30 articles, we further calculate more features the polarity of the articles. After that, we calculate Manhattan distance between the polarity value of the given article and all the other articles in our search results. We find the Jaccard's distance between the article we are searching for and all the other articles in the search list based on the publisher and category.

In step 3, we implement a fuzzy ranking engine. Using the similarity score from step 1, Jaccard's score, and the polarity scores, we use a fuzzy engine to rank the top 30 matches. The results are presented to the user in this ranked order.

Let's proceed to step 1, building a similarity index/matrix.

Building a similarity index

Our first step is to build a similarity index. We are going to leverage the **bag-of-words** representation of text, and then use the **vector space model** to create the similarity index.

Look at the overview diagram of this step:

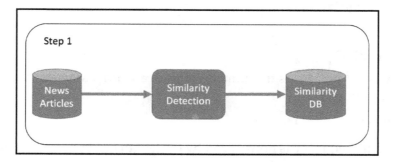

Bag-of-words

In bag-of-words representation, every document is represented as a collection of words present in the document, hence the name bag-of-words. The order in which the words occur are not considered in bag of words approach. A good way to organize these bag-of-words is using a matrix representation. Let's say we have 100 documents (also called a corpus). In order to build such a matrix, we first make a list of all the unique words present in those 100 documents. This is called the vocabulary of our text corpus. Say we have 5,000 unique words. Our matrix is now a 100 x 5,000 dimension, where the rows are the document and in the column, we have the words from our vocabulary. Such a matrix is called a document term matrix.

Consider the following example. Here we have a corpus of sentences:

1. **Sentence 1**: Dog chased cat
2. **Sentence 2**: Dog hates cat

When represented as a document term matrix, it looks like the following:

Document/word	hates	dog	chased	cat
Sentence 1	0	1	1	1
Sentence 2	1	1	0	1

We have represented each sentence as a vector here. We can now leverage the vector space model to find the similarity between these two sentences. Now let's look at the cell values of this matrix.

The example matrix is a binary matrix. A cell value of 1 indicates the presence of a word in a document and 0 indicates absence. We can have other weighting schemes. Let's look at some weighting schemes.

Term frequency

Term frequency, or `tf(w, d)`, is the number of times a word `w` appears in the document `d`. If we look at our example:

```
tf(dog, sentence 1) = 1
```

Sometimes the term frequency is normalized by the length of the document. If we normalize it in our example case, then:

```
tf(dog, sentence) = 1/3
```

The denominator is the number of words in sentence 1.

Document frequency

Document frequency or `df(w)` is the number of documents in the corpus in which this word occurs. In our example, `df(dog) = 2`, dog appears in both the sentences.

Inverse document frequency (IDF)

Let's say we have N documents in our corpus, then the inverse document frequency is defined as:

$$IDF(w) = log(\frac{N}{df(w)})$$

Rare words tend to have high IDFs. If we look at the equation above and ignore the log function, IDF is the total number of documents divided by the number of documents that the word is in. In effect, it is measuring how good the word is at identifying this document. If the word is only used in a small number of documents, then the denominator will be low, therefore the overall value will be high. The log is just used to normalize the result.

TFIDF

This is the product of a term frequency and inverse document frequency:

$$tfidf(w, d) = tf(w, d)idf(w)$$

TFIDF is a very popular weighting metric used in text mining.

To begin with, we separate our data into two data frames:

```
> title.df <- data.subset[,c('ID','TITLE')]
> others.df <- data.subset[,c('ID','PUBLISHER','CATEGORY')]
```

title.df stores the title and the article ID. others.df stores the article ID, publisher, and category.

We will be using the tm package in R to work with our text data:

```
library(tm)
title.reader <- readTabular(mapping=list(content="TITLE", id="ID"))
corpus <- Corpus(DataframeSource(title.df),
readerControl=list(reader=title.reader))
```

We create a data frame reader using readTabular. Next, we use the Corpus function to create our text corpus. To Corpus, we pass our title.df data frame, and the title.reader data frame reader.

Our next step is to do some processing of the text data:

```
> getTransformations()
[1] "removeNumbers"      "removePunctuation" "removeWords"
"stemDocument"       "stripWhitespace"
>
```

Calling getTransformation shows us the list of available functions that can be used to transform the text:

```
corpus <- tm_map(corpus, removePunctuation)
corpus <- tm_map(corpus, removeNumbers)
corpus <- tm_map(corpus, stripWhitespace)

corpus <- tm_map(corpus, content_transformer(tolower))
corpus <- tm_map(corpus, removeWords, stopwords("english"))
```

We remove punctuation, numbers, unnecessary white spaces, and stop words from our articles. Finally, we convert our text to lowercase.

Punctuation, numbers, and whitespace may not be a good feature to distinguish one article from another. Hence, we remove them.

Let's look at the list of `stopwords("english")` in the `tm` package:

```
stopwords("english")

   [1] "i"          "me"          "my"          "myself"      "we"
"our"          "ours"
   [8] "ourselves"  "you"         "your"        "yours"       "yourself"
"yourselves"   "he"
  [15] "him"        "his"         "himself"     "she"         "her"
"hers"         "herself"
  [22] "it"         "its"         "itself"      "they"        "them"
"their"        "theirs"
  [29] "themselves" "what"        "which"       "who"         "whom"
"this"         "that"
  [36] "these"      "those"       "am"          "is"          "are"
"was"          "were"
  [43] "be"         "been"        "being"       "have"        "has"
"had"          "having"
  [50] "do"         "does"        "did"         "doing"       "would"
"should"       "could"
  [57] "ought"      "i'm"         "you're"      "he's"        "she's"
"it's"         "we're"
  [64] "they're"    "i've"        "you've"      "we've"       "they've"
"i'd"          "you'd"
  [71] "he'd"       "she'd"       "we'd"        "they'd"      "i'll"
"you'll"       "he'll"
  [78] "she'll"     "we'll"       "they'll"     "isn't"       "aren't"
"wasn't"       "weren't"
  [85] "hasn't"     "haven't"     "hadn't"      "doesn't"     "don't"
"didn't"       "won't"
```

These words will be present again in most of the English text, no matter what the content is. They cannot act as a good feature to distinguish our articles. Hence, we remove such words.

We want our algorithms to treat the words `"dog"` and `"Dog"` the same way. Hence, we bring them to lowercase.

Furthermore, we could apply stemming to our words. Stemming reduces the word to its root form.

Finally, let's proceed to build our document term matrix:

```
> dtm <- DocumentTermMatrix(corpus, control=list(wordlenth = c(3,10)
,weighting = "weightTfIdf"))
> dtm
<<DocumentTermMatrix (documents: 2638, terms: 6628)>>
Non-/sparse entries: 18317/17466347
Sparsity           : 100%
Maximal term length: 21

> inspect(dtm[1:5,10:15])
<<DocumentTermMatrix (documents: 5, terms: 6)>>
Non-/sparse entries: 0/30
Sparsity           : 100%
Maximal term length: 9
Sample             :
        Terms
Docs     abbey abbvie abc abcs abdul abenomics
  180407     0      0   0    0     0         0
  306465     0      0   0    0     0         0
  371436     0      0   0    0     0         0
  38081      0      0   0    0     0         0
  410152     0      0   0    0     0         0
>
```

We use the `DocumentTermMatrix` function to create our matrix. We pass our text corpus and also pass a list to the parameter `control`. Inside the list, we say that we are interested only in words with length, so the number of characters between 3 and 10. For our cell values in our matrix, we want them to be TFIDF.

We can inspect the created document term matrix by calling the `inspect` function.

Having created a document term matrix, let's create the cosine distance between the articles:

```
sim.score <- tcrossprod_simple_triplet_matrix(dtm)/(sqrt( row_sums(dtm^2)
%*% t(row_sums(dtm^2)) ))
```

In the preceding code, we take a document term matrix and return a document matrix. We will be calling this a similarity matrix going forward. The cell values of this matrix correspond to the cosine similarity between two documents. The previous line of code implements this cosine similarity.

The cosine similarity between two vectors A and B of length n is given as:

$$C = \frac{\sum_{i=1}^{n} A_i B_i}{\sqrt{\sum_{i=1}^{n} A_i^2} \cdot \sqrt{\sum_{i=1}^{n} B_i^2}}$$

Look at the numerator of this equation. It's the inner product of both the vectors. In a vector space model, the inner product of two vectors gives the similarity between them. We divide this inner product by the l2 norm of the those individual vector. This makes the score bounded between -1 and 1. The similarity is hence a number between -1 and 1, where -1 indicates that two documents are completely different from each other. If both the vectors have non-negative numbers, then the similarity score is bounded between 0 and 1.

Why cosine similarity?

In the previous chapters we had leveraged pearson coefficient to find similarity. Why don't we use the same for text documents? Cosine similarity is non-invariant to changes in the magnitude of values. That is, if in one of the vectors we increase the value of its members, the cosine similarity will change. We need this behavior, as the vector contains the `tfidf` scores. A change in `tfidf` score means there is a change in the document. The document is no longer the same one we had before. Pearson coefficient is invariant to shifts in the vector. Hence for comparing similarities between documents, we use cosine as the metric.

Now, in our document term matrix, we have a row for each article. The columns are again the article IDs.

Let's peek into our similarity matrix:

```
> sim.score[1:10,1:10]
        Docs
Docs            38081 306465 371436 410152 180407 311113 263442 171310
116144      70584
   38081  1.0000000        0      0      0      0      0      0      0
0.1428571 0.1543033
  306465  0.0000000        1      0      0      0      0      0      0
0.0000000 0.0000000
  371436  0.0000000        0      1      0      0      0      0      0
0.0000000 0.0000000
  410152  0.0000000        0      0      1      0      0      0      0
```

```
0.0000000  0.0000000
   180407  0.0000000      0      0      0      1      0      0      0
0.0000000  0.0000000
   311113  0.0000000      0      0      0      0      1      0      0
0.0000000  0.0000000
   263442  0.0000000      0      0      0      0      0      1      0
0.0000000  0.0000000
   171310  0.0000000      0      0      0      0      0      0      1
0.0000000  0.0000000
   116144  0.1428571      0      0      0      0      0      0      0
1.0000000  0.0000000
    70584  0.1543033      0      0      0      0      0      0      0
0.0000000  1.0000000
```

Let's look at row 1, document number 38081. Looks like it's not close, with a lot of documents displayed there, except for 116144.

To learn more about the tm package, creating term document matrixes from different sources and other text manipulation functions, refer to the tm manual at https://cran.r-project.org/web/packages/tm/tm.pdf. To learn more about cosine similarity, refer to https://en.wikipedia.org/wiki/Cosine_similarity.

Searching

Having created our similarity matrix, we can leverage that matrix to find a match for any given document. Let's see how to leverage this matrix to perform the search function in this section.

Once again, the block diagram of step 2 is presented as follows:

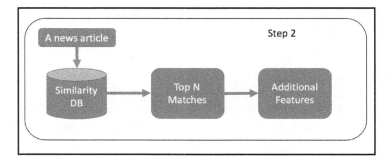

We will be using the `sim.score` created in the previous step to perform the search.

Let's say we want to find similar articles to article `38081`:

```
> match.docs <- sim.score["38081",]
> match.docs
    38081      306465      371436      410152      180407      311113      263442
171310      116144       70584
1.0000000  0.0000000  0.0000000  0.0000000  0.0000000  0.0000000  0.0000000
0.0000000  0.1428571  0.1543033
   228128      128325      263795      230506      326375      136203      166993
158814      417839      220118
0.0000000  0.0000000  0.0000000  0.1690309  0.0000000  0.0000000  0.0000000
0.1259882  0.0000000  0.0000000
   276048      307643       38069      349240      192743      131763      156247
16642      354055      410578
0.1336306  0.0000000  0.3779645  0.0000000  0.0000000  0.0000000  0.0000000
0.0000000  0.0000000  0.0000000
   196045      393546       35625      370930       41315       35049      104981
276610      196153      367915
0.0000000  0.0000000  0.0000000  0.0000000  0.0000000  0.0000000  0.0000000
0.0000000  0.0000000  0.0000000
```

We go to our `match.doc` similarity matrix and pick up row `38081`. Now, this row has all the other articles and their similarity scores.

Let's now take this row and make a data frame:

```
> match.df <- data.frame(ID = names(match.docs), cosine = match.docs,
stringsAsFactors=FALSE)

> match.df$ID <- as.integer(match.df$ID)
> head(match.df)
            ID cosine
38081    38081      1
306465  306465      0
371436  371436      0
410152  410152      0
180407  180407      0
311113  311113      0
```

Our `match.df` data frame now contains all the matching documents for `38081` and their cosine scores. No wonder the first row is `38081`; it has to match itself perfectly.

But as we said before, we are going to recommend only the top 30 matches:

```
> match.refined<-head(match.df[order(-match.df$cosine),],30)
> head(match.refined)
            ID    cosine
38081    38081 1.0000000
38069    38069 0.3779645
231136 231136 0.2672612
334088 334088 0.2672612
276011 276011 0.2519763
394401 394401 0.2390457
>
```

So let's order our `match.df` data frame in descending order of cosine similarity and extract the top 30 matches using the `head` function.

Now that we have the matching documents, we need to present them in a ranked order. In order to rank the results, we are going to calculate some additional measures and use fuzzy logic to get the final ranking score.

Before we go ahead and calculate the additional measures, let's merge `title.df` and `other.df` with `match.refined`:

```
> match.refined <- inner_join(match.refined, title.df)
Joining, by = "ID"
> match.refined <- inner_join(match.refined, others.df)
Joining, by = "ID"

> head(match.refined)

        ID    cosine
TITLE
1   38081 1.0000000                          PRECIOUS-Gold ticks lower,
US dollar holds near peak
2   38069 0.3779645 PRECIOUS-Bullion drops nearly 1 pct on dollar, palladium
holds near 2-1/2-yr high
3 231136 0.2672612                       Dollar steady near 3-1/2 month
lows vs. yen, Aussie weaker
4 334088 0.2672612                        Canadian dollar falls amid
lower than expected GDP data
5 276011 0.2519763                     Gold holds near four-month low as
ECB move on rates awaited
6 394401 0.2390457             Dollar Tree Will Buy Competitor
Family Dollar For $8.5 Billion
            PUBLISHER CATEGORY
1            Reuters         b
2            Reuters         b
```

```
3              NASDAQ        b
4            CTV News        b
5  Business Standard         b
6      The Inquisitr         b
```

We have all the information and the cosine similarity in one data frame now.

Polarity scores

We are going to leverage the `sentimentr` R package to learn the sentiments of the articles we have collected.

Let's look at how to score using the `sentiment` function :

```
> sentiment.score <- sentiment(match.refined$TITLE)
> head(sentiment.score)
   element_id sentence_id word_count    sentiment
1:          1           1          8   0.00000000
2:          2           1         11   0.00000000
3:          3           1          9  -0.13333333
4:          4           1          9  -0.08333333
5:          5           1         11   0.07537784
6:          6           1          9   0.00000000
>
```

The `sentiment` function in `sentimentr` calculates a score between -1 and 1 for each of the articles. In fact, if a text has multiple sentences, it will calculate the score for each sentence. A score of -1 indicates that the sentence has a very negative polarity. A score of 1 means that the sentence is very positive. A score of 0 refers to the neutral nature of the sentence.

However, we need the score at an article level and not at a sentence level, so we can take an average value of the score across all the sentences in a text.

Calculate the average value of the sentiment scores for each article:

```
> sentiment.score <- sentiment.score %>% group_by(element_id) %>%
+   summarise(sentiment = mean(sentiment))
> head(sentiment.score)
# A tibble: 6 x 2
  element_id    sentiment
       <int>        <dbl>
1          1   0.00000000
2          2   0.00000000
3          3  -0.13333333
4          4  -0.08333333
5          5   0.07537784
6          6   0.00000000
```

Here, the `element_id` refers to the individual article. By grouping `element_id` and calculating the average, we can get the sentiment score at an article level. We now have the scores for each article.

Let's update the `match.refined` data frame with the polarity scores:

```
> match.refined$polarity <- sentiment.score$sentiment
> head(match.refined)
      ID    cosine
TITLE
1  38081 1.0000000                          PRECIOUS-Gold ticks lower,
US dollar holds near peak
2  38069 0.3779645 PRECIOUS-Bullion drops nearly 1 pct on dollar, palladium
holds near 2-1/2-yr high
3 231136 0.2672612                     Dollar steady near 3-1/2 month
lows vs. yen, Aussie weaker
4 334088 0.2672612                     Canadian dollar falls amid
lower than expected GDP data
5 276011 0.2519763                     Gold holds near four-month low as
ECB move on rates awaited
6 394401 0.2390457               Dollar Tree Will Buy Competitor
Family Dollar For $8.5 Billion
           PUBLISHER CATEGORY    polarity
1            Reuters         b  0.00000000
2            Reuters         b  0.00000000
3             NASDAQ         b -0.13333333
4           CTV News         b -0.08333333
5 Business Standard         b  0.07537784
6      The Inquisitr         b  0.00000000
```

Before we move on, let's spend some time understanding the inner workings of our dictionary-based `sentiment` method. The `sentiment` function utilizes a sentiment lexicon (Jockers, 2017) from the lexicon package. It preprocesses the given text as follows:

- Paragraphs are split into sentences
- Sentences are split into words
- All punctuation is removed except commas, semicolons, and colons
- Finally, words are stored as tuples, for example, $w\_\{5,2,3\}$ means the third word in the second sentence of the fifth paragraph

Each word is looked up in the lexicon; positive and negative words are tagged with +1 and -1 respectively. Let's call the words which have received a score the polarized words. Not all words receive a score. Only those found in the lexicons receive a score. We can pass a customer lexicon through the `polarity_dt` parameter to the sentiment function. For each of the polarized words, *n* words before them and *n* words after them are considered, and together they are called **polarized context clusters**. The parameter n can be set by the user. The words in the polarized context cluster can be tagged as either of the following:

- neutral
- negator
- amplifier
- de-amplifier
- adversative conjunctions

A dictionary of these words can be passed through `parameter valence_shifter_dt`. Looking up this dictionary, the neighboring words can be tagged. The weights for these are passed through the `amplifier.weight` and `adversative.weight` parameters. Each polarized word is weighted now based on `polarity_dt`, and also weighted based on the number of valence shifters/words surrounding it, which are tagged either as amplifiers or adversative conjunctions. Neutrally tagged weights have no weights. For more details about weight and scoring refer to R function (`help`) for `sentiment` function.

Jaccard's distance

While ranking the matched articles, we want to also include the category and publisher columns.

Let's proceed to include those columns:

```
target.publisher <- match.refined[1,]$PUBLISHER
target.category <- match.refined[1,]$CATEGORY
target.polarity <- match.refined[1,]$polarity

target.title <- match.refined[1,]$TITLE
```

We need the publisher, category, and the sentiment details of the document we are searching for. Fortunately, the first row of our `match.refined` data frame stores all the details related to `38081`. We retrieve those values from there.

For the rest of the articles, we need to find out if they match the publisher and category of document `38081`:

```
match.refined$is.publisher <- match.refined$PUBLISHER == target.publisher
match.refined$is.publisher <- as.numeric(match.refined$is.publisher)
```

Now we can go into `match.refined` and create a new column called `is.publisher`, a Boolean column to say if the article's publisher is same as the publisher for the one we are searching for.

Now for the category:

```
match.refined$is.category <- match.refined$CATEGORY == target.category
match.refined$is.category <- as.numeric(match.refined$is.category)
```

Repeat the same for the category. We have created a new column called `is.category` to store the category match.

With the two new columns, we can calculate the Jaccard's distance between document `38081` and all the other documents in the `match.refined` data frame, as shown in the following code block:

```
match.refined$jaccard <- (match.refined$is.publisher +
match.refined$is.category)/2
```

Jaccards distance/index

The Jaccard index measures the similarity between two sets, and is a ratio of the size of the intersection and the size of the union of the participating sets. Here we have only have two elements, one for publisher and one for category, so our union is 2. The numerator, by adding the two Boolean variable, we get the intersection.

Finally, we also calculate the absolute difference (Manhattan distance) in the polarity values between the articles in the search results and our search article. We do a min/max normalization of the difference score as follows:

```
match.refined$polaritydiff <- abs(target.polarity -
match.refined$polarity$sentiment)

range01 <- function(x){(x-min(x))/(max(x)-min(x))}
match.refined$polaritydiff <- range01(unlist(match.refined$polaritydiff))
```

We proceed to do some cleaning:

```
> head(match.refined)
      ID      cosine
TITLE
1 419826 1.0000000                         Report: iWatch Expected at
Sept. 9 iPhone Event
2 137901 0.5000000            Local shops stocked with limited-
edition LPs for event
3 113526 0.5000000                                   Blood Moon
Event Will Begin Tonight
4 202272 0.5000000 Kim Kardashian attends USC SHOAH Foundation event
dedicated to Armenian  ...
5 420093 0.5000000  Apple iPad Air 2 To House 2 GB Of RAM; Apple iWatch
Likely To Function  ...
6 273675 0.4082483                     More iWatch release hints,
HealthKit lays groundwork
                   PUBLISHER CATEGORY polarity.element_id
polarity.sentence_id polarity.word_count
1                    PC Magazine        t                    1
1                   7
2        Huntington Herald Dispatch     e                    2
1                   8
3                 Design \\& Trend      t                    3
1                   6
4                  Armenpress.am        e                    4
1                  10
5 International Business Times AU        t                    5
1                  13
6                Product Reviews        t                    6
1                   7
   polarity.sentiment is.publisher is.category jaccard polaritydiff
1        0.00000000            1             1      1.0    0.00000000
2        0.00000000            0             0      0.0    0.00000000
3        0.00000000            0             1      0.5    0.00000000
4        0.28460499            0             0      0.0    0.17400235
5       -0.06933752            0             1      0.5    0.04239171
6        0.15118579            0             1      0.5    0.09243226
> match.refined$is.publisher = NULL
> match.refined$is.category = NULL
> match.refined$polarity = NULL
> match.refined$sentiment = NULL
> head(match.refined)
      ID      cosine
TITLE
1 419826 1.0000000                         Report: iWatch Expected at
Sept. 9 iPhone Event
2 137901 0.5000000            Local shops stocked with limited-
```

```
edition LPs for event
3 113526 0.5000000                                      Blood Moon
Event Will Begin Tonight
4 202272 0.5000000 Kim Kardashian attends USC SHOAH Foundation event
dedicated to Armenian  ...
5 420093 0.5000000  Apple iPad Air 2 To House 2 GB Of RAM; Apple iWatch
Likely To Function  ...
6 273675 0.4082483                        More iWatch release hints,
HealthKit lays groundwork
                      PUBLISHER CATEGORY jaccard polaritydiff
1                    PC Magazine        t     1.0  0.00000000
2       Huntington Herald Dispatch     e     0.0  0.00000000
3              Design \\& Trend         t     0.5  0.00000000
4                   Armenpress.am      e     0.0  0.17400235
5 International Business Times AU       t     0.5  0.04239171
6              Product Reviews          t     0.5  0.09243226
```

We remove some of the unwanted fields from the `match.refined` data frame. Finally, we have the ID, cosine distance, title, publisher, category, Jaccard score, and the polarity difference.

The last step is ranking these results.

Ranking search results

In the previous step, we finalized our top 30 results. In this step, we will be doing the ranking of the search results:

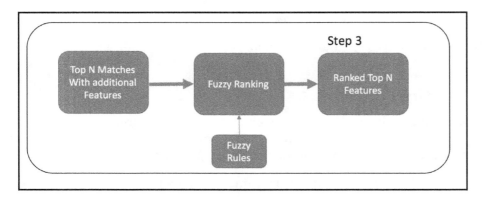

We need to perform our ranking based on the following metrics we have calculated:

- Cosine similarity
- Jaccard index
- Polarity difference

A standard way of doing this would be to come up with another score, which is a linear combination of the preceding three scores. We use that final score to sort the results.

However, we will leverage fuzzy logic programming to do the search result ranking.

Fuzzy logic

A detailed discussion on fuzzy logic is beyond the scope of this book. A short tutorial on fuzzy logic, `http://cs.bilkent.edu.tr/~zeynep/files/short_fuzzy_logic_tutorial.pdf`

We will give a short introduction here. Let us use an example from *Artificial Intelligence: A Guide to Intelligent Systems* book by Michael Negnevistky. Thanks to the article from `https://vpetro.io/`

- **Problem statement**: Estimate the level of risk involved in a software engineering project
- **Input**: Project funding and project staffing
- **Output**: Risk

Fuzzy logic programming works in three steps.

Let us explain each step using the above example.

Fuzzification

Fuzzification is the process where we convert our input and output to linguistic variables using ranges and membership functions.In this example, we want to convert our input, project funding and staffing, and output risk into linguistic variables:

- **Project funding**: Inadequate, marginal and adequate. These are the three linguistic variables we have for project funding. We will use a fuzzy cone membership function.
- **Project staffing**: Small and large, a fuzzy cone membership function
- **Risk:** low, normal and high.

We need some more defintions:

- **Linguistic Variable:** Variables whose values are words in a natural language. Let us take the example of Project Funding, the actual values of project funding in this example are percentages. So if we say the project funding is 50% then, 50% of the funding is still available. This 50% is now transalated to the linguistic variable, adequate, marginal or inadequate. The fuzzy system will use only these linguistc variables and not the original value.
- **Crisp Values:** The real values an input or output can take is a crisp value. For example, 50% is the crisp value Project funding can take.
- **Membership Function:** Its a function which defines how the crisp values are mapped to a membership value (degree of membership). These functions can be either linear or curved. For example,let us again take project funding,

Crisp input value for project funding is 60%

Membership function will translate this value into degree of membership for each of the linguistic variables. We will not show here the detail of how the membership function converts our crisp input values to linguistic variables, but will give a simple example to follow.

Let us say we are trying to evaluate the risk for the following crisp values,

Project funding = 35%

Project staffing = 60%

When we pass these values to the respective membership function we get the following results, Inadequate = 0.5, adequate = 0.0 and marginal = 0.2; similarly for project staffing we get small = 0.1 and large =0.7

The crisp input value for project funding 35%, cannot be represented by the linguistic variable adequate, hence membership value for adequate is 0.0. It does not belong completely to marginal linguistic variable, and hence we have 0.2 as the value.

Similarly 70% of project staffing has a high degree of membership with linguistic variable large, hence the value 0.7.

As you saw, fuzzification converts the crisp input values to fuzzy membership values to linguistic variables.

Defining the rules

After we define our linguistic variables for our input and output, we need to define the relationship between the input and output. This is where rules come to play. They are fuzzy rules as they deal with the linguistic variables and their values (degree of membership).

Rules define the interaction between our input variables to produce the output. Here we have three simple rules for our example:

1. If project funding is adequate or project staffing is small then risk is low.
2. If project funding is marginal and project staffing is large then risk is normal.
3. If project funding is inadequate then risk is high.

Evaluating the rules

If project funding is adequate or project staffing is small then risk is low.

This rule has an OR clause, its evaluated using UNION operator. Max operator in set is used to evaluate this rule. There are several other set operators such as ASUM or BSUM which can be used to evaluate the UNION (OR) operator.

Let us borrow the fuzzification results from the previous section. The fuzzification of project funding = adequate for crisp value 35% is 0.0. The fuzzification of project staffing = small for crisp value 60% is 0.1

Let us use the Max operator Maximum among them is taken as the results, hence the this rule evaluates to, Project Risk = low = 0.1

The next rule, If project funding is marginal and project staffing is large then risk is normal, has an AND and hence we use an intersection operator. Intersection operator can be handled using min, prod or bdif set operator.

The fuzzification of project funding = marginal for crisp value 35% is 0.2. The fuzzification of project staffing =large for crisp value 35% is 0.7. Let us use the min operator here. The minimum is 0.2, the rule evaluates to Project risk = normal = 0.2

Finally, the last rule, If project funding is inadequate then risk his high. We can directly say

Project Risk = high = 0.5, as this is the fuzzification value for project funding = inadequate for crisp value of 35%.

Now we need to combine these results. This process of evaluating the rules and combining them is called as inference.

We have, for project risk, low = 0.1, normal = 0.2, and high = 0.5. We will use these values to scale the membership function. The final decision plot is a summation of all these scaled values.

Let us look at the decision plot:

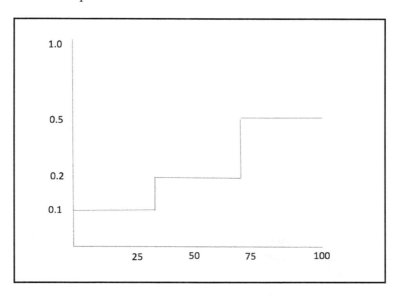

Defuzzification

In fuzzification, we converted the crisp values of our input to fuzzy degree of membership values for our linguistic variable. In defuzzification, we need to convert the degree of membership values for our output variable to its crisp value.

 Let us superimpose the membership function on top of the above decision plot. We have assumed a triangular membership function here. You can read more about triangular membership function and their importance in the paper why triangular memebership functions? http://www.sciencedirect.com/science/article/pii/0165011494900035

Decision plot with superimposed membership function:

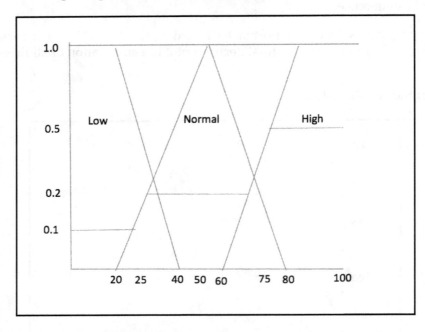

The most popular defuzzification method is the centroid method. It calculates the center of gravity for the area under the curve. The area under the green line represented in the graph. It is calculated as follows:

(0 + 10 + 20) * 0.1 accounts for the linguistic variable low.

(30 + 40 + 50 + 60) * 0.2 accounts for the linguistic variable normal.

(70 + 80 + 90 + 100) * 0.5 for the linguistic variable high.

Sum them all and divide by (0.1* 3+ 0.2 * 4 + 0.5 *4).

((0 + 10 + 20) * 0.1 + (30 + 40 + 50 + 60) * 0.2 + (70 + 80 + 90 + 100) * 0.5) / (0.1* 3+ 0.2 * 4 + 0.5 *4).

This is equal to 67.4.

Hence, we can conclude that the risk associated with the project is 67.4%.

Hopefully this gives an intuition about how to use fuzzy logic.

In our example, we want to convert our inputs are cosine, Jaccard and polarity score and our output is the ranking. We first convert them to linguistic variables. For example, let us take our cosine score:

- vlow = 0.2, indicating very low cosine score
- low = 0.4, low score
- medium = 0.6
- high =0.8

Then we define a `membership` function. The `membership` function is responsible for the fuzzy membership. Let us say we define a cone as our `membership` function with a radius of 0.2. There are no real mandates to choose the `membership` function. Refer to the membership plot appearing a little later in this chapter for fuzzy memberships. This is responsible for the fuzzification process. Let us say we pass our cosine score into this `membership` function it changes it to one of the linguistic values.

We follow the same process for polarity score and Jaccard's distance. Finally, we also define a final linguistic variable called ranking. This is our final ranking score or our output. Its defined in the same way as cosine, polarity, and Jaccards. It has a range and a `membership` function.

Having done the fuzzification process for our similarity scores, let us proceed to define the rules.

A simple rule can be as follows:

if cosine score = vlow, then ranking = low.

We can define more complex rules involving multiple linguistic variables. Refer to the code for different rules we have defined for this scenario. After all the rules are evaluated we can then proceed to inference process.

The last step is the defuzzification of the above result to a crisp value. We use the centroid method for defuzzification.

We will be using the `sets` R package for our fuzzy logic programming:

```
> library(sets, quietly = TRUE)

Attaching package: 'sets'

The following object is masked from 'package:dplyr':

    %>%

> sets_options("universe", seq(from = 0,
+                              to = 1, by = 0.1))
>
```

The first step is to set up our universe. We define the range of values and the granularity of the values we will be dealing with in our universe. Our cosine, Jaccard, and polarity are all normalized to have a value between zero and one. Hence, the range of our universe is set between zero and one.

The first step in fuzzy logic programming is to define the linguistic variables we will be dealing with:

```
variables <-
  set(cosine =
        fuzzy_partition(varnames =
                          c(vlow = 0.2, low = 0.4,
                            medium = 0.6, high = 0.8),
                        FUN = fuzzy_cone , radius = 0.2),
          jaccard =
          fuzzy_partition(varnames =
                            c(close = 1.0, halfway = 0.5,
                              far = 0.0),
                          FUN = fuzzy_cone , radius = 0.4),
        polarity =
        fuzzy_partition(varnames =
                          c(same = 0.0, similar = 0.3,close = 0.5,
                            away = 0.7),
                        FUN = fuzzy_cone , radius = 0.2),
        ranking =
        fuzzy_partition(varnames =
                          c(H = 1.0, MED = 0.7 , M = 0.5, L = 0.3),
                        FUN = fuzzy_cone , radius = 0.2
                        )
  )
```

For each variable, we define the various linguistic values and the fuzzy `membership` function. For example, for our linguistic variable cosine, the linguistic values include `vlow`, `low`, `medium`, and `high`. We define the `fuzzy_cone membership` function.

For this application, we have used a cone `membership` function throughout. There are other `membership` functions available.

Calling the R help for `fuzzy_cone`, the documentation will detail other available `membership` functions:

```
> help("fuzzy_cone")
```

We define the `jaccard` and `polarity` linguistic variables in the same way as `cosine`. The `ranking` lat linguistic variable defines the final score we need, which we can use to sort our results.

Based on the interaction between the linguistic variables `cosine`, `jaccard`, and `polarity`, the ranking linguistic variables are assigned different linguistic values. These interactions are defined as rules. Having defined the linguistic variables, the linguistic values, and the `membership` function, we proceed to write down our fuzzy rules:

```
rules <-
  set(
    ######### Low Ranking Rules ##################
    fuzzy_rule(cosine %is% vlow,
            ranking %is% L),
    fuzzy_rule(cosine %is% low || jaccard %is% far
            || polarity %is% away,
            ranking %is% L),
    fuzzy_rule(cosine %is% low || jaccard %is% halfway
            || polarity %is% away,
            ranking %is% L),

    fuzzy_rule(cosine %is% low || jaccard %is% halfway
            || polarity %is% close,
            ranking %is% L),
    fuzzy_rule(cosine %is% low || jaccard %is% halfway
            || polarity %is% similar,
            ranking %is% L),
    fuzzy_rule(cosine %is% low || jaccard %is% halfway
            || polarity %is% same,
            ranking %is% L),
    fuzzy_rule(cosine %is% medium || jaccard %is% far
            || polarity %is% away,
            ranking %is% L),
    ############## Medium Ranking Rules ################
```

```
      fuzzy_rule(cosine %is% low || jaccard %is% close
                || polarity %is% same,
                ranking %is% M),
      fuzzy_rule(cosine %is% low && jaccard %is% close
                && polarity %is% similar,
                ranking %is% M),
      ############## Median Ranking Rule ################
      fuzzy_rule(cosine %is% medium && jaccard %is% close
                && polarity %is% same,
                ranking %is% MED),
      fuzzy_rule(cosine %is% medium && jaccard %is% halfway
                && polarity %is% same,
                ranking %is% MED),
      fuzzy_rule(cosine %is% medium && jaccard %is% close
                && polarity %is% similar,
                ranking %is% MED),
      fuzzy_rule(cosine %is% medium && jaccard %is% halfway
                && polarity %is% similar,
                ranking %is% MED),
      ############## High Ranking Rule ###################
      fuzzy_rule(cosine %is% high,ranking %is% H)
    )
```

The rules define how the linguistic variables should be combined to make a decision. We have three groups of rules. Let's look at the first rule:

```
fuzzy_rule(cosine %is% vlow, ranking %is% L),
```

If the cosine linguistic value is `vlow`, the ranking is given as `L`, the lowest ranking. Similarly, each rule captures the interactions between the linguistic variables.

With the `rules` and linguistic `variables` defined, we can now put our complete fuzzy system together:

```
> ranking.system <- fuzzy_system(variables, rules)

> print(ranking.system)
A fuzzy system consisting of 4 variables and 14 rules.

variables:

jaccard(close, halfway, far)
polarity(same, similar, close, away)
ranking(H, MED, M, L)
cosine(vlow, low, medium, high)

rules:
```

```
cosine %is% low && jaccard %is% close && polarity %is% similar => ranking
%is% M
cosine %is% medium && jaccard %is% close && polarity %is% same => ranking
%is% MED
cosine %is% medium && jaccard %is% close && polarity %is% similar =>
ranking %is% MED
cosine %is% medium && jaccard %is% halfway && polarity %is% same => ranking
%is% MED
cosine %is% medium && jaccard %is% halfway && polarity %is% similar =>
ranking %is% MED
cosine %is% low || jaccard %is% far || polarity %is% away => ranking %is% L
cosine %is% low || jaccard %is% close || polarity %is% same => ranking %is%
M
cosine %is% low || jaccard %is% halfway || polarity %is% away => ranking
%is% L
cosine %is% low || jaccard %is% halfway || polarity %is% same => ranking
%is% L
cosine %is% low || jaccard %is% halfway || polarity %is% close => ranking
%is% L
cosine %is% low || jaccard %is% halfway || polarity %is% similar => ranking
%is% L
cosine %is% medium || jaccard %is% far || polarity %is% away => ranking
%is% L
cosine %is% high => ranking %is% H
cosine %is% vlow => ranking %is% L
> plot(ranking.system)
```

Let's look at the plot of our `membership` functions:

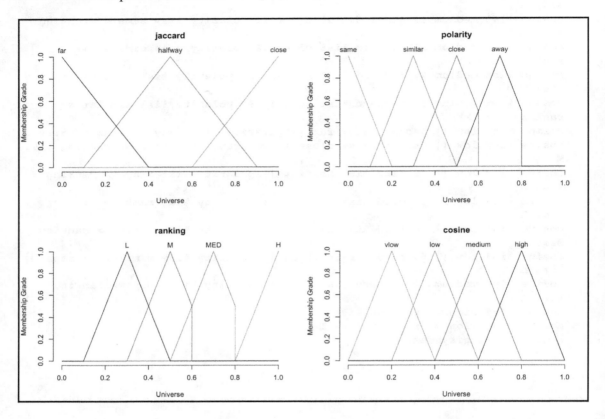

The final plot reveals the fuzziness in the boundary for different linguistic variables. Compare this with a hard-coded `if-else` logic system.

We can now proceed to use this system to do the ranking. Let's do the ranking on a single example:

```
fi <- fuzzy_inference(ranking.system, list(cosine = 0.5000000, jaccard = 0, polarity=0.00000000))

> gset_defuzzify(fi, "centroid")
[1] 0.4
> plot(fi)
```

The decision plot is as follows:

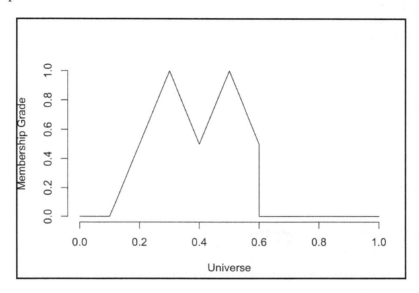

For given values of cosine, polarity, and Jaccard, we get a ranking score of 0.4. Now we can use this score to rank the results.

Let's generate the rankings for all the articles in match.refined:

```
> get.ranks <- function(dataframe){
+    cosine =  as.numeric(dataframe['cosine'])
+    jaccard = as.numeric(dataframe['jaccard'])
+    polarity = as.numeric(dataframe['polaritydiff'])
+    fi <- fuzzy_inference(ranking.system, list(cosine = cosine,  jaccard =
jaccard, polarity=polarity))
+    return(gset_defuzzify(fi, "centroid"))
+
+ }
>
> match.refined$ranking <- apply(match.refined, 1, get.ranks)
> match.refined <- match.refined[order(-match.refined$ranking),]
> head(match.refined)
         ID      cosine
TITLE
16  70584 0.1543033                            RPT-S.Africa stocks end
lower after volatile session
18 163775 0.1543033                     GLOBAL MARKETS-Shares, dollar
tumble on Ukraine anxiety
23 116144 0.1428571              PRECIOUS-Gold dives more than 2 pct as
selling hits precious metals
```

```
24 311314 0.1428571              PRECIOUS-Gold, silver hit multi-
month highs as stocks retreat
1    38081 1.0000000              PRECIOUS-Gold ticks lower,
US dollar holds near peak
2    38069 0.3779645 PRECIOUS-Bullion drops nearly 1 pct on dollar,
palladium holds near 2-1/2-yr high
   PUBLISHER CATEGORY jaccard polaritydiff ranking
16   Reuters       b       1    0.2962963     0.5
18   Reuters       b       1    0.8148148     0.5
23   Reuters       b       1    0.3098741     0.5
24   Reuters       b       1    0.6928995     0.5
1    Reuters       b       1    0.0000000     0.4
2    Reuters       b       1    0.0000000     0.4
```

The `get.ranks` function is applied in each row of `match.refined` to get the fuzzy ranking. Finally, we sort the results using this ranking.

This brings us to the end of our design and implementation of a simple fuzzy-induced content-based recommendation system.

Complete R Code

The complete R code is shown as follows:

```r
library(data.table)

wine.data <-
fread('https://archive.ics.uci.edu/ml/machine-learning-databases/wine/wine.
data')
head(wine.data)

table(wine.data$V1)

wine.type <- wine.data[,1]
wine.features <- wine.data[,-1]

wine.features.scaled <- data.frame(scale(wine.features))
wine.mat <- data.matrix(wine.features.scaled)

rownames(wine.mat) <- seq(1:dim(wine.features.scaled)[1])
wine.mat[1:2,]

wine.mat <- t(wine.mat)
cor.matrix <- cor(wine.mat, use = "pairwise.complete.obs", method =
"Pearson")
dim(cor.matrix)
```

```
cor.matrix[1:5,1:5]

user.view <- wine.features.scaled[3,]
user.view

sim.items <- cor.matrix[3,]
sim.items
sim.items.sorted <- sort(sim.items, decreasing = TRUE)
sim.items.sorted[1:5]

rbind(wine.data[3,]
,wine.data[52,]
,wine.data[51,]
,wine.data[85,]
,wine.data[15,]
)
```

```
library(tidyverse)
library(tidytext)
library(tm)
library(slam)


cnames <- c('ID' , 'TITLE' , 'URL' ,
            'PUBLISHER' , 'CATEGORY' ,
            'STORY' , 'HOSTNAME' ,'TIMESTAMP')

data <- read_tsv('newsCorpus.csv',
                col_names = cnames,
                col_types = cols(
                ID = col_integer(),
                TITLE = col_character(),
                URL = col_character(),
                PUBLISHER = col_character(),
                CATEGORY = col_character(),
                STORY = col_character(),
                HOSTNAME = col_character(),
                TIMESTAMP = col_double()
              )
              )
```

```
head(data)
data %>% group_by(PUBLISHER) %>% summarise()
data %>% group_by(CATEGORY) %>% summarise()


publisher.count <- data.frame(data %>% group_by(PUBLISHER) %>% summarise(ct
=n()))
head(publisher.count)
dim(publisher.count)
dim(publisher.count[publisher.count$ct <= 10,])


publisher.top <- head(publisher.count[order(-publisher.count$ct),],100)
head(publisher.top)

data.subset <- inner_join(publisher.top, data)
head(data.subset)
dim(data.subset)

title.df <- data.subset[,c('ID','TITLE')]
others.df <- data.subset[,c('ID','PUBLISHER','CATEGORY')]



######### Cosine Similarity #####################
title.reader <- readTabular(mapping=list(content="TITLE", id="ID"))

corpus <- Corpus(DataframeSource(title.df),
readerControl=list(reader=title.reader))
corpus

getTransformations()

corpus <- tm_map(corpus, removePunctuation)
corpus <- tm_map(corpus, removeNumbers)
corpus <- tm_map(corpus, stripWhitespace)
corpus <- tm_map(corpus, content_transformer(tolower))
corpus <- tm_map(corpus, removeWords, stopwords("english"))

stopwords("english")

dtm <- DocumentTermMatrix(corpus, control=list(wordlenth = c(3,10)
,weighting = "weightTfIdf"))
dtm
inspect(dtm[1:5,10:15])

sim.score <- tcrossprod_simple_triplet_matrix(dtm)/(sqrt( row_sums(dtm^2)
%*% t(row_sums(dtm^2)) ))
```

```
sim.score[1:10,1:10]

match.docs <- sim.score["38081",]
match.docs


match.df <- data.frame(ID = names(match.docs), cosine = match.docs,
stringsAsFactors=FALSE)
match.df$ID <- as.integer(match.df$ID)
head(match.df)
match.refined<-head(match.df[order(-match.df$cosine),],30)
head(match.refined)




################# Polarity score ##############

match.refined <- inner_join(match.refined, title.df)
match.refined <- inner_join(match.refined, others.df)

head(match.refined)

library(dplyr, quietly = TRUE)
library(sentimentr, quietly = TRUE)
sentiment.score <- sentiment(match.refined$TITLE)
head(sentiment.score)

sentiment.score <- sentiment.score %>% group_by(element_id) %>%
  summarise(sentiment = mean(sentiment))
head(sentiment.score)

match.refined$polarity <- sentiment.score$sentiment
head(match.refined)
help("sentiment")
#
target.publisher <- match.refined[1,]$PUBLISHER
target.category <- match.refined[1,]$CATEGORY
target.polarity <- match.refined[1,]$polarity
target.title <- match.refined[1,]$TITLE


#match.refined <- match.refined[-1,]
match.refined$is.publisher <- match.refined$PUBLISHER == target.publisher
match.refined$is.publisher <- as.numeric(match.refined$is.publisher)

match.refined$is.category <- match.refined$CATEGORY == target.category
match.refined$is.category <- as.numeric(match.refined$is.category)
```

```r
# Calcuate Jaccards
match.refined$jaccard <- (match.refined$is.publisher +
match.refined$is.category)/2
match.refined$polaritydiff <- abs(target.polarity - match.refined$polarity)

range01 <- function(x){(x-min(x))/(max(x)-min(x))}
match.refined$polaritydiff <- range01(unlist(match.refined$polaritydiff))


head(match.refined)
## clean up
match.refined$is.publisher = NULL
match.refined$is.category = NULL
match.refined$polarity = NULL
match.refined$sentiment = NULL


head(match.refined)


### Fuzzy Logic ########

library(sets, quietly = TRUE)
sets_options("universe", seq(from = 0,
                             to = 1, by = 0.1))


variables <-
  set(cosine =
        fuzzy_partition(varnames =
                          c(vlow = 0.2, low = 0.4,
                            medium = 0.6, high = 0.8),
                        FUN = fuzzy_cone , radius = 0.2),
      jaccard =
        fuzzy_partition(varnames =
                          c(close = 1.0, halfway = 0.5,
                            far = 0.0),
                        FUN = fuzzy_cone , radius = 0.4),
      polarity =
        fuzzy_partition(varnames =
                          c(same = 0.0, similar = 0.3,close = 0.5,
                            away = 0.7),
                        FUN = fuzzy_cone , radius = 0.2),
      ranking =
        fuzzy_partition(varnames =
                          c(H = 1.0, MED = 0.7 , M = 0.5, L = 0.3),
                        FUN = fuzzy_cone , radius = 0.2
                        )
```

```
  )

rules <-
  set(
    ######## Low Ranking Rules ##################
    fuzzy_rule(cosine %is% vlow,
               ranking %is% L),
    fuzzy_rule(cosine %is% low || jaccard %is% far
               || polarity %is% away,
               ranking %is% L),
    fuzzy_rule(cosine %is% low || jaccard %is% halfway
               || polarity %is% away,
               ranking %is% L),

    fuzzy_rule(cosine %is% low || jaccard %is% halfway
               || polarity %is% close,
               ranking %is% L),
    fuzzy_rule(cosine %is% low || jaccard %is% halfway
               || polarity %is% similar,
               ranking %is% L),
    fuzzy_rule(cosine %is% low || jaccard %is% halfway
               || polarity %is% same,
               ranking %is% L),
    fuzzy_rule(cosine %is% medium || jaccard %is% far
               || polarity %is% away,
               ranking %is% L),
    ############### Medium Ranking Rules #################
    fuzzy_rule(cosine %is% low || jaccard %is% close
               || polarity %is% same,
               ranking %is% M),
    fuzzy_rule(cosine %is% low && jaccard %is% close
               && polarity %is% similar,
               ranking %is% M),
    ############### Median Ranking Rule #################
    fuzzy_rule(cosine %is% medium && jaccard %is% close
               && polarity %is% same,
               ranking %is% MED),
    fuzzy_rule(cosine %is% medium && jaccard %is% halfway
               && polarity %is% same,
               ranking %is% MED),
    fuzzy_rule(cosine %is% medium && jaccard %is% close
               && polarity %is% similar,
               ranking %is% MED),
    fuzzy_rule(cosine %is% medium && jaccard %is% halfway
               && polarity %is% similar,
               ranking %is% MED),
    ############# High Ranking Rule ###################
    fuzzy_rule(cosine %is% high, ranking %is% H)
```

```
    )

ranking.system <- fuzzy_system(variables, rules)
print(ranking.system)

plot(ranking.system)

fi <- fuzzy_inference(ranking.system, list(cosine = 0.5000000,  jaccard =
0, polarity=0.00000000))
gset_defuzzify(fi, "centroid")
plot(fi)

get.ranks <- function(dataframe){
  cosine =  as.numeric(dataframe['cosine'])
  jaccard = as.numeric(dataframe['jaccard'])
  polarity = as.numeric(dataframe['polaritydiff'])
  fi <- fuzzy_inference(ranking.system, list(cosine = cosine,  jaccard =
jaccard, polarity=polarity))
  return(gset_defuzzify(fi, "centroid"))
}

match.refined$ranking <- apply(match.refined, 1, get.ranks)
match.refined <- match.refined[order(-match.refined$ranking),]
head(match.refined)
```

Summary

We started the chapter by introducing content-based filtering. We discussed how content based filtering methods can help with cold-start problems in recommendation systems. We then explained the new aggregator use case. We explored the data provided by the customer--various news articles from different publishers belonging to different categories. Based on the data, we came up with a design for our content-based recommendation system.

We implemented a similarity dictionary; given a news article, this dictionary would be able to provide the top N matching articles. The similarity was calculated based on the words present in the article. We leveraged the vector space model for text and ultimately used the cosine distance to find the similarities between articles.

We implemented a simple search based on the similarity dictionary to get a list of matching news articles. We introduced additional features for the matching document, sentiment, and polarity score.

Finally, we implemented fuzzy logic to rank the results.

In the next chapter, we will go into the details of various approaches to collaborative filtering algorithm. Collaborative filtering is the most powerful way to build recommender systems.

3
Collaborative Filtering

Given a database of user ratings for products, where a set of users have rated a set of products, collaborative filtering algorithms can give ratings for products yet to be rated by a particular user. This leverages the neighborhood information of the user to provide such recommendations. The input to collaborative filtering is a matrix, where the rows are users and the columns are items. Cell values are the ratings provided by the user for a product. Ratings of products are ubiquitous in today's internet world. IMDB, Yelp, Amazon, and similar systems today have a rating system deployed to capture user preferences. Preferences are typically captured by a rating system, where the ratings are defined as stars or a points system.

Based on the underlying technology, collaborative filtering can be:

- An online system, where the whole user product preference matrix is loaded into the memory to make recommendations for a user and his yet to be rated product combination
- A model-based system, where an approach similar to clustering is used to group users with similar preferences and later use those cluster centroids to make recommendations

In this chapter, we will cover the following:

- Introduction to collaborative filtering
- Introduction to the R package, recommenderlab, an extensible recommendation system framework in R
- Our use case and data
- Designing and implementing the steps involved in building a collaborative filtering project

The code for this chapter was written in RStudio Version 0.99.491. It uses R version 3.3.1. As we work through our example, we will introduce the R recommenderlab packages that we will be using. During our code description, we will be using some of the output printed in the console. We have included what will be printed in the console immediately after the statement that prints the information to the console, so as to not disturb the flow of the code.

Collaborative filtering

Given a user **rating matrix**, where several users have rated several products, the goal of collaborative filtering is as follows:

- Predict the ratings for all products unknown to the user
- Produce the ratings for the top-n list of products unknown to the user

The underlying premise of the collaborative filtering algorithm is that if two users agree on ratings for a large set of items, they may tend to agree for other items too. Let us use a small R code snippet to explain this concept. Assume we have seven products (A, B, C, D, E, F, G) and two users (user.a and user.b). We also have the ratings provided by both of the users for some of the products. The ratings are range of numbers from 1 to 5, with 1 indicating a poor rating, 5 indicating a good rating, and 0 indicating no rating.

The following is an R snippet for demonstration purposes:

```
> set.seed(100)

> products <- c('A','B','C','D','E','F','G')
> user.a <-   c( 3,  0,  2, 5, 5, 0,1)
> user.b <-   c( 3,  5,  3, 5, 4, 2, 1)
> ratings.matrix <- as.data.frame(list(user.a,user.b))
> names(ratings.matrix) <- c("user.a","user.b")
> rownames(ratings.matrix) <- products
> head(ratings.matrix)
```

	user.a	user.b
A	3	3
B	0	5
C	2	3
D	5	5
E	5	4
F	0	2

Both of the users agree on ratings for products A, C, D, and E. User user.a, has not seen and therefore not rated, products B and F. However, we see that user.b has rated those products. Since both the users agree on most of the products, we can use user.b ratings for product B, and F, and fill in these missing ratings for user.a

This is the fundamental working premise of collaborative filtering. The example is based on a user-based collaborative filtering approach. There are other approaches to collaborative filtering which are shown in the following diagram, but we hope this example serves to introduce the concept.

Having explained the hypothesis behind the algorithm, let us look at the approaches to collaborative filtering:

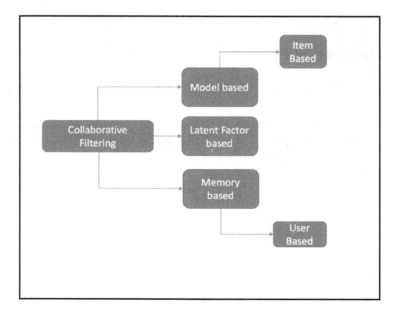

Memory-based approach

The memory-based approach to collaborative filtering loads the whole rating matrix into memory to provide recommendations, hence the name memory-based model. **User-based filtering** is the most prominent memory-based collaborative filtering model. The R snippet explained in the preceding section is the underlying principle by which memory-based methods work. As the user and product base grows, scalability is a big issue with memory-based models.

In the R snippet example, we used the ratings of `user.b` to fill in the missing ratings for `user.a`. In the real world, with thousands of users, the **user-based filtering** algorithm first proceeds as follows.

Let us say we have a set of users *{u₁,u₂.....uₙ}* and a set of products *{p₁,p₂...pₘ}*, and we are trying to predict the ratings for a single user, u_a.

Using a **similarity measure** such as **Pearson coefficient**, or **cosine distance**, we try to find **K** neighbors for u_a. For more on similarity measures, refer to `http://reference.wolfram.com/language/guide/DistanceAndSimilarityMeasures.html`:

- **Similarity measure**: A quantitative measure used to compare two vectors. They return large values for similar objects, and either zero or smaller values for dissimilar objects. Similarity measure is typically implemented as a real-valued function.
- **Pearson coefficient**: This measures the correlation between two variables. A value of +1 indicates that two variables are highly correlated and a value of -1 indicates negative correlation. The Pearson correlation score finds the ratio between the covariance and the standard deviation of both objects.
- **Cosine Similarity**: Cosine similarity between two vectors is the angle between them:

$$cos\theta = \frac{a.\,b}{|a|\,.\,|b|}$$

When the two vectors are centered (zero mean) their cosine similarity is same as the Pearson coefficient.

Let us say u_a does not have the ratings for p_5, p_7, and p_9. We take the average of ratings for these products from the K neighbors of u_a and use that as the ratings for u_a.

You can refer to *Chapter A, Comprehensive Survey of Neighborhood-based Recommendation Methods* in the book, Recommender System Handbook, at `https://link.springer.com/chapter/10.1007/978-0-387-85820-3_4`.

Model-based approach

The model based approach addresses the scalability problem seen in memory-based approaches. Compared to the user-based approach, where the recommendations came from leveraging a user's neighbors preference, the model-based approach leverages product similarity to make recommendations. The premise is that users will prefer those products similar to the ones they have already rated.

The first step in this approach is to calculate the product similarity matrix. Let us say there are a set of products: $\{p_1,p_2...p_m\}$. An $m \times m$ matrix is constructed to begin with. Once again **Pearson coefficient** or **cosine similarity** is used as a similarity measure. For efficiency purposes, instead of building a whole $m \times m$ matrix, a smaller $m \times k$ matrix is built, where $k \ll m$, k most similar items.

Let us write a small R snippet to explain this:

```
> products <- c('A','B','C')
> user.a <- c(2,0,3)
> user.b <- c(5,2,0)
> user.c <- c(3,3,0)
> ratings.matrix <- as.data.frame(list(user.a,user.b, user.c))
> names(ratings.matrix) <- c("user.a","user.b","user.c")
> rownames(ratings.matrix) <- products
> head(ratings.matrix)
  user.a user.b user.c
A      2      5      3
B      0      2      3
C      3      0      0
>
```

We have three users, `user.a`, `user.b`, `user.c`, and three products: A, B, C. We also have the ratings the users have provided for these products. The ratings are in a scale from 1 to 5. You should see the `ratings.matrix`, the final rating matrix summarizing the user product ratings.

Let us use this ratings matrix to build a product similarity matrix:

```
> ratings.mat <- (as.matrix(ratings.matrix))
> sim.mat <- cor(t(ratings.mat), method = "Pearson")
> sim.mat
            A           B           C
A   1.0000000   0.5000000  -0.7559289
B   0.5000000   1.0000000  -0.9449112
C  -0.7559289  -0.9449112   1.0000000
>
```

We have used the `cor` function from the `base` package to calculate the similarity matrix. Let us say we want to find the ratings for product B for `user.a`.

The most similar product to product B is A, as it has a higher score compared to C. In a real-world example, we will have multiple similar products. Now the score for B for `user.a` is calculated as follows:

$$(2 * 0.5 + 3 * -0.945) / (0.5 + (-0.945))$$

The predicted rating for product B for `user.a` is calculated using similarity measures between (B, A) and (B, C) weighted by the respective ratings given by `user.a` for A and C and scaling this weighted sum with the sum of similarity measures.

The similarity matrix of products are pre-computed and therefore it does not have the overhead of loading the whole user ratings matrix in memory. Amazon.com is successfully using item-based recommendations.

Latent factor approach

The latent factor approach leverages **matrix factorization** techniques to arrive at recommendations. Recently these methods have proved themselves superior to item-based and user-based recommender systems. This was one of the winning solutions in the famous Netflix recommendation competition. Edwin Chen's blog at `http://blog.echen.me/2011/10/24/winning-the-netflix-prize-a-summary/` is a good place to understand the various techniques used in the Netflix challenge.

Matrix factorization or matrix decomposition is the method of splitting a matrix into multiple matrices. The product of those matrices will produce the original matrix. For more on matrix decomposition, you can refer to `https://en.wikipedia.org/wiki/Matrix_decomposition`

Singular Value Decomposition (SVD) is a matrix factorization technique used in machine learning to reduce the dimension of the input data. The idea is to find the directions of maximum variances and retain only those as they can explain considerably the variation in the data. There is a wonderful article by Maler Maheb at `Medium.com`, which gives the intuition behind using SVD for recommender systems, at `https://medium.com/@m_n_malaeb/singular-value-decomposition-svd-in-recommender-systems-for-non-math-statistics-programming-4a622de653e9`

Let us say our original matrix is *m x n*, where we have *m* users and *n* products. Applying SVD on this matrix, we get:

- *m x f* matrix: for each user in *m*, we have *f* features/factors
- *n x f* matrix: for each product in *n*, we have *f* features/factors

Applying SVD matrices with missing values is not possible. Our ratings matrix will have a lot of missing values. Simon Funk proposed a new method, now called funk SVD, to do SVD on large matrices using numerical optimization methods and gradient descent. Funk SVD is implemented in the `recommenderlab` package. The dimension *f* in *m x f* and *n x f* represents the `latent factors`, hence the name of this method is the `latent factors` method. These `latent factors` represents some of the hidden features. For example in a movie database, where our items corresponds to movie, one or a couple of `latent factors` may point to the box office success of the movie.

Each user has a vector now from the *m x f* matrix. Similarly each product has a vector now from the *n x f* matrix. For a given user and item, multiplying their respective vectors gives the rating for that item specific to that user. Can you guess why? Here is where the features/factors comes to play. The features/factors are shared by both the matrices. The ratings in the original ratings matrix is now decomposed into a set of features. Thus when we multiply the user vector, *1 x f*, with the product vector *1 x f*, we get a scalar value, which is the rating for that product by that user.

Using this we can now predict the recommendation for unknown products for users.

Let us look at a quick R snippet :

```
> svd.coms <- svd(ratings.mat)
> user.a.vector <- svd.coms$u[1,]
> product.B.vector <- svd.coms$v[2,]
> ratings.user.a.prod.B <- user.a.vector %*% product.B.vector
> ratings.user.a.prod.B
          [,1]
[1,] 0.9574725
>
```

We use the `SVD` function from the base R package to decompose the `ratings.mat`.
`ratings.mat` is the same ratings matrix we used to explain item-based similarity.
`user.a.vector` is the vector representing `user.a`, and `product.B.vector` is the vector
representing the `product B`. `ratings.user.a.prod.B` is the product of these two
vectors representing the ratings of product B by `user.a`.

Now that we have explained all the three different approaches to build a collaborative
filtering method, let us proceed to look at the `recommenderlab` package.

Recommenderlab package

It will be very useful for the subsequent sections to get an overview of
the `recommenderlab` package. Let us quickly look at the `S4` objects inside the package and
see how we can use them to build collaborative filtering projects.

A high-level overview is shown in the following figure:

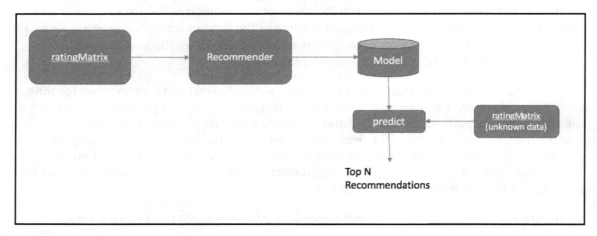

The `ratingMatrix` is an abstract object, used to store and manipulate the ratings matrix.
The term abstract is from object-oriented programming. `ratingMatrix` defines the
interfaces to develop a user `ratingsMatrix`, but does not implement them. There are two
concrete implementations of this object one for the real-valued matrix and the other one for
the binary matrix. The `Recommender` class is used to store the recommendation models. It
takes as an input a `ratingsMatrix` object and other parameters and builds the required
recommender model.

The `predict` function can produce recommendations for unseen/unknown data (where we don't know the recommendation) using the `Recommender` model.

Proceed to install `recommenderlab` if you have not already installed it:

```
install.packages("recommenderlab")
```

Create a binary rating matrix:

```
> library(recommenderlab, quietly = TRUE)
> bin.data <- sample(c(0,1), 20, replace = TRUE)
> bin.mat <- matrix(bin.data, nrow = 4, ncol = 5)
> bin.mat
     [,1] [,2] [,3] [,4] [,5]
[1,]    1    1    0    0    1
[2,]    0    1    1    1    1
[3,]    1    0    0    1    0
[4,]    1    1    0    0    0
> rating.mat <- as(bin.mat, "binaryRatingMatrix")
> rating.mat
4 x 5 rating matrix of class 'binaryRatingMatrix' with 11 ratings.
>
```

In the preceding code, we create a random binary matrix and coerce it to a `binaryRatingMatrix` object. Similarly, we can also create a `realRatingMatrix`.

Having built our `ratingsMatrix`, let us go ahead and create a simple `Recommender` model based on this matrix.

The `Recommender` model creation is as follows:

```
> model <- Recommender(data = rating.mat, method = "POPULAR")
> model
Recommender of type 'POPULAR' for 'binaryRatingMatrix'
learned using 4 users.
> str(model)
Formal class 'Recommender' [package "recommenderlab"] with 5 slots
  ..@ method  : chr "POPULAR"
  ..@ dataType: atomic [1:1] binaryRatingMatrix
  .. ..- attr(*, "package")= chr "recommenderlab"
  ..@ ntrain  : int 4
  ..@ model   :List of 1
  .. ..$ topN:Formal class 'topNList' [package "recommenderlab"] with 4
slots
  .. .. .. ..@ items     :List of 1
  .. .. .. .. ..$ : int [1:5] 1 2 4 5 3
  .. .. .. ..@ ratings   : NULL
  .. .. .. ..@ itemLabels: chr [1:5] "1" "2" "3" "4" ...
```

```
   .. .. .. ..@ n            : int 5
   ..@ predict :function (model, newdata, n = 10, data = NULL, type =
c("topNList"), ...)
>
```

We pass our ratings matrix to the `Recommender` class and select an approach called
popular. This creates our recommendation model.

Popular approach

This is a very simple strategy where the recommendations are based on the item popularity.
Among the products not rated by a user, the most popular ones among all the users are
suggested as recommendations.

There are several other implementations of the recommendation model available in this
package.

To get a list of the available recommendation models, apply the following:

```
> recommenderRegistry$get_entries(dataType = "binaryRatingMatrix")
$ALS_implicit_binaryRatingMatrix
Recommender method: ALS_implicit for binaryRatingMatrix
Description: Recommender for implicit data based on latent factors,
calculated by alternating least squares algorithm.
Reference: Yifan Hu, Yehuda Koren, Chris Volinsky (2008). Collaborative
Filtering for Implicit Feedback Datasets, ICDM '08 Proceedings of the 2008
Eighth IEEE International Conference on Data Mining, pages 263-272.
Parameters:
  lambda alpha n_factors n_iterations min_item_nr seed
1    0.1   10        10          10          1 NULL

$AR_binaryRatingMatrix
Recommender method: AR for binaryRatingMatrix
Description: Recommender based on association rules.
Reference: NA
Parameters:
  support confidence maxlen sort_measure sort_decreasing apriori_control
verbose
1    0.1        0.8      3 "confidence"            TRUE            list()
FALSE

$IBCF_binaryRatingMatrix
Recommender method: IBCF for binaryRatingMatrix
Description: Recommender based on item-based collaborative filtering
(binary rating data).
Reference: NA
```

```
Parameters:
   k    method normalize_sim_matrix alpha
1 30 "Jaccard"                    FALSE   0.5

$POPULAR_binaryRatingMatrix
Recommender method: POPULAR for binaryRatingMatrix
Description: Recommender based on item popularity.
Reference: NA
Parameters: None

$RANDOM_binaryRatingMatrix
Recommender method: RANDOM for binaryRatingMatrix
Description: Produce random recommendations (binary ratings).
Reference: NA
Parameters: None

$UBCF_binaryRatingMatrix
Recommender method: UBCF for binaryRatingMatrix
Description: Recommender based on user-based collaborative filtering.
Reference: NA
Parameters:
     method nn weighted sample
1 "jaccard" 25    TRUE   FALSE
```

Having created the `Recommender` model, let us see how to leverage it to produce the top N recommendations.

Producing the top N Recommendations involves the following:

```
> recomms <- predict(model, newdata = rating.mat, n =2)
> recomms@items
$`1`
[1] 4 3

$`2`
[1] 1

$`3`
[1] 2 5

$`4`
[1] 4 5

> recomms@ratings
NULL
```

We pass our `Recommender` model to the `predict` function. We are testing it on our input data, and therefore we have the `newdata` parameter set to our training data. Finally the parameter n decides how many recommendations we need. The recommendations are printed in the next line by calling `recomm@items`. Since our input is a binary matrix, we don't have any ratings.

Similarly, we can create a `realMatrix` either from an R matrix or a data frame and create a `Recommender` model and proceed with the recommendations.

This concludes our introduction to the `recommenderlab` package. Let us use this knowledge to solve the problem in hand for this chapter. For more information about `recommenderlab` visit `https://cran.r-project.org/web/packages/recommenderlab/index.html`

Use case and data

The `Jester5k` dataset is what we will be using to build our recommender system using collaborative filtering. It contains user ratings in the scale of -10 to 10 for several jokes. In this chapter, we will use these ratings as an input and produce ratings for jokes which the users have not seen or not rated before. For more information about the `Jester5k` dataset, visit: `http://www.ieor.berkeley.edu/%7Egoldberg/jester-data/`

Fortunately, a sample of this data is available with the `recommenderlab` package.

Let us quickly look at this data:

```
> library(recommenderlab, quietly = TRUE)
> data("Jester5k")

> str(Jester5k)
Formal class 'realRatingMatrix' [package "recommenderlab"] with 2 slots
  ..@ data       :Formal class 'dgCMatrix' [package "Matrix"] with 6 slots
  .. .. ..@ i       : int [1:362106] 0 1 2 3 4 5 6 7 8 9 ...
  .. .. ..@ p       : int [1:101] 0 3314 6962 10300 13442 18440 22513 27512
32512 35685 ...
  .. .. ..@ Dim     : int [1:2] 5000 100
  .. .. ..@ Dimnames:List of 2
  .. .. .. ..$ : chr [1:5000] "u2841" "u15547" "u15221" "u15573" ...
  .. .. .. ..$ : chr [1:100] "j1" "j2" "j3" "j4" ...
  .. .. ..@ x       : num [1:362106] 7.91 -3.2 -1.7 -7.38 0.1 0.83 2.91
-2.77 -3.35 -1.99 ...
  .. .. ..@ factors : list()
  ..@ normalize: NULL
```

```
> head(Jester5k@data[1:5,1:5])
5 x 5 sparse Matrix of class "dgCMatrix"
            j1    j2    j3    j4    j5
u2841     7.91  9.17  5.34  8.16 -8.74
u15547   -3.20 -3.50 -9.56 -8.74 -6.36
u15221   -1.70  1.21  1.55  2.77  5.58
u15573   -7.38 -8.93 -3.88 -7.23 -4.90
u21505    0.10  4.17  4.90  1.55  5.53
```

The data is stored as `realRatingMatrix`. We can examine the slots of this matrix by calling the `str()` function. Looking at the data slot of `realRatingMatrix`, we see that it's a matrix with 5,000 rows and 100 columns. The rows are the number of users and the columns represent the number of jokes. If all users have rated all jokes, we should have a total of 500,000 ratings. However, we see that we have 362,106 ratings.

As the name of the dataset suggests, `Jester5k` has 5 k users and their ratings for 100 jokes.

 s3, is R's object-oriented system. Refer to `http://adv-r.had.co.nz/S3.html` to get more details about the s3 object system.

Further, let's look at the first five rows and columns of `realRatingMatrix` to have a quick look at the ratings.

Let us look at the ratings provided by two random users, 1 and 100:

```
> Jester5k@data[1,]
    j1    j2    j3    j4    j5    j6    j7    j8    j9   j10   j11   j12
   j13   j14   j15   j16   j17   j18
  7.91  9.17  5.34  8.16 -8.74  7.14  8.88 -8.25  5.87  6.21  7.72  6.12
 -0.73  7.77 -5.83 -8.88  8.98 -9.32
   j19   j20   j21   j22   j23   j24   j25   j26   j27   j28   j29   j30
   j31   j32   j33   j34   j35   j36
 -9.08 -9.13  7.77  8.59  5.29  8.25  6.02  5.24  7.82  7.96 -8.88  8.25
  3.64 -0.73  8.25  5.34 -7.77 -9.76
   j37   j38   j39   j40   j41   j42   j43   j44   j45   j46   j47   j48
   j49   j50   j51   j52   j53   j54
  7.04  5.78  8.06  7.23  8.45  9.08  6.75  5.87  8.45 -9.42  5.15  8.74
  6.41  8.64  8.45  9.13 -8.79  6.17
   j55   j56   j57   j58   j59   j60   j61   j62   j63   j64   j65   j66
   j67   j68   j69   j70   j71   j72
  8.25  6.89  5.73  5.73  8.20  6.46  8.64  3.59  7.28  8.25  4.81 -8.20
  5.73  7.04  4.56  8.79  0.00  0.00
   j73   j74   j75   j76   j77   j78   j79   j80   j81   j82   j83   j84
   j85   j86   j87   j88   j89   j90
  0.00  0.00  0.00  0.00 -9.71  0.00  0.00  0.00  0.00  0.00  0.00  0.00
```

```
0.00   0.00   0.00   0.00   0.00   0.00
  j91    j92    j93    j94    j95    j96    j97    j98    j99   j100
 7.57  -9.42  -9.27   7.62   7.77   8.20   6.60   7.33   9.17   8.88


> Jester5k@data[100,]
   j1     j2     j3     j4     j5     j6     j7     j8     j9    j10    j11    j12
  j13    j14    j15    j16    j17    j18
-2.48   3.93   2.72  -2.67   1.75   3.35   0.73  -0.53  -0.58   3.88   3.16   1.17
 0.53   1.65   1.26  -4.08  -0.49  -3.79
  j19    j20    j21    j22    j23    j24    j25    j26    j27    j28    j29    j30
  j31    j32    j33    j34    j35    j36
-3.06  -2.33   3.59   0.58   0.39   0.53   2.38  -0.05   2.43  -0.34   3.35   2.04
 2.33   3.54  -0.19  -0.24   2.62   3.83
  j37    j38    j39    j40    j41    j42    j43    j44    j45    j46    j47    j48
  j49    j50    j51    j52    j53    j54
-2.52   5.19   1.75   0.00   0.39   1.75  -3.64  -2.28   2.33   3.16  -2.48   0.19
 2.82   4.22  -0.19   3.30  -0.53   3.45
  j55    j56    j57    j58    j59    j60    j61    j62    j63    j64    j65    j66
  j67    j68    j69    j70    j71    j72
-0.53   0.97  -2.91  -8.25  -0.29   2.52   4.66   3.50  -0.24   3.64  -0.05   1.21
-3.25   1.17  -2.57  -2.18  -5.44   2.67
  j73    j74    j75    j76    j77    j78    j79    j80    j81    j82    j83    j84
  j85    j86    j87    j88    j89    j90
 2.57  -4.03   2.96   3.40   1.12   1.36  -3.01   2.96   2.04  -3.25   1.94  -3.40
-3.50  -3.45  -3.06   2.04   3.20   3.06
  j91    j92    j93    j94    j95    j96    j97    j98    j99   j100
 2.86  -5.15   3.01   0.83  -6.21  -6.60  -6.31   3.69  -4.22   0.97
>
```

As we can see in the data, users don't have ratings for all the jokes. The two random users we have just shown have zero as the rating for some of the jokes.

A user will not have rated all the jokes. If they have not rated it, there will be a zero value. To get the number of jokes a user rated, we can run:

```
length(Jester5k@data[100,][Jester5k@data[100,]>0]) # answer = 58
```

Let us dig a little bit deeper to see this `zero.ratings` distribution:

```
> zero.ratings <- rowSums(Jester5k@data == 0)
> zero.ratings.df <- data.frame("user" = names(zero.ratings), "count" =
zero.ratings)
> head(zero.ratings.df)
           user count
u2841     u2841    19
u15547   u15547    29
u15221   u15221     0
u15573   u15573     0
u21505   u21505    28
u15994   u15994     1

> head(zero.ratings.df[order(-zero.ratings.df$count),], 10)
           user count
u3228     u3228    66
u5768     u5768    65
u10701   u10701    65
u7533     u7533    65
u19356   u19356    65
u7155     u7155    65
u7786     u7786    65
u7161     u7161    65
u15037   u15037    65
u7904     u7904    64
>
```

We are looking to see per user the count of jokes he has not rated. We can achieve this by doing the sum of rows of our ratings matrix. After summing it up, we create a dataframe, `zero.ratings.df`, with two columns; the first column is the user and the second column is the number of zero-entries they have in the ratings matrix, that is, the number of jokes where their ratings were zero. Further, we can order our dataframe zero ratings in descending order by the count. We can see that user u3228 has not rated 66 jokes.

Let us use this data to make a histogram to see the underlying distribution:

```
> hist(zero.ratings.df$count, main ="Distribution of zero rated jokes")
```

The histogram, shows the **Distribution of zero rated jokes**:

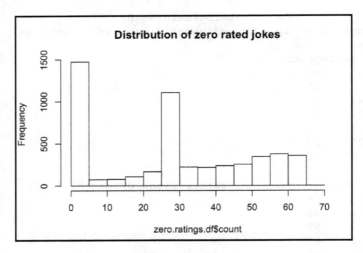

The histogram is showing the count of the zeros (that is, unrated jokes), so a low value on the x-axis means that users have rated more jokes. The bin 0-5 is a testimony to it. Out of 100 jokes, anything between 0 to 5 is left unrated. However, the distribution looks to have three modes.

A density plot may illustrate this more visually:

```
> zero.density <- density(zero.ratings.df$count)
> plot(zero.density)
```

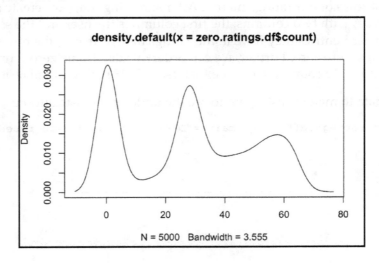

The three modes are evident from the density plot. We have three groups of users in our database. Those who have a low number for unrated jokes, another group which has around 25 jokes unrated and the final group which has around 65 jokes unrated.

> It's a good practice to have an overview of the underlying distribution of the data. In this case, it may be that we want to build three different models based on which group the user falls in.

We can further verify this empirically by using a clustering algorithm.

Let us use k-means to do an empirical verification:

```
> model <- kmeans(zero.ratings.df$count,3 )
> model$centers
        [,1]
1 54.845633
2  1.358769
3 29.366702
> model$size
[1] 1477 1625 1898
> model.df <- data.frame(centers = model$centers, size = model$size, perc =
(model$size / 5000) * 100)
> head(model.df)
    centers size  perc
1 54.845633 1477 29.54
2  1.358769 1625 32.50
3 29.366702 1898 37.96
```

We can fact check our user clusters by running a k-means algorithm on our data. We set the parameter k to the number of clusters and finally collect our results in a dataframe named `model.df`. The cluster centers reflect the number of jokes not rated. More information about R k-means can be found at `https://stat.ethz.ch/R-manual/R-devel/library/stats/html/kmeans.html`

Now that we've looked at the user distribution, let us proceed to look at the joke's ratings:

```
> Jester5k@data[,1]
  u2841 u15547 u15221 u15573 u21505 u15994    u238  u5809 u16636 u12843
 u17322 u13610   u7061 u23059   u7299
   7.91  -3.20  -1.70  -7.38   0.10   0.83   2.91  -2.77  -3.35  -1.99
  -0.68   9.17  -9.71  -3.16   5.58
 u20906   u7147   u6662   u4662   u5798   u7904   u7556   u3970    u999   u5462
 u20231 u13120 u22827 u20747   u1143
   9.08   0.00  -6.70   0.00   1.02   0.00  -3.01   5.87  -7.33   0.00
   7.48   0.00  -9.71   0.00   0.00
 u11381   u6617   u7602 u12658   u4519 u18953   u5021   u6457 u24750 u20139
 u13802 u16123   u7778 u15509   u8225
   0.00   6.55   0.00   0.00   0.78  -0.10   0.00   0.00   0.00  -6.65
   2.28   1.02   0.00  -8.35   5.53
 u12519 u16885 u12094   u6083 u19086   u1840   u7722 u17883 u12579   u3815
 u12563 u12313 u18725   u4354 u21146
 ..................
 [ reached getOption("max.print") -- omitted 4000 entries ]
>
> par(mfrow=c(2,2))
> joke.density <- density(Jester5k@data[,1][Jester5k@data[,1]!=0])
> plot(joke.density)

> joke.density <- density(Jester5k@data[,25][Jester5k@data[,25]!=0])
> plot(joke.density)

> joke.density <- density(Jester5k@data[,75][Jester5k@data[,75]!=0])
> plot(joke.density)

> joke.density <- density(Jester5k@data[,100]
  [Jester5k@data[,100]!=100])
> plot(joke.density)
```

We look at the first joke, `Jester5k@data[,1]`, for its scoring values; the output shown in the preceding code is truncated.

Further, we plot the density plot for four randomly selected jokes (1, 25, 75, and 100) and look at the distribution of scores.

The distribution graph is illustrated in the following figure:

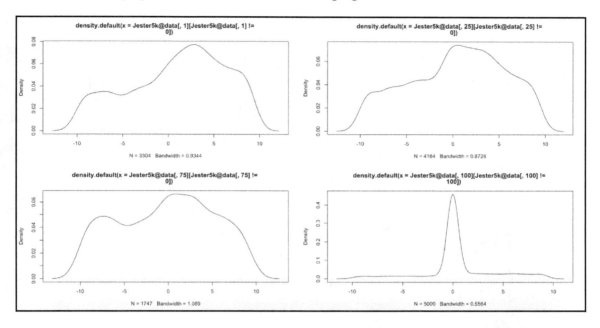

For all the four jokes, we see the rating is more than zero. The `recommenderlab` package provides a function, `getRatings`, which can work on the s3 object to retrieve the ratings.

Let us look at all of the `getRatings` function in our dataset:

```
hist(getRatings(Jester5k), main="Distribution of ratings")
```

The ratings distribution plot is shown in the following figure:

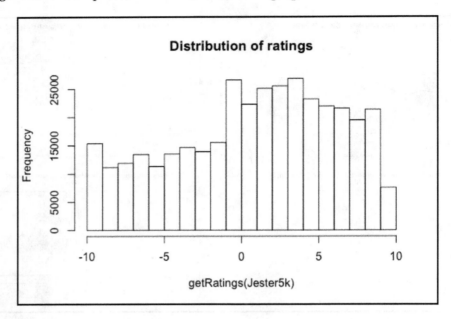

Let us now move on to see if we can find the most popular joke.

The R snippet to find the most popular joke is shown here:

```
> ratings.binary <- binarize(Jester5k, minRating =0)
> ratings.binary
5000 x 100 rating matrix of class 'binaryRatingMatrix' with 215798 ratings.
> ratings.sum <- colSums(ratings.binary)
> ratings.sum.df <- data.frame(joke = names(ratings.sum), pratings =
ratings.sum)
> head( ratings.sum.df[order(-ratings.sum.df$pratings), ],10)
     joke pratings
j50  j50      4081
j36  j36      4021
j32  j32      3914
j35  j35      3853
j27  j27      3846
j53  j53      3843
j29  j29      3820
j62  j62      3814
j49  j49      3762
j68  j68      3713
>
> tail( ratings.sum.df[order(-ratings.sum.df$pratings), ],10)
```

```
      joke pratings
j80   j80      1072
j90   j90      1057
j73   j73      1041
j77   j77      1012
j86   j86       994
j79   j79       934
j75   j75       895
j71   j71       796
j58   j58       695
j74   j74       689
>
```

We begin with binarizing our ratings matrix. In the new matrix, `ratings.binary`, the ratings with 0 or more will be considered as positive ratings and all the others will be considered as negative ratings. We create a dataframe, `ratings.sum.df`, with two columns: the joke name and the sum of the ratings received by the joke. Since we have binarized the matrix, this sum should be equal to the popularity of a joke. Displaying the matrix in descending order of the sum, we see the most popular jokes and the least popular jokes.

Finally, we are going to sample the datasets for 1,500 users and use that as our dataset for the rest of the chapter. Sampling is often used during exploration, by taking a smaller subset of the data, you can explore the data and produce the initial models quicker. Then when the time comes, you can apply the best approach to the entire dataset

Sampling the dataset looks like this:

```
data <- sample(Jester5k, 1500)
hist(getRatings(data), main="Distribution of ratings for 1500 users")
```

The following is the image for the distribution of ratings for 1500 users:

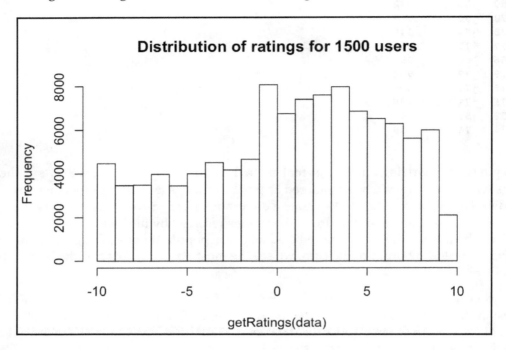

Hopefully, the data exploration we performed in this section has given you a good overview of the underlying dataset. Let us proceed now to build our joke recommendation system.

Designing and implementing collaborative filtering

We now have a good overview of the `recommenderlab` package and our `Jester5k` data. Our use case is to design a recommendation system for suggesting jokes to the users. We want to suggest to users the jokes they have either not seen or rated before. Let us begin with outlining the steps in our project.

The steps in designing our recommendation project are shown in the following figure:

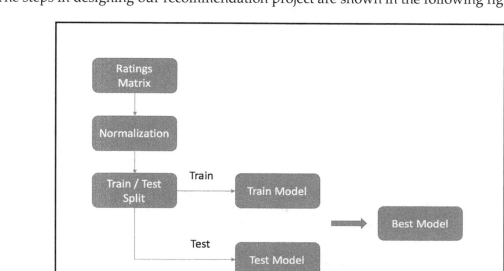

Ratings matrix

The first step is to obtain the ratings matrix. The `recommenderlab` expects the user rating matrix to be stored as either `binaryRatingsMatrix` or `realRatingsMatrix`.

The `realRatingsmatrix` s3 class has a slot called data where the actual ratings matrix is stored in a compressed format. The `getRatingMatrix` function is an easy way to extract this matrix from the s3 class.

Let us extract the ratings matrix from our dataset:

```
> data <- sample(Jester5k, 1500)
> ratings.mat <- getRatingMatrix(data)
> str(ratings.mat)
Formal class 'dgCMatrix' [package "Matrix"] with 6 slots
  ..@ i       : int [1:108531] 0 1 2 3 7 8 9 10 11 12 ...
  ..@ p       : int [1:101] 0 984 2083 3083 4026 5525 6743 8243 9743 10691
...
  ..@ Dim     : int [1:2] 1500 100
```

```
   ..@ Dimnames:List of 2
   .. ..$ : chr [1:1500] "u24377" "u11509" "u6569" "u19311" ...
   .. ..$ : chr [1:100] "j1" "j2" "j3" "j4" ...
   ..@ x        : num [1:108531] 7.72 0.68 8.35 -1.94 -4.61 2.18 7.96 2.23
8.06 -0.53 ...
   ..@ factors : list()
>
```

First we take a sample of 1,500 users from our dataset. Using `getRatingMatrix`, we extract the `realRatingsMatrix`, our ratings matrix from this dataset. We see that it's stored as `dgCMatrix`, a compressed matrix form.

Use the slot data to extract the matrix, as follows:

```
> str(data@data)
Formal class 'dgCMatrix' [package "Matrix"] with 6 slots
   ..@ i        : int [1:108531] 0 1 2 3 7 8 9 10 11 12 ...
   ..@ p        : int [1:101] 0 984 2083 3083 4026 5525 6743 8243 9743 10691
...
   ..@ Dim      : int [1:2] 1500 100
   ..@ Dimnames:List of 2
   .. ..$ : chr [1:1500] "u24377" "u11509" "u6569" "u19311" ...
   .. ..$ : chr [1:100] "j1" "j2" "j3" "j4" ...
   ..@ x        : num [1:108531] 7.72 0.68 8.35 -1.94 -4.61 2.18 7.96 2.23
8.06 -0.53 ...
   ..@ factors : list()
>
```

As you can see, using the `slot` data from our dataset, we can extract the ratings matrix.

Now that we have obtained the ratings matrix, we proceed to the next step of normalization.

When you have your own dataset, you can either create a matrix or a dataframe out of your dataset and coerce them to `realRatingsMatrix` or `realBinaryMatrix`, as shown in the previous section where we introduced the `recommenderlab` infrastructure.

Normalization

Our next step is to normalize the ratings. Currently, our ratings range from -10 to 10. For some of the underlying algorithms to work efficiently, it is generally a good practice to normalize the data. One reason for normalizing the data is to account for the different biases people use when rating items. Users do not rate items consistently, one user may mainly only recommend items they such as, (that is, mostly 4/5, 5/5) whereas another user may use rate across the range. Normalizing the data accounts for these biases.

Two normalization techniques are available with `recommenderlab`:

1. The first one is centering; it removes the row bias by subtracting the row mean value from all the row values.
2. The second one is the z-score normalization; a z-score is obtained by subtracting the mean from individual scores and dividing it by the standard deviation.

Centering as the name indicates makes the mean zero. It does not change the scale of the variable. If all the variables in the dataset were measured in the same scale, we can adopt centering as our normalization technique.

On the contrary, z-score normalization changes the scale in addition to centering the data. Now a unit change in the data is a one standard deviation change in the data. When the variables are measured in different scale, it makes sense to use z-score normalization.

Let us normalize our ratings:

```
data.norm    <- normalize(data, method = "center")
data.norm.z <- normalize(data, method = "Z-score")
par(mfrow=c(3,1))
plot(density(getRatings(data)), main = "Raw")
plot(density(getRatings(data.norm)), main = "Normalized")
plot(density(getRatings(data.norm.z)), main = "Z-score normalized")
par(mfrow=c(1,1))
```

The `normalize` function is used to normalize the data. The `method` parameter dictates if we need to use the centering or z-score normalizing approach. We further proceed to plot the ratings distribution.

The plots of the raw, normalized, and z-score normalized ratings are shown in the following figure:

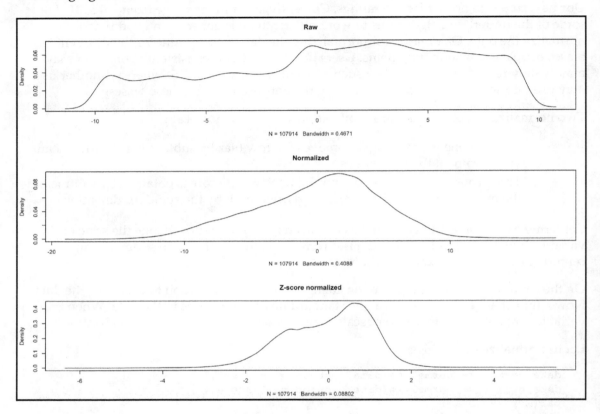

From the plots, we can see that we have brought the data close to a normal distribution from its original distribution.

More information about z-score normalization can be found at `https://en.wikipedia.org/wiki/Standard_score`

Let's proceed to the next step, where we want to arrange our data in such a way that we can evaluate the performance of our `Recommender` model.

Train test split

Once we have built our recommendation engine using collaborative filtering, we don't want to wait till the model is deployed in production to get to know it's performance. We want to produce the best performing recommendation engine. Therefore, during the development process, we can split our data into a training set and a test set. We can build our algorithm on the training set and test it against our test set to validate or infer the performance of our collaborative filtering method.

The `recommenderlab` package provides the necessary infrastructure to achieve this. The `evaluationScheme` class is provided to help us create a train/test strategy. It takes a `ratingsMatrix` as an input and provides several schemes including simple split, bootstrap sampling, and k-fold cross-validation to create an evaluation scheme.

Let us invoke the `evaluationScheme` with our input matrix:

```
> plan <- evaluationScheme(data, method="split", train=0.9, given=10,
goodRating=2)
> plan
Evaluation scheme with 10 items given
Method: 'split' with 1 run(s).
Training set proportion: 0.900
Good ratings: >=5.000000
Data set: 1500 x 100 rating matrix of class 'realRatingMatrix' with 107914
ratings.
```

Using the `evaluationScheme` method, we allocate 90% of our data to training. The given parameter achieves the following. From the test data, it takes 10 jokes for each user and keeps them aside for evaluation.The model will predict the rating for these ten jokes of the test records and these can be compared to the actual values. That way we can evaluate the performance of our recommender systems. Finally, the parameter `goodRating`, defines the threshold for good rating, here we say any rating greater than or equal to 1 is a positive rating. This is critical for evaluating our classifier. Let us say if we want to find the accuracy of our recommender system, then we need to find out the number of ratings where our predictions matched with the actual. So if the ratings of both actual and predicted is greater than or equal to 1, then they are considered as a match. We choose 2 here looking at the density plot of z-score normalized data.

The `method` parameter is very important as this decides the evaluation scheme. In our example, we have used split. In `split` it randomly assigns objects to train or test based on the proportion given.

Another important parameter we did not include is k. By default, the value of k is set to 1 for the `split` method. It decides the number of times to run the evaluation scheme. If we had selected k-fold cross-validation as our method, k defaults to 10. A total of 10 different models will be built for 10 splits of the data and the performance will be an average of all the 10 models.

The following figure compares the split and k-fold schemes:

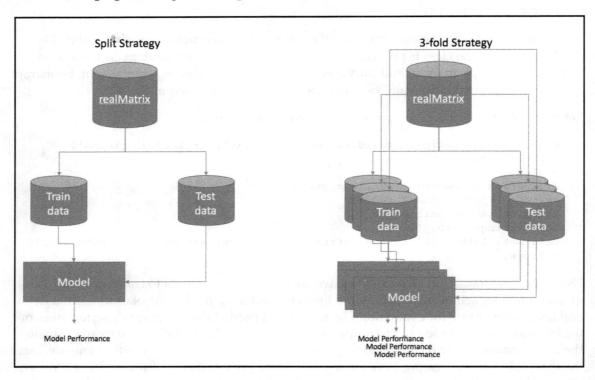

As you can see in a three-fold validation, we have three splits of our train and test data. The model is evaluated against all the three splits.

Refer to `https://en.wikipedia.org/wiki/Cross-validation_(statistics)` to find out more about cross-validation and, specifically, about k-fold cross-validation.

You can evoke R Help for the documentation:

```
help("evaluationScheme")
```

Now that we have built our scheme, we can use the scheme to extract our test and train dataset.

Extract the train and test data as follows:

```
> set.seed(100)
> data = normalize(data, method ="Z-score")

> train <- getData(plan, type = "train")
> train
1350 x 100 rating matrix of class 'realRatingMatrix' with 96678 ratings.

> test <- getData(plan, type = "unknown")
> test
150 x 100 rating matrix of class 'realRatingMatrix' with 9736 ratings.
>
> test.known <- getData(plan, "known")
> test.known
150 x 100 rating matrix of class 'realRatingMatrix' with 1500 ratings.
>
```

The getData function is used to extract the train, and test dataset. The type parameter returns different datasets. The train type returns the training dataset. The known type returns the known ratings from the test dataset. The unknown type returns the ratings used for evaluation of the dataset.

This is a standard technique followed in any machine learning algorithm development. The train dataset is used to train the model and the test dataset is used to test the performance of the model. If the model performs poorly, we go back to using the train dataset and tune the model. Tuning may involve either changing the approach (that is, instead of using user-based models, let us say we move to latent-based models and evaluate the performance) or we start changing some of the parameters of our existing approach. Say in the case of user-based filtering, we change the number of neighbors.

Our test dataset is further divided into test.known and test. The dataset test.known, the ratings for 10 products. Using those ratings, our recommender system will predict the recommendations. These recommendations can be now compared with the actual value from test data set.

Let us look at our test data set:

```
> dim(train@data)
[1] 1350   100
> dim(test@data)
[1] 150 100
```

Out of a total of 1,500 users, 90% of the data (that is 1,350), is allocated to train. A set of 150 users are reserved for the purpose of testing.

Train model

We have our data split into the following:

- `train`: The user matrix we will use to build our recommendation model.
- `test.known`: We will feed this for our predict method along with our model. The output can now be compared to our test dataset.
- `test`: The test dataset is used for evaluating our model

Using these, let us go ahead and build our recommender system. For the first model, we are going to build a random model.

Building the **random model looks** as follows:

```
> random.model <- Recommender(train, "RANDOM")
> random.model
Recommender of type 'RANDOM' for 'realRatingMatrix'
learned using 1350 users.
> getModel(random.model)
$range
[1] -5.998287  5.224277

$labels
    [1]  "j1"   "j2"   "j3"   "j4"   "j5"   "j6"   "j7"   "j8"   "j9"   "j10"
 "j11"  "j12"  "j13"  "j14"
   [15]  "j15"  "j16"  "j17"  "j18"  "j19"  "j20"  "j21"  "j22"  "j23"  "j24"
 "j25"  "j26"  "j27"  "j28"
   [29]  "j29"  "j30"  "j31"  "j32"  "j33"  "j34"  "j35"  "j36"  "j37"  "j38"
 "j39"  "j40"  "j41"  "j42"
   [43]  "j43"  "j44"  "j45"  "j46"  "j47"  "j48"  "j49"  "j50"  "j51"  "j52"
 "j53"  "j54"  "j55"  "j56"
   [57]  "j57"  "j58"  "j59"  "j60"  "j61"  "j62"  "j63"  "j64"  "j65"  "j66"
 "j67"  "j68"  "j69"  "j70"
   [71]  "j71"  "j72"  "j73"  "j74"  "j75"  "j76"  "j77"  "j78"  "j79"  "j80"
 "j81"  "j82"  "j83"  "j84"
   [85]  "j85"  "j86"  "j87"  "j88"  "j89"  "j90"  "j91"  "j92"  "j93"  "j94"
 "j95"  "j96"  "j97"  "j98"
   [99]  "j99"  "j100"

>
```

```
> random.predict <- predict(random.model, test.known, n = 5, type =
"topNList")
> random.predict@items[1]
[[1]]
[1] 81 96 47 28 65

> random.predict@ratings[1]
[[1]]
[1] 2.516658 2.139329 1.921027 1.900945 1.845772
```

Using the `Recommender` function, we have built a random model. Inspecting the model, we see that this model will produce a random number between -5.9 and 5.2 as defined by the range. The model does not learn anything, except the range of the ratings in the training set and produces the requested rating.

The `predict` function is used to predict the ratings. We need the top N predictions, that is the top five jokes the user would have rated. Is it the top 5 jokes of the 10 known (i.e. holdout) jokes for a specific user? This is specified by the `n` parameter and the `type` parameter. Finally, we can look into our predictions, `random.predict`, to find our recommendations and ratings for an individual user. In the preceding code snippet, we look for user 1. We see that jokes `81`, `96`, `47`, `28`, and `65` are recommended for this user.

Its a best practice to build a reference model to begin with before we start building our actual models. When we have our first model, we can compare it with our reference model to see some performance gain. Any good model should be better than a random model. Once we have a good model we can replace the random model with the good model and proceed to find better models. Random models, since they are very easy to create are typically used as the first reference model.

Let us build a more sensible model. The one we have seen in the previous sections, called the `popular` model.

Building `popular` model looks as follows:

```
> popular.model <- Recommender(train, "POPULAR")
> popular.model
Recommender of type 'POPULAR' for 'realRatingMatrix'
learned using 1350 users.
>
```

We build a model using the `popular` type. We have trained it with 1,350 user data.

Let us predict using this model:

```
> popular.model
Recommender of type 'POPULAR' for 'realRatingMatrix'
learned using 1350 users.
> popular.predict <- predict(popular.model, test.known, n = 5, type =
"topNList")
> popular.predict@items[1]
$u24654
[1] 50 36 27 32 35

> popular.predict@ratings[1]
$u4027
[1] 3.472511 3.218649 3.157963 3.011908 2.976325

>
```

Using the `predict` function and using the `test.known` dataset, we try to predict the top five recommendations for users in the `test` dataset. Remember that in the `known` parameter, we had reserved 10 recommendations for each user, stored in `test.known`. Using that we are now predicting other jokes for the user.

Before we proceed to build a better model, let us introduce the `evaluate` function.

Till now we had explicitly invoked the `Recommender` and create a recommender object. Further passed that model to `predict` function to get our predictions. This is the correct way of implementing a model. However, when are evaluating different models, we need a convenient way to run and test multiple models.

With `evaluate` function, we don't have to do those explicit steps.

The `evaluate` function can take an evaluation scheme and apply it to a given model and produce the performance of the recommendation model. The performance is given using multiple metrics.

Let us see how the `evaluate` function is used:

```
> results <- evaluate(plan, method = "POPULAR", type = "topNList", n = 5 )
POPULAR run fold/sample [model time/prediction time]
    1   [0.012sec/0.215sec]
> getConfusionMatrix(results)
[[1]]
         TP        FP        FN        TN precision     recall       TPR
FPR
5 1.993333 3.006667 12.29333 72.70667 0.3986667 0.1626843 0.1626843
0.03823596


>
```

As you can see, we have passed the `plan`, which is our evaluation scheme and the method. We request five recommendation for each user using parameters `k` and `type`.

The `getConfusionMatrix` function is used to provide us with different metrics to evaluate our recommendation engine. Using the test known data set and the constructed model, predictions are made. These predictions are compared with the test unknown dataset. Let us say we have a user A in test known and test unknown. The 10 items, defined by the given parameter, and their ratings in test known are used to find the recommendations for this user. The recommended items are compared against the test unknown dataset for that user.

While comparing the ratings, the parameter `goodRating` is used. Let us say we have set our `goodRating` parameter to 5. If the predicted rating is 5.1 and the actual rating is 7.1, they are considered as a match. Our recommendation is considered as a match with the test set. This way we can calculate the metrics we have detailed.

TP stands for **True Positive**, the number of instances where our recommendation matched with the actual recommendation.

FP stands for **False Positive**, the number of instances where we made a recommendation, but the actual data shows otherwise.

FN stands for **False Negative**, where we did not recommend, but the actual data shows otherwise.

TN stands for **True Negative**, where we did not recommend and the actual data was in agreement with us.

Precision is the ratio of the number of correct recommendations out of the total recommendations.

Recall is the ratio of the number of correct recommendations out of the total correct recommendations.

TPR stands for **True Positive Rate**, the number of true positives to the total positives (true positive + false negative).

FPR stands for **False Positive Rate**, the ratio of false positives to the sum of false positives and true negatives.

Refer to https://en.wikipedia.org/wiki/Confusion_matrix for more information about the confusion matrix.

Until now we have used the split scheme; now let us use the **n fold cross-validation scheme**. Further, we will be only using the evaluate function to find the performance of our recommendation model.

The n fold cross-validation is as follows:

```
> plan <- evaluationScheme(data, method="cross", train=0.9, given = 10,
goodRating=5)
> results <- evaluate(plan, method = "POPULAR", type = "topNList", n =
c(5,10,15) )
POPULAR run fold/sample [model time/prediction time]
      1   [0.013sec/0.216sec]
      2   [0.011sec/0.219sec]
      3   [0.011sec/0.232sec]
      4   [0.013sec/0.224sec]
      5   [0.013sec/0.217sec]
      6   [0.011sec/0.205sec]
      7   [0.012sec/0.223sec]
      8   [0.016sec/0.226sec]
      9   [0.011sec/0.22sec]
      10  [0.012sec/0.233sec]
> avg(results)
```

	TP	FP	FN	TN	precision	recall	TPR
FPR							
5	2.056000	2.944000	14.35467	70.64533	0.4112000	0.1672573	0.1672573
0.03842095							
10	3.962667	6.037333	12.44800	67.55200	0.3962667	0.3088684	0.3088684
0.07883053							
15	5.644000	9.356000	10.76667	64.23333	0.3762667	0.4214511	0.4214511
0.12230877							

Instead of the train test split scheme, here we are doing a cross-validation. By default, it does a 10-fold cross-validation. Finally, our results is an average of 10 cross-validations for three different top Ns. As you can see, we have passed n a vector with three values, 5, 10, and 15, so we can generate 5, 10, or 15 recommendations.

User-based models

We discussed the the user-based model in the previous sections. Let us do a quick recap here. The user-based model for collaborative filtering tries to mimic the word-of-mouth approach in marketing. It is a memory-based model. The premise of this algorithm is that similar users will have a similar taste in jokes. Therefore, they will rate jokes in a more or less similar manner. It's a two-step process, in the first step for a given user, the algorithm finds his neighbors. A similarity distance measure, such as Pearson coefficient, or cosine distance, is used to find the neighbors for a given user. For an item not rated by the user, we look at whether the user's neighbors have rated that item. If they have rated an average of his the neighbors' ratings are considered as the ratings for this user.

Let us prepare the data:

```
set.seed(100)
data <- sample(Jester5k, 1500)
plan <- evaluationScheme(data, method="split", train=0.9, given = 10,
goodRating=1)
train <- getData(plan, "train")
test <- getData(plan, "unknown")
test.known <- getData(plan, "known")
```

With our input data prepared, let us proceed to build the model.

Building a user-based model looks like this:

```
> plan <- evaluationScheme(data, method="cross", train=0.9, given = 10,
goodRating=5)
> results <- evaluate(plan, method = "UBCF", type = "topNList", n =
c(5,10,15) )
UBCF run fold/sample [model time/prediction time]
```

```
        1    [0.017sec/0.268sec]
        2    [0.016sec/0.267sec]
        3    [0.01sec/0.284sec]
        4    [0.01sec/0.273sec]
        5    [0.009sec/0.273sec]
        6    [0.009sec/0.272sec]
        7    [0.009sec/0.508sec]
        8    [0.009sec/0.236sec]
        9    [0.009sec/0.268sec]
        10   [0.01sec/0.262sec]
> avg(results)
            TP          FP          FN          TN precision      recall         TPR
FPR
5   2.024000 2.976000 14.40600 70.59400 0.4048000 0.1586955 0.1586955
0.03877853
10 3.838667 6.161333 12.59133 67.40867 0.3838667 0.2888018 0.2888018
0.08048999
15 5.448000 9.552000 10.98200 64.01800 0.3632000 0.3987303 0.3987303
0.12502479
>
```

Using our framework defined in the previous model, we can create a user-based recommendation system, as shown in the previous code, and evaluate its performance. We have used the cross-validation scheme to evaluate our model's performance.

We call the `evaluate` method with our cross-validation scheme and specify the user-based model by the parameter method. **UBCF** stands for **user-based recommendation**. Once again we are interested only in the top N recommendation and our N is now an array of three values: 5, 10, and 15. We want to evaluate our model for all the three Ns. Therefore, we have passed an array of values. Finally, when we see the model performance using the `results` object, the performance is averaged across 10 models, for all the three Ns we have supplied.

An alternate way to evaluate the model is to make the model do the recommendation for all the unknown items in the test data. Now compare the difference between the predicted and actual ratings and show a metric, such as root mean square error, or mean absolute error or squared error.

Find all the ratings:

```
> results.1 <- evaluate(plan, method ="UBCF", type ="ratings")
UBCF run fold/sample [model time/prediction time]
        1    [0.01sec/0.395sec]
        2    [0.011sec/0.223sec]
        3    [0.01sec/0.227sec]
        4    [0.011sec/0.247sec]
```

```
      5    [0.01sec/0.221sec]
      6    [0.009sec/0.213sec]
      7    [0.013sec/0.247sec]
      8    [0.009sec/0.401sec]
      9    [0.011sec/0.242sec]
     10    [0.009sec/0.243sec]
> avg(results.1)
          RMSE        MSE        MAE
res 4.559954 20.80655 3.573544
>
```

We can further improve the model by changing the parameters:

```
param=list(normalize="center",method="Pearson",nn=10)
```

Here we are saying for our user-based model, we need to normalize the data. Sine the scale of the rating is same across the users (from -10 to +10) we want to only bring the data to a zero mean. Further, we want to use the Pearson coefficient as our distance measure. Finally, we want to use 10 neighbors to get our recommendation.

Also since we have 100 jokes, we can have around 30 jokes in our test.known.

Let us make these changes and evaluate our model:

```
> plan <- evaluationScheme(data, method="cross", train=0.9, given = 30,
goodRating=5)
> results.1 <- evaluate(plan, method ="UBCF", param=param, type ="ratings")
UBCF run fold/sample [model time/prediction time]
      1    [0.01sec/0.223sec]
      2    [0.014sec/0.23sec]
      3    [0.008sec/0.402sec]
      4    [0.009sec/0.24sec]
      5    [0.011sec/0.245sec]
      6    [0.01sec/0.233sec]
      7    [0.009sec/0.227sec]
      8    [0.009sec/0.232sec]
      9    [0.009sec/0.209sec]
     10    [0.014sec/0.218sec]
> avg(results.1)
          RMSE        MSE        MAE
res 4.427301 19.61291 3.503708
```

We can see that our RMSE has gone down. Similarly, we can make some more changes and tune our model.

Item-based models

This is a model-based approach. From a given ratings matrix, this method explores the relationship between the items. Based on the ratings, different users provide different items, and an item-to-item similarity matrix is derived. Once again, as in the user-based model, Pearson coefficient or cosine distance is used as a similarity metric. For each item, we store the top K similar items, rather than storing all the items for efficiency purposes. A weighted sum idea is used to finally make a recommendation for a user. Refer to the paper from Amazon for more about item-based filtering: https://dl.acm.org/citation.cfm?id= 642471

The following code shows how to perform item-based recommendations:

```
> plan <- evaluationScheme(data, method="cross", train=0.9, given = 10,
goodRating=5)
> results <- evaluate(plan, method = "IBCF", type = "topNList", n =
c(5,10,15) )
IBCF run fold/sample [model time/prediction time]
      1  [0.096sec/0.038sec]
      2  [0.086sec/0.028sec]
      3  [0.092sec/0.032sec]
      4  [0.098sec/0.035sec]
      5  [0.347sec/0.03sec]
      6  [0.093sec/0.026sec]
      7  [0.099sec/0.033sec]
      8  [0.087sec/0.03sec]
      9  [0.094sec/0.035sec]
      10 [0.1sec/0.03sec]
> avg(results)
           TP        FP        FN       TN precision      recall        TPR
FPR
5   0.7533333  4.246667 15.68600 69.31400 0.1506667 0.03764956 0.03764956
0.05794888
10  1.5920000  8.408000 14.84733 65.15267 0.1592000 0.09053889 0.09053889
0.11464379
15  2.5126667 12.487333 13.92667 61.07333 0.1675111 0.14731668 0.14731668
0.16999810
```

As you can see, the class structure of `recommenderlab` is very elegant; the only change we made was to use IBCF as the value to the `method` parameter.

Let us also look at the RMSE metrics for this model:

```
> results.1 <- evaluate(plan, method = "IBCF", type = "ratings" )
> avg(results.1)
         RMSE       MSE       MAE
res 5.352557 28.67655 4.154455
```

The RMSE is higher than the user-based model. Which is not surprising. Item-based model typically performs slightly poorer than the user-based model. The trade off is memory usage. User-based model consumes more memory but gives better results.

Factor-based models

Factor-based models leverage matrix decomposition techniques to predict recommendations for unrated items.

A model using funkSVD from recommenderlab is shown here:

```
> plan <- evaluationScheme(data, method="cross", train=0.9, given = 10,
goodRating=5)

> results <- evaluate(plan, method = "SVDF", type = "topNList", n =
c(5,10,15) )
SVDF run fold/sample [model time/prediction time]
     1  [31.933sec/2.148sec]
     2  [29.701sec/1.405sec]
     3  [31.053sec/1.534sec]
     4  [30.957sec/1.323sec]
     5  [31.157sec/1.321sec]
     6  [30.675sec/1.306sec]
     7  [30.701sec/1.508sec]
     8  [30.479sec/1.283sec]
     9  [31.163sec/1.354sec]
     10  [31.164sec/1.328sec]
> avg(results)
          TP        FP        FN       TN precision    recall       TPR
FPR
5  1.358667  3.641333 14.19933 70.80067 0.2717333 0.1047871 0.1047871
0.04796178
10 2.712000  7.288000 12.84600 67.15400 0.2712000 0.2021191 0.2021191
0.09596163
15 3.951333 11.048667 11.60667 63.39333 0.2634222 0.2896861 0.2896861
0.14562328
>
```

Once again the steps are the same, except the value for the method parameter.

Again let us see the performance from a RMSE perspective:

```
> results.1 <- evaluate(plan, method = "SVDF", type = "ratings" )
SVDF run fold/sample [model time/prediction time]
     1  [42.193sec/1.974sec]
     2  [37.083sec/1.543sec]
```

```
     3    [33.355sec/1.456sec]
     4    [34.085sec/1.505sec]
     5    [33.442sec/1.356sec]
     6    [34.764sec/1.328sec]
     7    [33.307sec/1.232sec]
     8    [34.139sec/1.484sec]
     9    [33.132sec/1.359sec]
    10    [35.274sec/1.342sec]
> avg(results.1)
        RMSE       MSE       MAE
res 5.086455 25.88602 3.853208
>
```

Our RMSE error is much higher than both the item-based and the user-based models.

In this case, we are better of using an user-based model.

Let us now build a complete model, using our knowledge from the above three experiments.

To being with let us normalize the data and then split it into test and train:

```
data <- Jester5k
data <- normalize(data, method = "center")
plan <- evaluationScheme(data, method="split", train=0.9, given = 10,
goodRating=5)
train <- getData(plan, "train")
test <- getData(plan, "unknown")
test.known <- getData(plan, "known")
```

Let us build the user-based recommendation model:

```
> param=list(method="Pearson",nn=10)
> final.model <- Recommender(train, method = "UBCF", param = param)
Warning message:
In .local(x, ...) : x was already normalized by row!
> final.model
Recommender of type 'UBCF' for 'realRatingMatrix'
learned using 4500 users.
```

We saw that, Pearson with 10 nearest neighbors worked well, we will use those to build our final model.

Let us get the top-N recommendation:

```
> final.predict <- predict(final.model, test, n = 5, type = "topNList")
> final.predict@items[1]
$u7147
```

```
[1] 66 36 35 54 42

> final.predict@ratings[1]
$u7147
[1] 2.746771 2.742437 2.722453 2.297228 1.974920
```

We have shown in this section, how to build all three types of recommender systems. We finally chose the user-based system as it out-performed all the other systems in RMSE.

The next section gives the complete list of code we have used in this chapter.

Complete R Code

The complete project code is as follows:

```
set.seed(100)
products <- c('A','B','C','D','E','F','G')
user.a <-    c( 3,  0,  2,  5,  5,  0,1)
user.b <-    c( 3,  5,  3,  5,  4,  2,  1)

ratings.matrix <- as.data.frame(list(user.a,user.b))
names(ratings.matrix) <- c("user.a","user.b")
rownames(ratings.matrix) <- products
head(ratings.matrix)

products <- c('A','B','C')
user.a <- c(2,0,3)
user.b <- c(5,2,0)
user.c <- c(3,3,0)
ratings.matrix <- as.data.frame(list(user.a,user.b, user.c))
names(ratings.matrix) <- c("user.a","user.b","user.c")
rownames(ratings.matrix) <- products
head(ratings.matrix)


ratings.mat <- (as.matrix(ratings.matrix))
sim.mat <- cor(t(ratings.mat), method = "Pearson")
sim.mat

svd.coms <- svd(ratings.mat)
user.a.vector <- svd.coms$u[1,]
product.B.vector <- svd.coms$v[2,]

ratings.user.a.prod.B <- user.a.vector %*% product.B.vector
ratings.user.a.prod.B
```

```
svd.coms$u[1,] %*% svd.coms$v[2,]

install.packages("recommenderlab")


library(recommenderlab, quietly = TRUE)

# Binary Rating Matrix
bin.data <- sample(c(0,1), 20, replace = TRUE)
bin.mat <- matrix(bin.data, nrow = 4, ncol = 5)
bin.mat
rating.mat <- as(bin.mat, "binaryRatingMatrix")
rating.mat

# A quick recommender
model <- Recommender(data = rating.mat, method = "POPULAR")
model
str(model)

recommenderRegistry$get_entries(dataType = "binaryRatingMatrix")

# Quick Prediction
recomms <- predict(model, newdata = rating.mat, n =2)
recomms@items
recomms@ratings


data("Jester5k")
str(Jester5k)
head(Jester5k@data[1:5,1:5])


# Users
Jester5k@data[1,]
Jester5k@data[100,]

zero.ratings <- rowSums(Jester5k@data == 0)
zero.ratings.df <- data.frame("user" = names(zero.ratings), "count" =
zero.ratings)
head(zero.ratings.df)
head(zero.ratings.df[order(-zero.ratings.df$count),], 10)
hist(zero.ratings.df$count, main ="Distribution of zero rated jokes")
zero.density <- density(zero.ratings.df$count)
plot(zero.density)

model <- kmeans(zero.ratings.df$count,3 )
model$centers
model$size
```

```
model.df <- data.frame(centers = model$centers, size = model$size, perc =
(model$size / 5000) * 100)
head(model.df)


# Ratings
Jester5k@data[,1]

par(mfrow=c(2,2))
joke.density <- density(Jester5k@data[,1][Jester5k@data[,1]!=0])
plot(joke.density)

joke.density <- density(Jester5k@data[,25][Jester5k@data[,25]!=0])
plot(joke.density)

joke.density <- density(Jester5k@data[,75][Jester5k@data[,75]!=0])
plot(joke.density)

joke.density <- density(Jester5k@data[,100][Jester5k@data[,100]!=100])
plot(joke.density)


par(mfrow=c(1,1))
nratings(Jester5k)
hist(getRatings(Jester5k), main="Distribution of ratings")

# Popular joke
# Binarize the ratings
ratings.binary <- binarize(Jester5k, minRating =0)
ratings.binary
ratings.sum <- colSums(ratings.binary)
ratings.sum.df <- data.frame(joke = names(ratings.sum), pratings =
ratings.sum)
head( ratings.sum.df[order(-ratings.sum.df$pratings), ],10)
tail( ratings.sum.df[order(-ratings.sum.df$pratings), ],10)



# Sample
data <- sample(Jester5k, 1500)
hist(getRatings(data), main="Distribution of ratings for 1500 users")


##
data <- sample(Jester5k, 1500)
ratings.mat <- getRatingMatrix(data)
str(ratings.mat)
```

```
str(data@data)


# Normalize the data
data.norm   <- normalize(data, method = "center")
data.norm.z <- normalize(data, method = "Z-score")

par(mfrow=c(3,1))
plot(density(getRatings(data)), main = "Raw")
plot(density(getRatings(data.norm)), main = "Normalized")
plot(density(getRatings(data.norm.z)), main = "Z-score normalized")
par(mfrow=c(1,1))


# Train test split
set.seed(100)
data = normalize(data, method ="Z-score")
plan <- evaluationScheme(data, method="split", train=0.9, given = 10,
goodRating=1)
plan
train <- getData(plan, "train")
train
test <- getData(plan, "unknown")
test
test.known <- getData(plan, "known")
test.known

# Look at the data
dim(train@data)
dim(test@data)


# Base line model
random.model <- Recommender(train, "RANDOM")
random.model
getModel(random.model)

random.predict <- predict(random.model, test.known, n = 5, type =
"topNList")
random.predict@items[1]
random.predict@ratings[1]

test.known@data[1,c(81, 96 ,47 ,28, 65)]

# Popular Model
popular.model <- Recommender(train, "POPULAR")
popular.model
```

```
popular.predict <- predict(popular.model, test.known, n = 5, type =
"topNList")
popular.predict@items[1]
popular.predict@ratings[1]

test.known@data[1,c(50,36,27,32,35)]



# Evaluate the results
results <- evaluate(plan, method = "POPULAR", type = "topNList", n = 5 )
getConfusionMatrix(results)


# Cross validation
plan <- evaluationScheme(data, method="cross", train=0.9, given = 10,
goodRating=5)
results <- evaluate(plan, method = "POPULAR", type = "topNList", n =
c(5,10,15) )
avg(results)



# User based models
set.seed(100)
data <- sample(Jester5k, 1500)
plan <- evaluationScheme(data, method="split", train=0.9, given = 10,
goodRating=1)
train <- getData(plan, "train")
test <- getData(plan, "unknown")
test.known <- getData(plan, "known")


plan <- evaluationScheme(data, method="cross", train=0.9, given = 10,
goodRating=5)
results <- evaluate(plan, method = "UBCF", type = "topNList", n =
c(5,10,15) )
avg(results)


param=list(normalize="center",method="Pearson",nn=10)
plan <- evaluationScheme(data, method="cross", train=0.9, given = 30,
goodRating=5)
results.1 <- evaluate(plan, method ="UBCF", param=param, type ="ratings")
avg(results.1)

# Item based models
plan <- evaluationScheme(data, method="cross", train=0.9, given = 10,
```

```
      goodRating=5)
      results <- evaluate(plan, method = "IBCF", type = "topNList", n =
      c(5,10,15) )
      avg(results)

      results.1 <- evaluate(plan, method = "IBCF", type = "ratings" )
      avg(results.1)


      # factor based models
      plan <- evaluationScheme(data, method="cross", train=0.9, given = 10,
      goodRating=5)
      results <- evaluate(plan, method = "SVDF", type = "topNList", n =
      c(5,10,15) )
      avg(results)

      results.1 <- evaluate(plan, method = "SVDF", type = "ratings" )
      avg(results.1)

      # final model
      data <- Jester5k

      data <- normalize(data, method = "center")
      plan <- evaluationScheme(data, method="split", train=0.9, given = 10,
      goodRating=5)
      train <- getData(plan, "train")
      test <- getData(plan, "unknown")
      test.known <- getData(plan, "known")


      param=list(method="Pearson",nn=10)
      final.model <- Recommender(train, method = "UBCF", param = param)
      final.model

      final.predict <- predict(final.model, test, n = 5, type = "topNList")
      final.predict@items[1]
      final.predict@ratings[1]

      test@data[1,]

      test@data[1,c(45,80,10,25,77)]

      final.predict <- predict(final.model, test, type = "ratings")
      final.predict@items[1]
      final.predict@ratings[1]
```

Summary

We looked at what is a collaborative filtering method and went into different collaborative filtering strategies. We introduced the R package `recommenderlab` to perform collaborative filtering. We leveraged the Jester5k dataset to demonstrate a collaborative filtering algorithm. We looked at the random model, popular model, item-based similarity, user-based similarity models, and factor models. We introduced the concept of evaluating the performance of a recommender system before deploying it. We demonstrated the steps to split the datasets in order to evaluate our model performance.

In the next chapter, we will be looking to build Deep Neural networks using the `MXNet` package for time series data. We will introduce the package `MXNet` R and proceed to build a deep neural network.

4
Taming Time Series Data Using Deep Neural Networks

With the advent of the Internet of Things, more and more devices are being added to the World Wide Web every day. Today's world is rapidly becoming inundated with intelligence devices. These devices are producing data at a rapid pace which we have never seen before. The storage cost has significantly come down, allowing companies to store this massive data in a cheap manner. Smart City projects have been kick-started by various governments. These Smart City projects rely heavily on this instrumentation. Technology companies and governments now want to leverage this massive data, generated from these smart devices, to perform analytics and produce data-enabled applications. The end use cases of these analytics are limitless. The data is characterized by three factors:

- **Volume**: The amount of data generated
- **Variety**: The different types of data
- **Velocity**: The speed at which this data is generated

Among all the different varieties of data, data from sensors is the most widespread and is referred to as time series data.

A time series is a series of data points indexed (or listed or graphed) in time order. Most commonly, a time series is a sequence taken at successive equally spaced points in time. Thus it is a sequence of discrete-time data.

Time series data is not a new type of data. For decades, financial industries have been using this data for various market-related purposes. Algorithmic trading is the use of computer programs to generate and follow a defined set of instructions to trade in the market. This allows profit to be generated at a greater speed and frequency compared to a human trader. Algorithmic trading leverages time series data. The traditional approach to time series data involves analyzing it in frequency domains or temporal domains. Today, deep learning has opened up a whole new door to analyzing time series data at a never before seen speed and level of precision.

Time series data is not just limited to sensor data and financial data. In many other real-world applications, such as speech recognition, machine translation, and sequence generation, data is captured in a temporal fashion. Two points in a time series may look identical, but they may have different temporal dependencies, thus making them belong to two different categories.

Deep learning allows us to build sophisticated models, which can capture non-linear relationships in the data in a much more efficient and faster manner. Deep learning can be defined in two ways.

Any neural network with more than three hidden layers can be defined as a deep learning network. Different layers in the network capture different properties of the data. The nature of deep learning is very valuable to time series analysis.

The other definition is the series of hacks performed on these networks to incorporate bagging and boosting functionalities, thus allowing us to build an ensemble of models through a single network. Once again, each model in the ensemble is now capable of understanding different regions of the data. This is very useful for analyzing time series data.

The aim of this chapter is to introduce MXNet R to our readers and show them how fully connected deep networks can be effective in predicting time series data. Our treatment of traditional time series data analysis will be very limited. We will provide sufficient references for traditional time series analysis.

In this chapter, we will do the following:

- Introduce time series data and traditional approaches to solve them
- Provide an overview of deep neural networks
- Introduce the MXNet R package
- Go over time series use cases and data
- Build a deep learning solution for our time series problem

The code for this chapter was written in RStudio version 0.99.491. It uses R version 3.3.1. As we work through our example, we will introduce the MXNet R package that we will be using. During our code descriptions, we will be using some of the output printed in the console. We have included what was printed in the console immediately following the statement that prints the information to the console, to not disturb the flow of the code.

Time series data

Let us quickly look at some examples of time series data. We will use some data from Rob J Hyndman, from https://robjhyndman.com/TSDL/.

We will use the age of death of successive kings of England dataset.

Let us store the time series data as a ts object:

```
> kings <- scan("http://robjhyndman.com/tsdldata/misc/kings.dat",skip=3)
Read 42 items
> king.ts <- ts(kings)
> king.ts
Time Series:
Start = 1
End = 42
Frequency = 1
 [1] 60 43 67 50 56 42 50 65 68 43 65 34 47 34 49 41 13 35 53 56 16 43 69
59 48 59 86 55 68 51 33 49 67 77
[35] 81 67 71 81 68 70 77 56
>
```

Using the scan function, we get the data from the URL. Following that, we create a time series object using ts.

Let us plot the time series:

```
plot(king.ts)
```

The standard R `plot` function knows how to plot time series data. The time series plot is as shown in the following diagram:

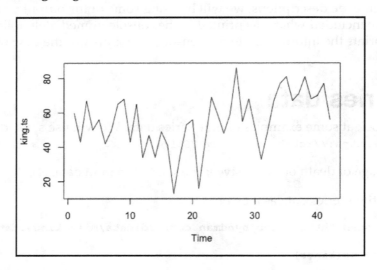

Time series can be either non-seasonal or seasonal.

Non-seasonal time series

Non-seasonal time series tend to have a trend component and an error component. We say a trend exists in the time series when there is a long-term increase or decrease in the data. It does not have to be linear.

An additive model is used to estimate the trend of a non-seasonal time series. The time series can be smoothed to remove the trend using methods such as moving averages. The trend can be either increasing or decreasing.

Let us perform smoothing using a simple moving average:

```
library(TTR)

par(mfrow=c(2 ,2))
plot(SMA(king.ts, n=2), main = "n=2")
plot(SMA(king.ts, n=5), main = "n=5")
plot(SMA(king.ts, n=10), main = "n=10")
plot(SMA(king.ts, n=15), main = "n=15")
par(mfrow=c(1,1)
```

The `TTR` library provides the `SMA` function to perform the smoothing of the data. The n parameter defines the order of the moving average, which means how many points we want to consider to do our moving average.

Let's look at the plots of the smoothed time series:

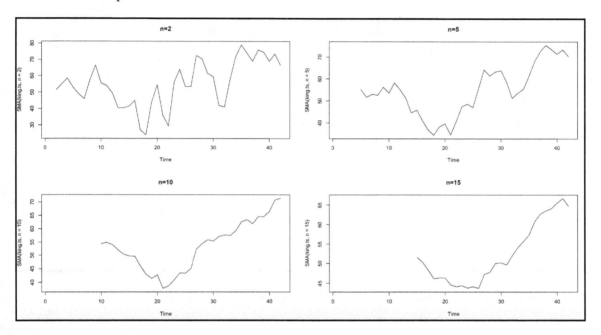

Seasonal time series

Seasonal time series have a trend, error, and a seasonality component. Consider the sales figures of winter clothing. They tend to rise during winter and flat ten out during summer and other seasons. This is the seasonality effect. Seasonality is always of a fixed and known period.

We will use another small dataset to show seasonality—the number of births per month in New York City from January 1946 to December 1959:

```
> births <- scan("http://robjhyndman.com/tsdldata/data/nybirths.dat")
Read 168 items
> births.ts <- ts(births, frequency = 12)
> births.comps <- decompose(births.ts)
```

Using the `decompose` function, we split the trend, seasonality, and error from the time series. Let us now plot these components using `plot(births.comps)`:

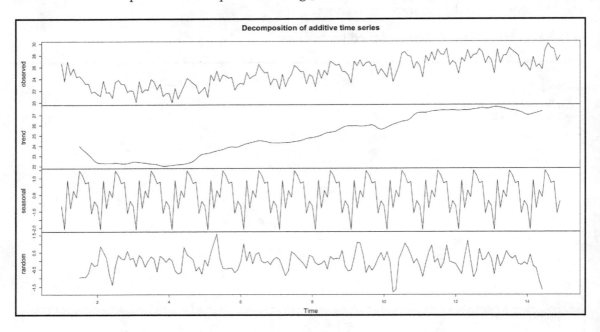

We see the individual components, trends, seasonality, and errors in the graph.

Time series as a regression problem

Another machine learning approach is to treat time series problems as regression problems.

In the previous section, we looked at non-seasonal time series with trend and error components, and seasonal time series with an additional seasonal component. These are non-stationary aspects of the time series. The time series has to be made stationary before we use any regression methods.

Statistical stationarity
A stationary time series is one whose statistical properties, such as mean, variance, autocorrelation, and so on, are all constant over time.

Let us do a simple regression exercise with our time series data. We are going to predict the age of death of a king based on the age of death of the previous king. It's a simple example and hence may sound very strange. The idea is to show how regression is used to do time series forecasting.

Let us smooth the data to make it stationary:

```
> smooth.king <- SMA(king.ts, n=5)
> smooth.king
Time Series:
Start = 1
End = 42
Frequency = 1
 [1]   NA   NA   NA   NA 55.2 51.6 53.0 52.6 56.2 53.6 58.2 55.0 51.4 44.6
45.8 41.0 36.8 34.4 38.2 39.6
[21] 34.6 40.6 47.4 48.6 47.0 55.6 64.2 61.4 63.2 63.8 58.6 51.2 53.6 55.4
61.4 68.2 72.6 75.4 73.6 71.4
[41] 73.4 70.4
```

We used the SMA function to perform the smoothing.

Let us now create our x values:

```
> library(zoo)
> library(quantmod)
>
> data <- as.zoo(smooth.king)
> x1 <- Lag(data,1)
> new.data <- na.omit(data.frame(Lag.1 = x1, y = data))
> head(new.data)
    Lag.1    y
6    55.2 51.6
7    51.6 53.0
8    53.0 52.6
9    52.6 56.2
10   56.2 53.6
11   53.6 58.2
>
```

We are using the quantmod package to get the lag of the time series. Our predictor is the age of death of the previous king. Hence, we take a lag of 1. Finally, our data frame, new.data, holds our x and y.

Let us now build our linear regression model:

```
> model <- lm(y ~ Lag.1, new.data)
> model

Call:
lm(formula = y ~ Lag.1, data = new.data)

Coefficients:
(Intercept)        Lag.1
     2.8651       0.9548

>
```

By using the `lm` function, we have built our linear regression model:

$$y = 2.8651 + 0.9548(age\,of\,death\,of\,previous\,king)$$

Let us quickly plot our model:

```
plot(model)
```

Several plots are generated. Let us look at the `qq` plot:

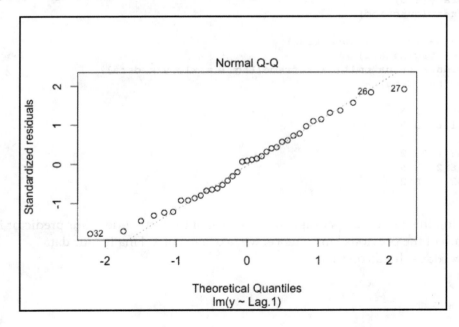

This plot shows whether or not the residuals are normally distributed. The residuals follow a straight line.

Let us look at the residual plot:

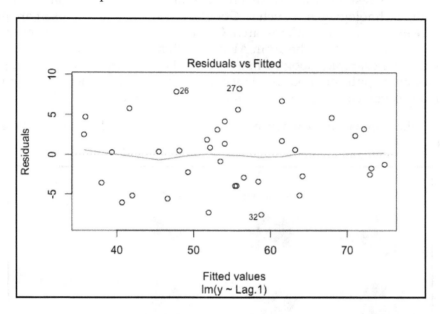

This plot shows whether or not the residuals have non-linear patterns. We can see equally spread residuals around the red horizontal line, without distinct patterns, which is a good indication that we don't have non-linear relationships.

We will stop this section here. Hopefully, it gave you an idea about how to rearrange time series data to suit a regression problem. Some of the techniques shown here, such as lag, will be used later when we build our deep learning model.

For more about time series regression, refer to the book *Forecasting: Principles and Practices* at https://www.otexts.org/fpp/4/8. It introduces some basic time series definitions. More curious readers can refer to *A Little Book of R for Time Series* at https://a-little-book-of-r-for-time-series.readthedocs.io/en/latest/src/timeseries.html.

Deep neural networks

Neural networks are extremely popular today, thanks to major research advancement over the last 10 years. The result of this research has culminated in deep learning algorithms and architecture. Big technology giants such as Google, Facebook, and Microsoft are heavily investing in deep learning network research. Complex neural networks powered by deep learning are considered state of the art in AI and machine learning. We see them being used in everyday life. For example, Google's image search is powered by deep learning. Google Translate is another application powered by deep learning today. The field of computer vision has made several advancements thanks to deep learning.

The following diagram is a typical neural network, commonly called a **multi-layer perceptron**:

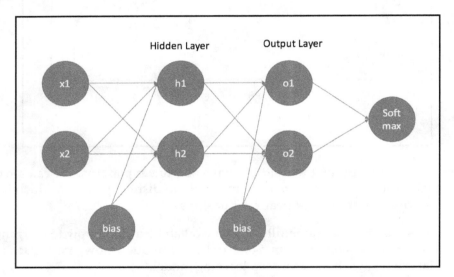

This network architecture has a single hidden layer with two nodes. The output layer is activated by a `softmax` function. This network is built for a classification task. The hidden layer can be activated by `tanh`, `sigmoid`, `relu`, or `soft relu activation` functions. The `activation` function performs the key role of introducing non-linearity in the network. The product of weight and the input from the previous layer summed up with the bias is passed to these activation functions.

Let's compare this network to a deeper network.

The following is a deep network architecture:

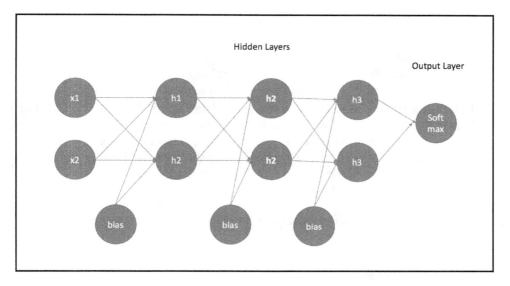

Compared to the multi-layer perceptron, we can see that there are several hidden layers. For the sake of clarity in the diagram, we have only two nodes in each hidden layer, but in practice there may be several hundred nodes.

As you can see, the deep learning networks are different from their sibling single-hidden-layer neural networks in terms of their **depth**, that is, the number of hidden layers. The input data is now passed through multiple hidden layers, on the assumption that each layer will learn some aspects of the input data.

So when do we call a network deep? Networks with more than three layers (including input and output) can be called deep neural network.

As previously mentioned, in deep learning networks the nodes of each hidden layer learn to identify a distinct set of features based on the previous layer's output. Subsequent hidden layers can understand more complex features as we aggregate and recombine features from the previous layer:

- **Feature hierarchy**: The previously mentioned phenomenon of subsequent layers in a deep network understands more complex features as a result of aggregation. The recombination of features by the previous layer is called a **feature hierarchy**. This allows the network to handle very large and complex datasets.
- **Latent features**: Latent features are the hidden features in the dataset. The feature hierarchy allows deep neural networks to discover the latent features in the data. This allows them to work on unlabeled data efficiently to discover anomalies, structures, and other features embedded in the data, without any human intervention. For example, we can take a million images and cluster them according to their similarities.

Let us see how intuitively a feedforward neural network learns from the data.

Let us consider a simple network with:

- One input layer and two nodes
- One hidden layer and two nodes
- One output layer and two nodes

Say we are solving a classification task. Our input X is a 2 x 2 matrix and our output Y is a vector of the binary response, either one or zero.

We initialize the weights and biases to begin with.

The two nodes in our input layer are fully connected to the two nodes in the hidden layer. We have four weights going from our input node to our hidden node. We can represent our weights using a 2 x 2 matrix. We have bias across the two nodes in our hidden layer. We can represent our bias using a 1 x 2 matrix.

Again, we connect our hidden nodes fully to the two nodes of our output layer. The weight matrix is again 2 x 2 and the bias matrix is again 1 x 2.

Let us look at our network architecture:

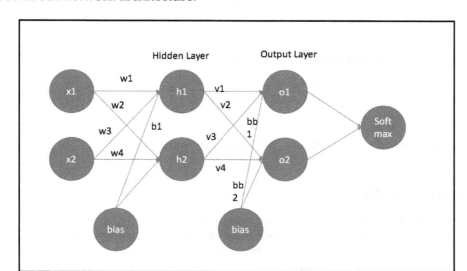

{w1,w2,w3,w4} and {b1,b2} are the weights and bias for the input to hidden nodes.

{v1,v2,v3,v4} and {bb1,bb2} are the weights and bias for the hidden to output nodes.

It is very important to initialize the weights and bias randomly. **Xavier initialization** is a popular initialization used widely today. See this blog for a very intuitive explanation on Xavier initialization, at http://andyljones.tumblr.com/post/110998971763/an-explanation-of-xavier-initialization.

Forward cycle

The input x1, x2 is multiplied by the weights *w1..w4* in each node and the respective bias is added. This is the linear transformation:

$$h1 = W^T X + b$$

An activation function is applied on top to make it a non-linear transformation. A sigmoid transformation looks like this:

$$a1 = \frac{1}{(1 + e^{-h1})}$$

Now these activations are multiplied by *v1..v4* and the respective bias is added:

$$h2 = V^T a1 + bb$$

Once again, the activation is applied on top of it:

$$a2 = \frac{1}{(1 + e^{-h2})}$$

A `softmax` function is applied, finally, to get the prediction output.

Backward cycle

The training of the network happens in the backward cycle, hence the name backpropagation algorithm. The difference between the actual and predicted value error is calculated. This error is walked back over the model and the weights in the model are adjusted. The derivative of the errors with respect to these weights gives us an idea as to how much these weights contributed to the overall error. That percentage of contribution is adjusted in the weight. Refer to `https://en.wikipedia.org/wiki/Backpropagation` to learn more.

Hopefully, this gave you an intuitive explanation on how neural networks learn from data. Let us go to the next section to learn more about the `MXNet` R library we will be using to build our deep learning network.

Introduction to the MXNet R package

We will use the package `MXNet` R to build our neural networks. It implements state-of-the-art deep learning algorithms and enables efficient GPU computing. We can work in our familiar R environment and at the same time harness the power of the GPUs (though access to GPU is available through the Python API now, we still need to wait for it to be available for R). It will be useful to give you a small overview about the basic building blocks of `MXNet` before we start using it for our time series predictions.

 Refer to the `https://github.com/apache/incubator-mxnet/tree/master/R` package for more details on the `MXNet` R package.

In MXNet, NDArray is the basic operation unit. It's a vectorized operation unit for matrix and tensor computations. All operations on this operation unit can be run on either the CPU or GPUs. The most important point is that all these operations are parallel. It's the basic data structure for manipulating and playing around with data in MXNet. It supports a wide range of mathematical operations, allowing for the writing of machine learning programs in an imperative fashion. Let us look at some basic NDArray operations.

The following code demonstrates the creation of matrices:

```
> library(mxnet)
>
> zero.matrix <- mx.nd.zeros(c(3,3))
> zero.matrix
     [,1] [,2] [,3]
[1,]    0    0    0
[2,]    0    0    0
[3,]    0    0    0
> ones.matrix <- mx.nd.ones(c(3,3))
> ones.matrix
     [,1] [,2] [,3]
[1,]    1    1    1
[2,]    1    1    1
[3,]    1    1    1
```

We have created two matrices of size *3 x 3*, one filled with zeros and the other filled with ones.

The context defines where the code is executed, either in the CPU or GPU. Let us look at the context:

```
> mx.ctx.default()
$device
[1] "cpu"

$device_id
[1] 0

$device_typeid
[1] 1

attr(,"class")
[1] "MXContext"
```

As my machine does not include a GPU, the only context available is CPU.

To create an array in a specified context, we use the following:

```
zero.matrix.gup <- mx.nd.zeros(c(3,3), mx.gpu(0))
```

We pass the context while creating the arrays. Here, we have passed the GPU context, specifying that we need this *3 x 3* zero filled array to be created in the GPU.

Data can be copied between contexts/devices as shown in the following code:

```
zero.copy <- mx.nd.copyto(zero.matrix, mx.cpu())
```

We copy the data to the CPU by passing the GPU context.

Let us see some matrix operations and sampling:

```
> mx.nd.dot(ones.matrix, ones.matrix)
     [,1] [,2] [,3]
[1,]   3    3    3
[2,]   3    3    3
[3,]   3    3    3
> mx.nd.elemwise.add(ones.matrix,ones.matrix)
     [,1] [,2] [,3]
[1,]   2    2    2
[2,]   2    2    2
[3,]   2    2    2
```

The code demonstrates matrix multiplication and element-wise addition in the matrix.

Let us look at some sampling:

```
> mu <- mx.nd.array(c(0.0,2.5))
> sigma <- mx.nd.array(c(1,3))
> mx.nd.sample.normal(mu = mu, sigma = sigma)
[1] 0.5613724 0.4520042
>
```

The code generates data from a normal distribution for a given mean and standard deviation.

We previously saw the imperative operations on NDArrays. MXNet supports symbolic inferences through its symbolic API. In symbolic programming, the operations are not executed in a sequential manner. The first step is to define a computation graph. This graph contains placeholders for input and output. Compiling this graph provides a function. This function can be bound to the NDArrays and executed. The biggest advantage of using a symbolic graph is that functions can be optimized for execution before they are run.

More on the MXNet symbolic API can be found at `https://mxnet.incubator.apache.org/tutorials/basic/symbol.html`.

Symbolic programming in MXNet

Let us do some symbolic declaration:

```
> a <- mx.symbol.Variable("a")
> a
C++ object <0x11dea3e00> of class 'MXSymbol' <0x10c0a79b0>
> b <- mx.symbol.Variable("b")
> b
C++ object <0x10fecf330> of class 'MXSymbol' <0x10c0a79b0>
> c <- a + b
> c
C++ object <0x10f91bba0> of class 'MXSymbol' <0x10c0a79b0>
>
```

As you can see, they are MXSymbol objects.

We need an executor to supply data to it and to get the results:

```
> arg_lst <- list(symbol = c, ctx = mx.ctx.default(), a = dim(ones.matrix),
+                 b= dim(ones.matrix), grad.req="null")
> pexec <- do.call(mx.simple.bind, arg_lst)
> pexec
C++ object <0x11d852c40> of class 'MXExecutor' <0x101be9c30>
> input_list <-  list(a = ones.matrix,b = ones.matrix)
> mx.exec.update.arg.arrays(pexec, input_list)
> mx.exec.forward(pexec)
> pexec$arg.arrays
$a
     [,1] [,2] [,3]
[1,]    1    1    1
[2,]    1    1    1
[3,]    1    1    1

$b
     [,1] [,2] [,3]
[1,]    1    1    1
[2,]    1    1    1
[3,]    1    1    1

> pexec$outputs
$`_plus4_output`
     [,1] [,2] [,3]
```

```
[1,]    2    2    2
[2,]    2    2    2
[3,]    2    2    2
```

We create an executor by calling `mx.simple.bind` for our symbol c. In order to create it, we need to tell the executor the shape of a and b, which are arguments to c. After that, using `mx.exec.update.arg.arrays`, we push the real data into the executor for it to execute the symbol c. The output slot of the executor has the results stored.

Let us look at another example, where we create a symbol d, which is a dot product of two matrices:

```
> d <- mx.symbol.dot(a, b)
> arg_lst <- list(symbol = d, ctx = mx.ctx.default(), a = dim(ones.matrix),
+                 b= dim(ones.matrix), grad.req="null")
> pexec <- do.call(mx.simple.bind, arg_lst)
> pexec
C++ object <0x1170550a0> of class 'MXExecutor' <0x101be9c30>
> input_list <-  list(a = ones.matrix,b = ones.matrix)
> mx.exec.update.arg.arrays(pexec, input_list)
> mx.exec.forward(pexec)
> pexec$arg.arrays
$a
     [,1] [,2] [,3]
[1,]    1    1    1
[2,]    1    1    1
[3,]    1    1    1

$b
     [,1] [,2] [,3]
[1,]    1    1    1
[2,]    1    1    1
[3,]    1    1    1

> pexec$outputs
$dot3_output
     [,1] [,2] [,3]
[1,]    3    3    3
[2,]    3    3    3
[3,]    3    3    3
```

Again, we bind an executor using `mx.simple.bind` to c. Using `mx.exec.update.arg.arrays`, we provide the actual data to a and b. Finally, using `mx.exec.forward`, we execute the executor to get the results.

Refer to `https://github.com/apache/incubator-mxnet/tree/master/R-package/vignettes` for R vignettes and other operations using `MXNet`.

With this background in imperative and symbolic use of `MXNet` R, let us go ahead and build a simple multi-layer perceptron to solve the famous XOR gate problem. We want the network to learn the XOR truth table:

X	Y	Z
0	0	0
0	1	1
1	0	1
1	1	0

Our network architecture is as follows:

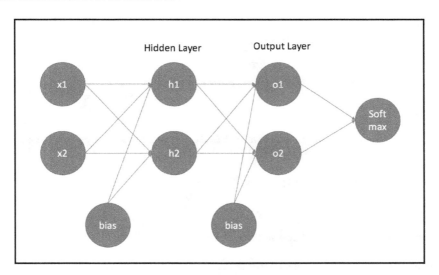

Let us generate some training data:

```
############   XOR Learning   ###########
mx.set.seed(1)

### Generate some data.
x.1 <- mx.nd.sample.normal(mu = mx.nd.array(c(0,0)),
sigma = mx.nd.array(c(0.001,0.001)), shape = (1000))
y.1 <- rep(0, 1000)
x.2 <- mx.nd.sample.normal(mu = mx.nd.array(c(0,1)),
```

```
sigma = mx.nd.array(c(0.001,0.001)), shape = (1000))
y.2 <- rep(1,1000)
x.3 <- mx.nd.sample.normal(mu = mx.nd.array(c(1,0)),
sigma = mx.nd.array(c(0.001,0.001)), shape = (1000))
y.3 <- rep(1,1000)
x.4 <- mx.nd.sample.normal(mu = mx.nd.array(c(1,1)),
sigma = mx.nd.array(c(0.001,0.001)), shape = (1000))
y.4 <- rep(0,1000)

X <- data.matrix(mx.nd.concat(list(x.1,x.2,x.3,x.4)) )
Y <- c(y.1,y.2,y.3,y.4)
```

We have used four normal distributions to generate our data points. Finally, we combine them into one array, X. The labels are stored in the Y variable.

Now let us go ahead and define our network architecture to solve our XOR problem:

```
############### Define the Network #########

# Input layer
data <- mx.symbol.Variable("data")

# Hidden Layer
hidden.layer <- mx.symbol.FullyConnected(data = data
                                         , num_hidden = 2)

# Hidden Layer Activation
act <- mx.symbol.Activation(data = hidden.layer, act_type = "relu")

# Output Layer
out.layer <- mx.symbol.FullyConnected(data = act
                                      , num.hidden = 2)

# Softmax of output
out <- mx.symbol.SoftmaxOutput(out.layer)
```

We have created two hidden layers using mx.symbol.FullyConnected. The num_hidden parameter is where we specify the number of hidden layers.

We use relu activation for this layer. mx.symbol.Activation is used to create this activation. We pass the previous hidden layer to this to say this activation function is tied to the previous hidden layer.

Our output layer is defined by mx.symbol.FullyConnected has two nodes. The activation for our output layer is a softmax activation layer defined by mx.symbol.SoftmaxOutput.

Softmax activation

Softmax activation is most frequently used for classification tasks. Softmax rescales the output from the previous layer. First, it calculates the exponential of the input to its neuron and then it divides the total sum of input with all of the neurons in the layer, so that the activation sums up to one and lies between zero and one.

The softmax equation looks like this:

$$y_k = \frac{exp(h_k)}{\sum exp(h_k)}$$

Softmax activation is used as the last layer in a deep learning neural network for multi-class classification. The layer has the same number of nodes as the number of classes and it rescales the output so that it adds up to 1.0, therefore calculating the probability for each class, that is P(y|x).

Let us build our model and test it on an XOR truth table:

```
> model <- mx.model.FeedForward.create(out, X=X
+                                       , y=Y
+                                       , ctx = mx.ctx.default()
+                                       , array.layout = "rowmajor"
+                                       , learning.rate = 0.01
+                                       , momentum = 0.9
+                                       , array.batch.size = 50
+                                       , num.round = 20
+                                       , eval.metric = mx.metric.accuracy
+       #                                , initializer =
mx.init.normal(c(0.0,0.1))
+ )
Start training with 1 devices
[1] Train-accuracy=0.506075949367089
[2] Train-accuracy=0.497
[3] Train-accuracy=0.497
[4] Train-accuracy=0.5095
[5] Train-accuracy=0.558
[6] Train-accuracy=0.67625
[7] Train-accuracy=0.74075
[8] Train-accuracy=0.75
[9] Train-accuracy=0.75
[10] Train-accuracy=0.75
[11] Train-accuracy=0.75
[12] Train-accuracy=0.75
[13] Train-accuracy=0.75
```

```
[14] Train-accuracy=0.912
[15] Train-accuracy=1
[16] Train-accuracy=1
[17] Train-accuracy=1
[18] Train-accuracy=1
[19] Train-accuracy=1
[20] Train-accuracy=1
> X_test = data.matrix(rbind(c(0,0),c(1,1),c(1,0),c(0,1) ) )
> preds = predict(model, X_test, array.layout = "rowmajor")
> pred.label <- max.col(t(preds)) -1
> pred.label
[1] 0  0 1 1
```

We complete our model building by calling `mx.model.FeedForward.Create`. We pass our final output layer out to this function. We also pass our training dataset and set up some parameters for the multi-layer perceptron.

Finally, we pass the model to the `predict` function to see the predictions.

Wow, we have finished building a neural network with 100% accuracy for our training data. You can look at the prediction results from the model for a simple XOR truth table.

We can further investigate our model by looking at the graph generated by our symbolic programming:

```
> graph.viz(model$symbol)
> model$arg.params
$fullyconnected4_weight
           [,1]       [,2]
[1,] -1.773083 1.751193
[2,] -1.774175 1.751324

$fullyconnected4_bias
[1]   1.769027 -1.754247

$fullyconnected5_weight
           [,1]       [,2]
[1,] 2.171195 -2.166867
[2,] 2.145441 -2.132973

$fullyconnected5_bias
[1] -1.662504  1.662504

>
```

The computational graph is shown in the following diagram:

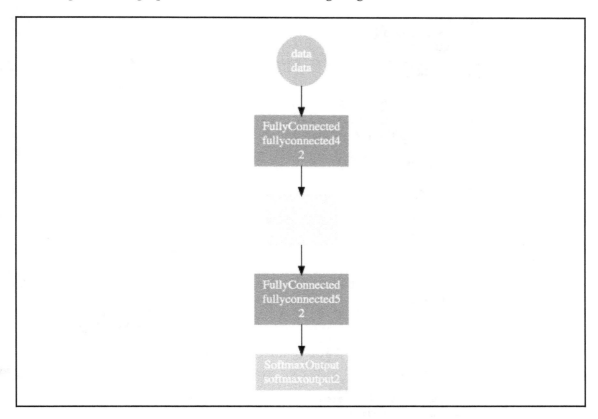

Furthermore, we can look into the weights our model has generated for this network.

Hopefully, this section gave you a good overview of the Mxnet R package. Using this knowledge, let us go ahead and solve our time series problem.

Use case and data

We want to build a deep neural network model to predict the movement of certain stocks. The problem is very difficult. Before we move onto building our network, let us look at our data.

To retrieve stock price data, do the following:

```
> library(ggplot2)
> stock.data <- new.env()
> tickers <- ('AAPL')
> stock.data <- getSymbols(tickers, src = 'yahoo', from = '2000-01-01', env
= FALSE, auto.assign = F)
```

We leverage the package `quantmod`. The `getSymbols` function in `quantmod` can fetch stock information from sources such as Yahoo and Google. As you can see, we are fetching Apple's stock price data using their *AAPL* ticker.

Let us look at the fetched data:

```
> data <- stock.data$AAPL.Close
> head(data)
            AAPL.Close
2000-01-03    3.997768
2000-01-04    3.660714
2000-01-05    3.714286
2000-01-06    3.392857
2000-01-07    3.553571
2000-01-10    3.491071
```

We are interested only in the close price. We take the closing price out and peek at the top rows.

Let us now plot the close price:

```
plot.data <- na.omit(data.frame(close_price = data))
names(plot.data) <- c("close_price")
ggplot(plot.data, aes(x = seq_along(close_price))) + geom_line(aes(y =
close_price, color ="Close Price"))
```

We pull the data into a data frame called `plot.data`, so as to pass this conveniently to `ggplot`.

The `ggplot` line graph is as follows:

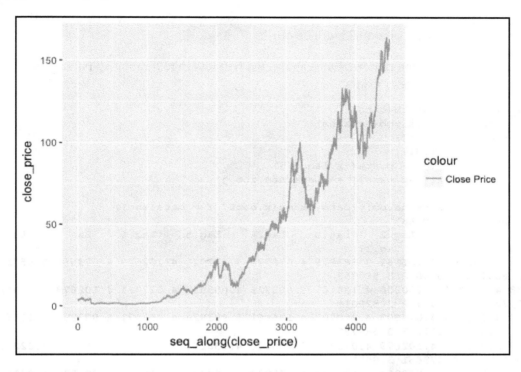

The graph shows the time series of the stock prices. It's a non-stationery time series with a definite trend and error component.

Deep networks for time series prediction

If you remember the initial regression problem for time series forecasting, we used the previous kings' ages at the time of their deaths to predict the next king's age at his time of death. We are going to do something similar here.

We are going to use a rolling window approach.

Our first training record will be constructed as follows:

- The closing price from day 1 in our dataset, up to day 31, will be our X. The day 32 closing price will be our Y.

Now, our second training record will be as follows:

- The closing price from day 2 in our dataset, up to day 32, will be our X. The closing price on day 33 will be our Y.

We will follow the same pattern. Once again, we will leverage `quantmod` package's `Lag` functionality to prepare our data:

```
> data.ts <- as.ts(data)
> data.zoo <- as.zoo(data.ts)
> x.data <- list()
> for (j in 1:31){
+     var.name <- paste("x.lag.",j)
+     x.data[[var.name]] <- Lag(data.zoo,j)
+ }
> final.data <- na.omit(data.frame(x.data, Y = data.zoo))
> head(final.data)
        Lag.1    Lag.2    Lag.3    Lag.4    Lag.5    Lag.6    Lag.7    Lag.8
Lag.9    Lag.10    Lag.11
32 4.250000 4.136161 3.883929 4.053571 4.022321 4.102679 4.073661 3.857143
3.689732 3.529018 3.580357
33 4.075893 4.250000 4.136161 3.883929 4.053571 4.022321 4.102679 4.073661
3.857143 3.689732 3.529018
34 4.102679 4.075893 4.250000 4.136161 3.883929 4.053571 4.022321 4.102679
4.073661 3.857143 3.689732
35 3.973214 4.102679 4.075893 4.250000 4.136161 3.883929 4.053571 4.022321
4.102679 4.073661 3.857143
36 4.064732 3.973214 4.102679 4.075893 4.250000 4.136161 3.883929 4.053571
4.022321 4.102679 4.073661
37 4.151786 4.064732 3.973214 4.102679 4.075893 4.250000 4.136161 3.883929
4.053571 4.022321 4.102679
        Lag.12   Lag.13   Lag.14   Lag.15   Lag.16   Lag.17   Lag.18   Lag.19
Lag.20    Lag.21    Lag.22
32 3.705357 3.629464 3.928571 3.935268 4.008929 3.794643 3.975446 4.053571
3.805804 3.712054 3.587054
33 3.580357 3.705357 3.629464 3.928571 3.935268 4.008929 3.794643 3.975446
4.053571 3.805804 3.712054
34 3.529018 3.580357 3.705357 3.629464 3.928571 3.935268 4.008929 3.794643
3.975446 4.053571 3.805804
35 3.689732 3.529018 3.580357 3.705357 3.629464 3.928571 3.935268 4.008929
3.794643 3.975446 4.053571
36 3.857143 3.689732 3.529018 3.580357 3.705357 3.629464 3.928571 3.935268
4.008929 3.794643 3.975446
37 4.073661 3.857143 3.689732 3.529018 3.580357 3.705357 3.629464 3.928571
3.935268 4.008929 3.794643
        Lag.23   Lag.24   Lag.25   Lag.26   Lag.27   Lag.28   Lag.29   Lag.30
Lag.31          Y
```

```
32 3.455357 3.113839 3.312500 3.491071 3.553571 3.392857 3.714286 3.660714
3.997768 4.075893
33 3.587054 3.455357 3.113839 3.312500 3.491071 3.553571 3.392857 3.714286
3.660714 4.102679
34 3.712054 3.587054 3.455357 3.113839 3.312500 3.491071 3.553571 3.392857
3.714286 3.973214
35 3.805804 3.712054 3.587054 3.455357 3.113839 3.312500 3.491071 3.553571
3.392857 4.064732
36 4.053571 3.805804 3.712054 3.587054 3.455357 3.113839 3.312500 3.491071
3.553571 4.151786
37 3.975446 4.053571 3.805804 3.712054 3.587054 3.455357 3.113839 3.312500
3.491071 4.114397
>
```

We start by creating an empty x.data list. Inside the for loop we invoke the Lag function to get the last 31 closing prices.

We combine this list with our original data and omit all the rows with NA values. Now we are ready with our dataset.

Training test split

Let us split our data into training and test datasets. Out of the whole time series, we will use 80% of the data for training and the rest for testing. We need to keep the order of the time series intact while splitting it.

Split the data as follows:

```
train.perc = 0.8
train.indx = 1:as.integer(dim(final.data)[1] * train.perc)

train.data <- final.data[train.indx,]
test.data  <- final.data[-train.indx ,]
```

train.data contains 80% of our data and test.data now contains the final 20%.

Let us now split the data into the dependent variable, y, and independent variable, x:

```
train.x.data <- data.matrix(train.data[,-1])
train.y.data <- train.data[,1]

test.x.data <- data.matrix(test.data[,-1])
test.y.data <- test.data[,1]
```

We convert our x values to matrix form in both `test` and `train`.

Let us now build our deep learning model:

```
> mx.set.seed(1000)
> mx.set.seed(100)
> deep.model <- mx.mlp(data = train.x.data, label = train.y.data,
+                      hidden_node = c(1000,500,250)
+                      ,out_node = 1
+                      ,dropout = 0.50
+                      ,activation = c("relu", "relu","relu")
+                      ,out_activation = "rmse"
+                      , array.layout = "rowmajor"
+                      , learning.rate = 0.01
+                      , array.batch.size = 100
+                      , num.round = 100
+                      , verbose = TRUE
+                      , optimizer = "adam"
+                      , eval.metric = mx.metric.mae
+
+
+
+ )
Start training with 1 devices
[1] Train-mae=15.2418377055816
[2] Train-mae=5.98307889670961
[3] Train-mae=5.7484189195517
[4] Train-mae=5.6041526859502
[5] Train-mae=6.04107117950916
[6] Train-mae=5.36318696523706
[7] Train-mae=5.72930882248614
[8] Train-mae=6.00756897252467
[9] Train-mae=5.67507700107164
[10] Train-mae=5.25129721558756
[11] Train-mae=5.42784706542889
[12] Train-mae=4.4136934593651
[13] Train-mae=4.43816334171428
[14] Train-mae=4.23920807351669
[15] Train-mae=4.23434906916486
[16] Train-mae=3.81724757853481
[17] Train-mae=4.10677673581574
[18] Train-mae=3.82710250659121
[19] Train-mae=4.00823825577895
[20] Train-mae=4.13603322044015
[21] Train-mae=4.39080083830489
[22] Train-mae=3.89751798558566
[23] Train-mae=3.91841303234299
[24] Train-mae=3.82613876476884
```

```
[25]  Train-mae=3.91980588843425
[26]  Train-mae=3.86194357938237
[27]  Train-mae=4.2168276017242
[28]  Train-mae=3.97845429400603
[29]  Train-mae=3.76002277152406
[30]  Train-mae=3.83593577626679
[31]  Train-mae=3.71273083243105
[32]  Train-mae=3.6195217209061
[33]  Train-mae=3.87637294858694
[34]  Train-mae=3.79551469782988
[35]  Train-mae=3.66272431297435
[36]  Train-mae=3.81557290663322
[37]  Train-mae=3.73366007523404
[38]  Train-mae=3.57986994018157
[39]  Train-mae=3.48014950540331
[40]  Train-mae=3.70377947661612
[41]  Train-mae=3.57618864927027
[42]  Train-mae=3.52039705213573
[43]  Train-mae=3.55409083919393
[44]  Train-mae=3.64251783867677
[45]  Train-mae=3.45834989514616
[46]  Train-mae=4.0749755111999
[47]  Train-mae=3.71578220281336
[48]  Train-mae=3.50679727282789
[49]  Train-mae=4.14914410233498
[50]  Train-mae=3.7334080057674
[51]  Train-mae=3.70052516341209
[52]  Train-mae=3.91092829631435
[53]  Train-mae=3.67670645170742
[54]  Train-mae=3.63808277865251
[55]  Train-mae=3.6711657425099
[56]  Train-mae=3.45309603734149
[57]  Train-mae=3.6100285096301
[58]  Train-mae=3.47404639359977
[59]  Train-mae=3.48650643053982
[60]  Train-mae=3.44442329986228
[61]  Train-mae=3.76036083085669
[62]  Train-mae=3.61709513925844
[63]  Train-mae=3.50891292694542
[64]  Train-mae=3.74455126540528
[65]  Train-mae=3.58543863587909
[66]  Train-mae=3.46644685930676
[67]  Train-mae=3.54323410050737
[68]  Train-mae=3.64015973226892
[69]  Train-mae=3.75287163681454
[70]  Train-mae=3.48837021980021
[71]  Train-mae=3.57296027570963
[72]  Train-mae=3.77685429851214
```

```
[73]   Train-mae=3.63230897545815
[74]   Train-mae=3.46640953759352
[75]   Train-mae=3.42612222330438
[76]   Train-mae=3.59378631307019
[77]   Train-mae=3.71207889818483
[78]   Train-mae=3.67349873264631
[79]   Train-mae=3.91540269825194
[80]   Train-mae=3.75410354889101
[81]   Train-mae=3.74548216611147
[82]   Train-mae=3.48044820434517
[83]   Train-mae=3.45057798130645
[84]   Train-mae=3.56516027308173
[85]   Train-mae=3.82901276187764
[86]   Train-mae=3.57472546464867
[87]   Train-mae=3.5186486049162
[88]   Train-mae=3.48254795942042
[89]   Train-mae=3.5777530745003
[90]   Train-mae=3.46502910438511
[91]   Train-mae=3.50481863598029
[92]   Train-mae=3.94887298007806
[93]   Train-mae=3.85228754586644
[94]   Train-mae=3.39591218464904
[95]   Train-mae=3.32976617760129
[96]   Train-mae=3.46257649577326
[97]   Train-mae=3.74387675043609
[98]   Train-mae=3.49124042812321
[99]   Train-mae=3.49357031944725
[100]  Train-mae=3.66018298261695
```

`mx.mlp` is a convenience function provided by `MXNet` R to create and train a feedforward deep neural network. We built a three-layer network, with three hidden layers of size 100, 500, and 250 respectively. We passed a vector to the `hidden_node` parameter. We specified that we need a single output node and our output node is to be a regression node. By specifying the `out_activation` parameter as `rmse`, we indicate that our output node is a regression node. `rmse` stands for root mean square error. All our hidden nodes use a `relu` `activation` function.

For more details about the parameters, please refer to the `MXNet` R's documentation.

Let us now write a small function to evaluate the performance of our model:

```
> model.evaluate <- function(deep.model, new.data, actual){
+    preds = predict(deep.model, new.data, array.layout = "rowmajor")
+    error <- actual - preds
+      return(mean(abs(error)))

+
+ }
>
```

The `model.evaluate` function takes the model, predicts the output, and compares the output prediction with the actual values. It calculates and returns the mean absolute error.

Let us look at the error in the training dataset:

```
> print("Train Error")
[1] "Train Error"
> model.evaluate(deep.model,train.x.data, train.y.data)
[1] 0.6641051
> print("Test Error")
[1] "Test Error"
> model.evaluate(deep.model,test.x.data, test.y.data)
[1] 1.478305
```

We have a mean absolute error of 0.66 in our training data and 1.478 in the test data. This is the average of the absolute difference between the actual stock close price and our prediction. It's good to get such a low MAE. The plot of our predictions should show us the best of this model.

Let us assemble our actual and predicted values in a data frame:

```
> preds = predict(deep.model,  train.x.data, array.layout = "rowmajor")
> plot.data <- data.frame(actual = train.y.data, predicted = preds[1,])
```

Using the `plot.data` frame, let us plot the actual and predicted values:

```
ggplot(plot.data,aes(x = seq_along(actual))) + geom_line(aes(y = actual,
color = "Actual")) + geom_line(aes(y = predicted, color = "Predicted"))
```

Let us look at the plot:

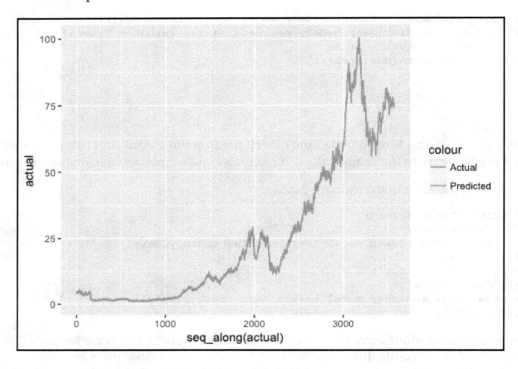

Not bad, our model is trained well with the training data.

Let us now predict the test data and plot it:

```
> preds = predict(deep.model,  test.x.data, array.layout = "rowmajor")
> plot.data <- data.frame(actual = test.y.data, predicted = preds[1,])
> ggplot(plot.data,aes(x = seq_along(actual))) + geom_line(aes(y = actual,
color ="actual")) + geom_line(aes(y = predicted, color ="predicted"))
>
```

Once again, we pack the actual and predicted values in a `plot.data` frame for ease of plotting. Let us look at the prediction plot:

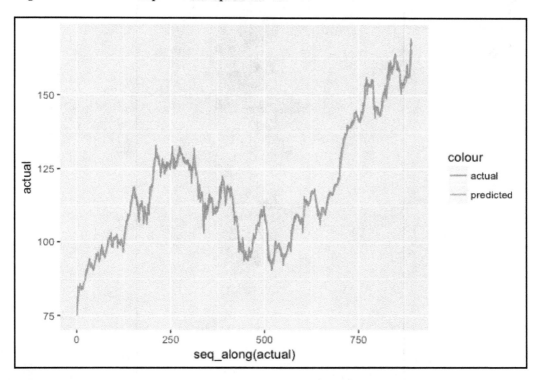

Great, we can see great performance with our test data too.

Let us look at the model graphically by calling `graph.viz(deep.model$symbol)`:

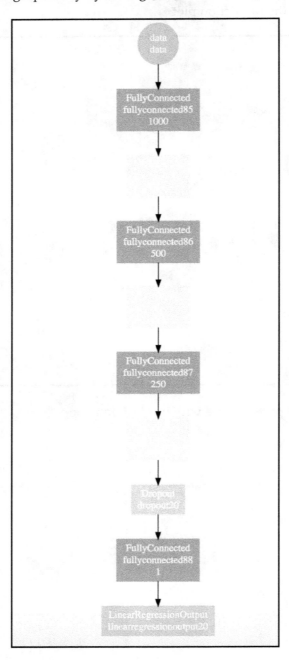

We can look into the weights learned in each of the layers. Let us look at the weights of the first hidden layer:

```
> deep.model$arg.params$fullyconnected18_weight
                  [,1]           [,2]           [,3]           [,4]           [,5]
 [,6]             [,7]
 [1,] -0.0083999438   8.485802e-04   0.0036450755  -0.05046703   8.365825e-03
 8.337282e-03  -0.0087173656
 [2,]  0.0013683429  -6.198279e-03  -0.0083191348  -0.05300714  -3.504494e-03
-5.474154e-03   0.0020545013
                  [,8]           [,9]          [,10]          [,11]          [,12]
 [,13]           [,14]          [,15]
 [1,] -6.238837e-04  -0.02354868   -0.02122656    0.0090157799  -0.02873407
-0.05015010   -0.06675677   -0.02245500
 [2,] -2.801131e-03  -0.01479008   -0.01589586   -0.0063846195  -0.02265893
-0.05025507   -0.06229784   -0.02008835
                  [,16]          [,17]          [,18]          [,19]          [,20]
 [,21]           [,22]          [,23]
 [1,] -0.09068959    0.0078839101  -0.05393362   -0.0087832464  -0.02230835
-0.02040787   -0.08998983   -6.150414e-03
 [2,] -0.09574232    0.0016337502  -0.06588018   -0.0046719122  -0.02494662
-0.03023234   -0.07455231   -1.322337e-03
                  [,24]          [,25]          [,26]          [,27]          [,28]
 [,29]           [,30]          [,31]
 [1,] -0.1390225    -0.01965304   -0.02212325   -0.01884965   -0.0020784298
-0.02215839   -0.06166138   -0.06153671
 [2,] -0.1502734    -0.01914297   -0.02417008   -0.02372178   -0.0086792232
-0.02916201   -0.06242901   -0.06657734
                  [,32]          [,33]          [,34]          [,35]          [,36]
 [,37]           [,38]          [,39]
 [1,] -9.309854e-03  -0.06228027   -0.08344175   -0.05109306   -0.0040911064
-0.09716180   -5.205772e-03  -0.04241674
 [2,] -8.990907e-03  -0.05343428   -0.08138016   -0.05199971   -0.0090623405
-0.08794980   -1.023613e-03  -0.05040253
                  [,40]          [,41]          [,42]          [,43]          [,44]
 [,45]           [,46]          [,47]
 [1,] -0.05714688   -0.02148283   -0.06252886   -0.06428687   -0.06470018
-8.545434e-04  -0.05015615   -0.06178543
 [2,] -0.06344762   -0.01426465   -0.06747299   -0.06294472   -0.07089290
-2.695541e-03  -0.05909692   -0.06171135
                  [,48]          [,49]          [,50]          [,51]          [,52]
 [,53]           [,54]
 [1,] -0.02646469   -6.758149e-03  -0.0091832494  -0.0094310865  -0.03371038
-0.05042901   -0.1533335
 [2,] -0.03239496    4.416389e-03   0.0053570746  -0.0086173108  -0.01760352
-0.05314169   -0.1448236
```

We have truncated the output. Similarly, other weights can be viewed. Note that your weights may not be the same as the ones printed here.

The bias can also be viewed the same way:

```
> deep.model$arg.params$fullyconnected18_bias
  [1]  0.000000000  0.000000000  0.000000000 -0.059611209  0.000000000
0.000000000  0.000000000
  [8]  0.000000000 -0.024556005 -0.023876512  0.000000000 -0.024011787
-0.042338740 -0.058526210
 [15]  0.005647324 -0.091564119  0.037828133 -0.059977122  0.000000000
-0.030254431 -0.024757026
 [22] -0.078628004  0.000000000 -0.138698250 -0.024626205 -0.044002995
-0.024062941  0.000000000
 [29] -0.023961084 -0.059944697 -0.060011234  0.000000000 -0.059861079
-0.080372341 -0.059978724
 [36]  0.000000000 -0.088168561  0.000000000 -0.051067013 -0.059992053
-0.024269760 -0.059945188
 [43] -0.059870388 -0.070009373  0.000000000 -0.060004737 -0.059908539
-0.024218539  0.000000000
 [50]  0.000000000  0.000000000 -0.025039205 -0.060019433 -0.164350569
0.000000000  0.000000000
 [57] -0.057100140 -0.056344267 -0.025078535  0.000000000 -0.059744403
0.000000000  0.000000000
 [64] -2.256225824  0.000000000  0.000000000 -0.024597727  0.000000000
-0.024030440 -0.101686195
 [71] -0.024144597 -0.024073172 -0.059996437  0.000000000 -0.060016021
0.000000000 -0.059985686
```

Again, we have truncated the output here.

Sometimes, looking at the learned weights of a neural network can provide insight into the learning behavior. For example, if weights look unstructured, maybe some were not used at all, or if very large coefficients exist, maybe regularization was too low or the learning rate too high.

Plot the weights as follows:

```
library(Matrix)
weights <- deep.model$arg.params$fullyconnected18_weight
dim(weights)
image(as.matrix(weights))
```

According to the diagram, the x axis corresponds to the row number and the y axis to the column number, with column 1 at the bottom.

Let us look at the graph:

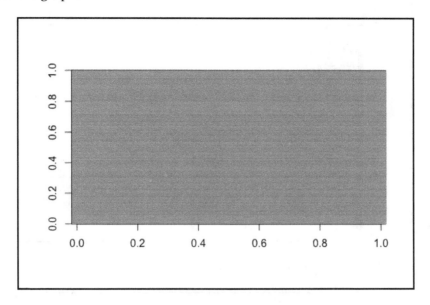

Similarly, we can plot other weights:

```
weights.1 <- deep.model$arg.params$fullyconnected19_weight
dim(weights.1)
image(as.matrix(weights.1))

weights.2 <- deep.model$arg.params$fullyconnected20_weight
dim(weights.2)
image(as.matrix(weights.2))
```

Their plots look like the following diagram:

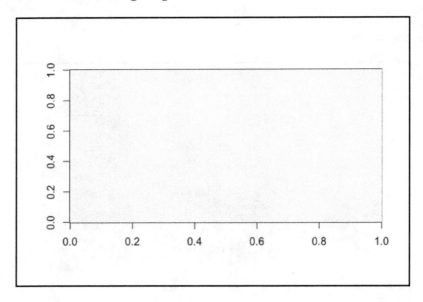

The plot of the last-but-one layer is as follows:

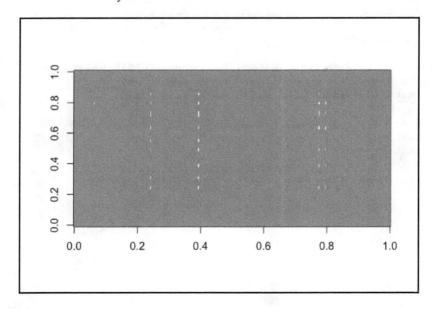

This one has some small sparks spread about. It's better than the previous ones.

Finally, let us talk about tuning the model. There are several knobs to be tuned in this model, and some of them are:

1. Number of hidden layers.
2. Number of nodes in each hidden layer.
3. Activation function in each hidden layer.
4. Learning rate.
5. Dropout percentage.
6. Batch normalization rate.
7. Optimizer (sgd or adam).

It's typically suggested to use random search in parameter space to search for the parameters. Grid search is not recommended for deep learning networks.

We provide a function here which can be used to perform a random search across different parameters:

```
random.search <- function(){

    # Sample layers
    count.layers <- sample(2:5, 1)
    no.layers <- c()
    activations <- c()
    for (i in 1:count.layers-1){
        # Sample node per layers
        no.nodes <- sample(10:50,1)
        no.layers[i] <- no.nodes
        activations[i] <- "relu"
    }
    no.layers <- append(no.layers, 1)
    activations <- append(activations, "relu")
    deep.model <- mx.mlp(data = train.x.data, label = train.y.data,
                        hidden_node = no.layers
                        , out_node = 1
                        , dropout = 0.50
                        , activation = activations
                        ,out_activation = "rmse"
                        , array.layout = "rowmajor"
                        , learning.rate = 0.01
                        , array.batch.size = 100
                        , num.round = 10
                        , verbose = TRUE
                        , optimizer = "adam"
```

```
                              , eval.metric = mx.metric.mae
  )
  train.error <- model.evaluate(deep.model,train.x.data, train.y.data)
  test.error <- model.evaluate(deep.model,test.x.data, test.y.data)
  output <- list(layers = no.layers, activations <- activations
                  , train.error = train.error, test.error = test.error)
  return(output)
}

final.output = list()
for (i in 1:2){
  out <- random.search()
  final.output[[i]] <- out
}
```

You can go head and modify the code for other parameters too, such as dropout, learning rate, and other parameters, to see how the models evolve.

Before we conclude, let us have some discussion around the suitability of deep learning networks for time series analysis. Earlier, when we discussed time series, we referred to the trend, seasonality, and error components in time series data. These lead to the non-stationary aspect of time series data. We suggested that we should remove the seasonality and the trend component from the time series data to use them for prediction in regression models. When it comes to using a neural network for time series predictions, there are several options available:

- **Data Preprocessing**:
    1. Remove the trend and seasonality and use the non-stationary data for prediction.
    2. Arrange the data in a way that includes the seasonality correlation in the input fed to the network.
    3. Use a scheme of rolling windows as shown in this chapter.
- **Network**:
    1. Deep neural networks formed my multiple hidden layers.
    2. **Recurrent neural networks (RNN)**.
    3. LSTM networks--a variation of the RNN network.

In our example, we didn't do any data preprocessing to remove trend and seasonality. There are several research papers available on this topic. Most of them are empirical studies using well known time series data to analyze the effect of data preprocessing in prediction output. One paper is an empirical study conducted by Sharda and Patil. They compared prediction using ARIMA and Neural Networks on 75 time series data and found Neural Network predictions to be more accurate. You can access the paper at `https://link.springer.com/article/10.1007/BF01577272`.

We have successfully created a fully connected regression deep learning network to predict the stock price. RNN and LTSM network APIs are currently not available with MXNet. Hopefully, they should be available soon.

Complete R code

The following is the complete R code:

```
# Time series data
kings <- scan("http://robjhyndman.com/tsdldata/misc/kings.dat",skip=3)
king.ts <- ts(kings)
king.ts

install.packages("TTR")
library(TTR)

par(mfrow=c(2 ,2))
plot(SMA(king.ts, n=2), main = "n=2")
plot(SMA(king.ts, n=5), main = "n=5")
plot(SMA(king.ts, n=10), main = "n=10")
plot(SMA(king.ts, n=15), main = "n=15")
par(mfrow=c(1,1))

smooth.king <- SMA(king.ts, n=5)
smooth.king

births <- scan("http://robjhyndman.com/tsdldata/data/nybirths.dat")
births.ts <- ts(births, frequency = 12)
births.comps <- decompose(births.ts)
plot(births.comps)


library(zoo)
library(quantmod)

data <- as.zoo(smooth.king)
```

```
x1 <- Lag(data,1)
new.data <- na.omit(data.frame(Lag.1 = x1, y = data))
head(new.data)

model <- lm(y ~ Lag.1, new.data)
model
plot(model)


plot(king.ts)
# Introducing MXNet library
library(mxnet)

zero.matrix <- mx.nd.zeros(c(3,3))
zero.matrix
ones.matrix <- mx.nd.ones(c(3,3))
ones.matrix

# Context
mx.ctx.default()

# To create a matrix in GPU
zero.matrix.gup <- mx.nd.zeros(c(3,3), mx.gpu(0))

# Moving data between devices
help("mx.nd.copyto")
zero.copy <- mx.nd.copyto(zero.matrix, mx.cpu())

# Operations
mx.nd.dot(ones.matrix, ones.matrix)
mx.nd.elemwise.add(ones.matrix,ones.matrix)

# Sampling
mu <- mx.nd.array(c(0.0,2.5))
sigma <- mx.nd.array(c(1,3))
mx.nd.sample.normal(mu = mu, sigma = sigma)


# Symbolic Programming
a <- mx.symbol.Variable("a")
a
b <- mx.symbol.Variable("b")
b
c <- a + b
c

arg_lst <- list(symbol = c, ctx = mx.ctx.default(), a = dim(ones.matrix),
                b= dim(ones.matrix), grad.req="null")
```

```
pexec <- do.call(mx.simple.bind, arg_lst)
pexec

input_list <-  list(a = ones.matrix,b = ones.matrix)

mx.exec.update.arg.arrays(pexec, input_list)

mx.exec.forward(pexec)

pexec$arg.arrays

pexec$outputs

######## Another operation ##############

d <- mx.symbol.dot(a, b)

arg_lst <- list(symbol = d, ctx = mx.ctx.default(), a = dim(ones.matrix),
                b= dim(ones.matrix), grad.req="null")

pexec <- do.call(mx.simple.bind, arg_lst)
pexec

input_list <-  list(a = ones.matrix,b = ones.matrix)

mx.exec.update.arg.arrays(pexec, input_list)
mx.exec.forward(pexec)

pexec$arg.arrays
pexec$outputs


############# XOR Learning ###########
mx.set.seed(1)

### Generate some data.
x.1 <- mx.nd.sample.normal(mu = mx.nd.array(c(0,0)),
                           sigma = mx.nd.array(c(0.001,0.001)), shape =
(1000))
y.1 <- rep(0, 1000)
x.2 <- mx.nd.sample.normal(mu = mx.nd.array(c(0,1)),
                           sigma = mx.nd.array(c(0.001,0.001)), shape =
(1000))
y.2 <- rep(1,1000)
x.3 <- mx.nd.sample.normal(mu = mx.nd.array(c(1,0)),
                           sigma = mx.nd.array(c(0.001,0.001)), shape =
(1000))
y.3 <- rep(1,1000)
```

```
x.4 <- mx.nd.sample.normal(mu = mx.nd.array(c(1,1)),
                            sigma = mx.nd.array(c(0.001,0.001)), shape =
(1000))
y.4 <- rep(0,1000)

X <- data.matrix(mx.nd.concat(list(x.1,x.2,x.3,x.4)) )
Y <- c(y.1,y.2,y.3,y.4)


############## Define the Network #########

# Input layer
data <- mx.symbol.Variable("data")

# Hidden Layer
hidden.layer <- mx.symbol.FullyConnected(data = data
                                    , num_hidden = 2)

# Hidden Layer Activation
act <- mx.symbol.Activation(data = hidden.layer, act_type = "relu")

# Output Layer
out.layer <- mx.symbol.FullyConnected(data = act
                                    , num.hidden = 2)

# Softmax of output
out <- mx.symbol.SoftmaxOutput(out.layer)

# Build the model


model <- mx.model.FeedForward.create(out, X=X
                            , y=Y
                            , ctx = mx.ctx.default()
                            , array.layout = "rowmajor"
                            , learning.rate = 0.01
                            , momentum = 0.9
                            , array.batch.size = 50
                            , num.round = 20
                            , eval.metric = mx.metric.accuracy
        #                   , initializer =
mx.init.normal(c(0.0,0.1))
)

# Perform Predictions
X_test = data.matrix(rbind(c(0,0),c(1,1),c(1,0),c(0,1) ) )
preds = predict(model, X_test, array.layout = "rowmajor")
pred.label <- max.col(t(preds)) -1
```

```
pred.label


# Visualize the model
graph.viz(model$symbol)
model$arg.params


##########################################


######### Regression Neural Network ###########

# Prepare the data
library(mxnet)
library(quantmod, quietly = TRUE)
library(ggplot2)

stock.data <- new.env()
tickers <- ('AAPL')
stock.data <- getSymbols(tickers, src = 'yahoo', from = '2000-01-01', env =
FALSE, auto.assign = F)

data <- stock.data$AAPL.Close
head(data)


plot.data <- na.omit(data.frame(close_price = data))
names(plot.data) <- c("close_price")
ggplot(plot.data,aes(x = seq_along(close_price))) + geom_line(aes(y =
close_price, color ="Close Price"))


# Feature generation
data.ts <- as.ts(data)
data.zoo <- as.zoo(data.ts)


x.data <- list()
  for (j in 1:31){
    var.name <- paste("x.lag.",j)
    x.data[[var.name]] <- Lag(data.zoo,j)
  }

final.data <- na.omit(data.frame(x.data, Y = data.zoo))
head(final.data)


set.seed(100)
```

```
# Train/test split
train.perc = 0.8
train.indx = 1:as.integer(dim(final.data)[1] * train.perc)

train.data <- final.data[train.indx,]
test.data  <- final.data[-train.indx ,]

train.x.data <- data.matrix(train.data[,-1])
train.y.data <- train.data[,1]

test.x.data <- data.matrix(test.data[,-1])
test.y.data <- test.data[,1]



mx.set.seed(100)
deep.model <- mx.mlp(data = train.x.data, label = train.y.data,
                    hidden_node = c(1000,500,250)
                    ,out_node = 1
                    ,dropout = 0.50
                    ,activation = c("relu", "relu","relu")
                    ,out_activation = "rmse"
                    , array.layout = "rowmajor"
                    , learning.rate = 0.01
                    , array.batch.size = 100
                    , num.round = 100
                    , verbose = TRUE
                    , optimizer = "adam"
                    , eval.metric = mx.metric.mae
)


model.evaluate <- function(deep.model, new.data, actual){
  preds = predict(deep.model, new.data, array.layout = "rowmajor")
  error <- actual - preds
  return(mean(abs(error)))
}

print("Train Error")
model.evaluate(deep.model,train.x.data, train.y.data)


print("Test Error")
model.evaluate(deep.model,test.x.data, test.y.data)


preds = predict(deep.model,  train.x.data, array.layout = "rowmajor")
```

```
plot.data <- data.frame(actual = train.y.data, predicted = preds[1,])
ggplot(plot.data,aes(x = seq_along(actual))) + geom_line(aes(y = actual,
color = "Actual")) + geom_line(aes(y = predicted, color = "Predicted"))

preds = predict(deep.model,  test.x.data, array.layout = "rowmajor")
plot.data <- data.frame(actual = test.y.data, predicted = preds[1,])
ggplot(plot.data,aes(x = seq_along(actual))) + geom_line(aes(y = actual,
color ="actual")) + geom_line(aes(y = predicted, color ="predicted"))

graph.viz(deep.model$symbol)

library(Matrix)
# Look at the graph plot for the name of each layer
# alternatively call deep.model$arg.params$  to see the name
weights <- deep.model$arg.params$fullyconnected85_weight
dim(weights)
image(as.matrix(weights))

weights.1 <- deep.model$arg.params$fullyconnected19_weight
dim(weights.1)
image(as.matrix(weights.1))

weights.2 <- deep.model$arg.params$fullyconnected20_weight
dim(weights.2)
image(as.matrix(weights.2))




random.search <- function(){

  # Sample layers
  count.layers <- sample(2:5, 1)
  no.layers <- c()
  activations <- c()
  for (i in 1:count.layers-1){
    # Sample node per layers
    no.nodes <- sample(10:50,1)
    no.layers[i] <- no.nodes
    activations[i] <- "relu"
  }
  no.layers <- append(no.layers, 1)
  activations <- append(activations, "relu")
  deep.model <- mx.mlp(data = train.x.data, label = train.y.data,
                       hidden_node = no.layers
                       , out_node = 1
```

```
                         , dropout = 0.50
                         , activation = activations
                        ,out_activation = "rmse"
                         , array.layout = "rowmajor"
                         , learning.rate = 0.01
                         , array.batch.size = 100
                         , num.round = 10
                         , verbose = TRUE
                         , optimizer = "adam"
                         , eval.metric = mx.metric.mae
    )
    train.error <- model.evaluate(deep.model,train.x.data, train.y.data)
    test.error <- model.evaluate(deep.model,test.x.data, test.y.data)
    output <- list(layers = no.layers, activations <- activations
                    , train.error = train.error, test.error = test.error)
    return(output)
}

final.output = list()
for (i in 1:2){
  out <- random.search()
  final.output[[i]] <- out
}
```

Summary

We started the chapter by introducing time series data and the traditional approaches to solving them. We gave you an overview of deep learning networks and information on how they learn. Furthermore, we introduced the MXNet R package. Then we prepared our stock market data so that our deep learning network could consume it. Finally, we built two deep learning networks, one for regression, where we predicted the actual closing price of the stock, and one for classification, where we predicted whether the stock price would move up or down.

In the next chapter, we will deal with sentiment mining. We will show how to extract tweets in R, process them and use a dictionary based method to find the sentiments of the tweets. Finally using those scored tweets as datasets we will build a Naive Bayes model based on Kernel density estimate.

5

Twitter Text Sentiment Classification Using Kernel Density Estimates

Twitter and other social media applications are generating a lot of unstructured text today at a great velocity. Today's product companies look at these social media applications as a great source to give them an understanding of how consumers feel about their products or services. Hence, the analysis of these unstructured texts has become very important for these companies.

Text mining as field is gaining importance day by day. The invention of techniques such as bag-of-words, `word2vec` embedding has made text data suitable for processing by most machine learning algorithms. Analyzing the sentiment in a text is an active field of research.

 Sentiment analysis, also called opinion mining, is the field of study that analyzes people's opinions, sentiments, evaluations, appraisals, attitudes, and emotions towards entities such as products, services, organizations, individuals, issues, events, topics, and their attributes. Liu, *Bing. Sentiment Analysis and Opinion Mining* (Kindle Locations 199-201). Morgan and Claypool Publishers.

We will look at how to pre-process text so it can be efficiently used by machine learning algorithms. We will introduce a recently published state of the art word weighting scheme called Delta TFIDF. Delta TFIDF is a variation of the traditional `tfidf` weighting scheme, specially designed for sentiment classification tasks. Sentiment classification can be done using either a dictionary method or a machine learning approach. We will show you examples of both.

Given a text, the model should predict the sentiment of the text as either positive or negative.

Any data we analyze is generated from a process. The underlying process emits the data following a probability distribution. **Kernel density** estimate techniques help find the underlying probability distribution. It helps find the probability density function for the given sample of data. Once we have an idea about the distribution of the data, we can leverage this understanding of the data to make decisions further down the line based on the application.

In this chapter, our application is to classify a given text as either positive sentiment oriented or negative sentiment oriented. In our training set, we will have both positively oriented and negatively oriented sentences. We will be using **kernel density estimation** (**KDE**) for this classification task. Using KDE, we can find the distribution for positively oriented text and negatively oriented text. The assumption is that these two distributions should be different.

We will explore the following in this chapter:

- Introducing kernel density estimation
- Extracting tweets using the `twitteR` package in R
- The sentiment classification overview and approach
- Dictionary-based scoring
- Text pre-processing using the `tm` package
- Building a sentiment classifier in R using KDE
- Assembling an `RShiny` application

The code for this chapter was written in RStudio Version 0.99.491. It uses R version 3.3.1. As we work through our example we will introduce the R packages `twitteR`, `sentimentr`, `tidyr`, `tm`, and `naivebayes`, which we will be using. During our code description, we will be using some of the output printed in the console. We have included what will be printed in the console immediately following the statement which prints the information to the console, so as to not disturb the flow of the code.

Kernel density estimation

In order to explain KDE, let us generate some one-dimensional data and build some histograms. Histograms are a good way to understand the underlying probability distribution of the data.

We can generate histograms using the following code block for reference:

```
> data <- rnorm(1000, mean=25, sd=5)
> data.1 <- rnorm(1000, mean=10, sd=2)
> data <- c(data, data.1)
> hist(data)
> hist(data, plot = FALSE)
$breaks
 [1]  0  5 10 15 20 25 30 35 40 45

$counts
[1]   8 489 531 130 361 324 134  22   1

$density
[1] 0.0008 0.0489 0.0531 0.0130 0.0361 0.0324 0.0134 0.0022 0.0001

$mids
[1]  2.5  7.5 12.5 17.5 22.5 27.5 32.5 37.5 42.5

$xname
[1] "data"

$equidist
[1] TRUE

attr(,"class")
[1] "histogram"
```

This code creates two artificial data-sets and combines them. Both datasets are based on the normal distribution; the first has a mean of 25 and standard deviation of 5, the second has a mean of 10 and standard deviation of 2. If we recall from basic statistics, a normal distribution is in a bell shape centered at the mean value, and 99% of the values are between the mean-(3*sd) and mean+(3*sd). By combining these data from these two distributions, the new dataset will have two peaks and a small area of overlap.

Let us look at the first histogram generated:

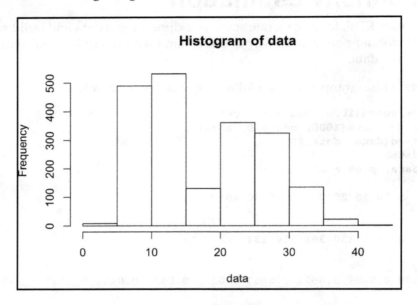

The output in R shows the bin size and the locations. Look at $breaks and $mids in the R output.

What if we change the bin sizes as follows:

```
> hist(data, breaks = seq(0,50,2))
```

We provide the hist function with the breaks parameter, which is a sequence from 0 to 50, with a step size of two. We want our bin size to be two rather than 10—the default value R is selected.

Let us look at the histogram:

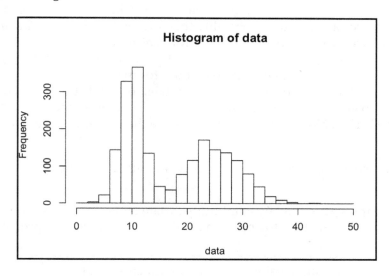

As you can see, by varying the bin size, the representation of the data changes. You can test the same effect by varying the bin locations or $mids. The histogram depends on having the right bin size and bin location.

The alignment of the bins with the data points decide the height of a bar in the histogram. Ideally, this height should be based on actual density of the nearby points. Can we stack the bar in such way that the height is proportional to the points they represent. This is where KDE one-ups the histogram.

A discrete random variable takes on a finite number of possible values. We can determine the probability for all the possible value of that random variable using a probability mass function. A continuous random variable takes on infinite number of possible values. We cannot find the probability of a particular value, instead we find the probability that a value falls in some interval. A probability density function (PDF) is used to find the probability of a value falling in an interval for a continuous random variable.

Let us look at an example:

```
mean=25
sd=5
1-(2*pnorm(mean+(2*sd), mean=mean,sd=sd, lower.tail=FALSE))

[1]0.9544997
```

pnorm is the function to get the cumulative probability distribution function for normal distributions, i.e. the probability that a given value is within a range of a normal distribution. Here we calculate the probability that a value falls between 2 standard deviations of the mean value, which we know from basic statistics is 95%. We can calculate this probability by looking at the probability that the given value is greater than the mean+(2*sd); we then multiply that by 2 (to account for the values less than mean-(2*sd)). This gives us the probability the values are in the "tails" of the distribution, so we subtract this value from 1 to get the probability that the values lie between mean +/- (2*sd) to give the answer of 0.9544997. Note that even if you change the values of mean and sd, the result is always 0.9544997.

There is also an excellent plot here: https://en.wikipedia.org/wiki/Probability_density_function

For a set of N samples generated by a uni/multivariate and continuous random variable kernel density, the estimate tries to approximate the random variable's probability density function.

Let us see a univariate example using the density function to approximate the PDF of the given data:

```
# Kernel Density estimation
kde = density(data)
plot(kde)
```

Let us look at the density plot:

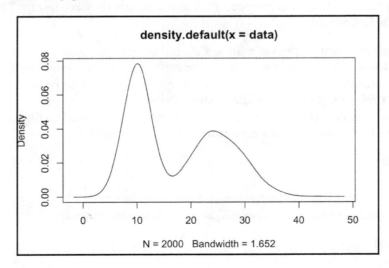

This smoothed out plot from KDE gives us a better idea about the distribution of the underlying data. The `density` function in R uses a Gaussian kernel by default for each point in the data. The parameters of KDE are the kernel, which is used at every point to decide the shape of the distribution at each point, and the bandwidth, which defines the smoothness of the output distribution.

Why use a kernel instead of calculating the density at each point and them summing it up?

We can calculate the density at each point x_0 as follows:

$$\hat{f}(x_0) = \frac{n^{-1} \sum_i I(|x_i - x_0| \le h)}{2h}$$

Where h is the distance threshold. This may give a bumpy plot as each point x_i in the neighborhood defined by h receives the same weight.

So instead, we use a kernel.

$$\hat{f}(x_0) = \frac{1}{nh} \sum_i K\left(\frac{x_i - x_0}{h}\right),$$

Where K is the kernel and h is the smoothing parameter. The kernel gives weight to each point x_i based on its proximity to x_0.

Look at the R `help` function to learn more about the `density` function:

```
help(density)
```

Hopefully, this section gives an understanding of how to use kernel density estimate to approximate the probability density function of the underlying dataset. We will be using this PDF to build our sentiment classifier.

Refer to Chapter 6's, *Kernel Smoothing methods* section in *The Elements of Statistical Learning*, by Trevor Hastie, Robert Tibshirani and Jerome Friedman for a rigorous discussion on kernel density estimates.

Twitter text

We will leverage the `twitteR` package to extract tweets. Refer to `https://cran.r-project.org/web/packages/twitteR/index.html` to get more information about this package.

In order to use this package, you need a Twitter account. With the account, sign in to `https://app.twitter.com` and create an application. Use the consumer key, consumer secret key, access token, and access token security keys from that page to authenticate into Twitter.

Authorizing with keys into Twitter is done as follows:

```
library(twitteR, quietly = TRUE)
setup_twitter_oauth(consumer.key, consumer.secret, access.token,
token.secret)
```

We are ready to extract some tweets.

We will retrieve only the English tweets using the `searchTwitter` function provided by the `twitteR` package:

```
tweet.results <- searchTwitter("@apple", n=1000,lang = "en")
tweet.df <- twListToDF(tweet.results)
```

Using the function `twListToDF`, we convert our extracted tweets from Twitter to a dataframe, `tweet.df`. Out of all the fields extracted, we are most interested in the name text column.

Let us remove all the retweets:

```
> tweet.df <- tweet.df[tweet.df$isRetweet == FALSE, ]
```

```
> tweet.df <- data.frame(tweet.df['text'])
```

We have removed all the retweets from our results and retain just the text column. Our `tweet.df` data frame now only has a single text column.

Let us clean our tweet text:

```
> library(stringr)
> tweet.df$text =str_replace_all(tweet.df$text,"[\\.\\,\\;]+",  " ")
> tweet.df$text =str_replace_all(tweet.df$text,"http\\w+",  "")
> tweet.df$text =str_replace_all(tweet.df$text,"@\\w+",  " ")
> tweet.df$text =str_replace_all(tweet.df$text,"[[:punct:]]",  " ")
> tweet.df$text =str_replace_all(tweet.df$text,"[[:digit:]]",  " ")
> tweet.df$text =str_replace_all(tweet.df$text,"^ ",  " ")
> tweet.df$text =str_replace_all(tweet.df$text,"[<].*[>]",  " ")
```

We have removed the URLs, spaces, Unicode characters, and so on from our tweets.

Having extracted and cleaned up this Twitter text, let us proceed to build our text classification.

Sentiment classification

Sentiment in text can be either positive or negative. We will stick to this definition for this chapter. Sentiment mining is an active field of research. A starting point for someone to learn the various aspects of sentiment mining is through the book *Sentiment Analysis and Opinion Mining*, by Bing Liu.

Broadly speaking, sentiment mining problems are solved using the following techniques:

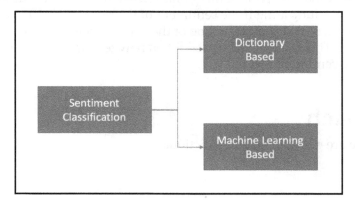

Dictionary methods

Sentiment lexicons, in which words are categorized as positive and negative, are used in this technique. There are several lexicons available today:

- `SocialSent` is a domain specific lexicon available from Stanford University: `https://nlp.stanford.edu/projects/socialsent/`
- Wordnet is a lexical database for English from Princeton: `http://wordnet.princeton.edu/`
- There are several sentiment annotated datasets available at Bing Liu's website: `https://www.cs.uic.edu/~liub/FBS/sentiment-analysis.html`

We match these lexicons to the tokens (words) in the input data and we can then calculate an overall sentiment, for example, based on the proportion of positive words to negative words.

The `tidyr` package has three sentiment lexicons. In the book *Text Mining with R: The Tidy Approach*, there is a full chapter on sentiment mining using lexicons: `http://tidytextmining.com/sentiment.html`.

Machine learning methods

Machine learning methods expect a training dataset. We need a set of tuples, where our x is the text and y is a label indicating if the sentiment of the tweet is positive or negative. We build features from these texts and train one of the existing classification algorithms, such as naive-bayes or SVM. This model can be used when new text arrives to classify it as either a positive or negative sentiment text.

Our approach

In this chapter, we are going to leverage dictionary and machine learning methods.

Look at the steps we are going to follow:

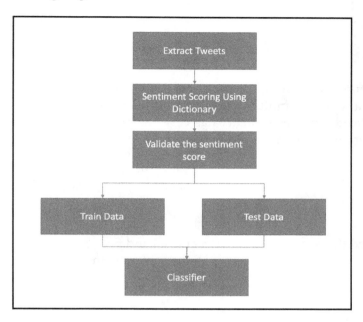

After extracting our text, we are going to use the dictionary-based approach to first give sentiment scores to the extracted tweets. Later, we will manually verify if the scores are good. This is our gold set of data for building a classifier. We divide this data into two sets, one we will use for training our classifier, and the other we will use to test our classifier. Since we don't have any pre-labeled tweet data, we are following this approach.

Let us now proceed to build our gold dataset using a sentiment dictionary.

Dictionary based scoring

As described in the steps we outlined for our approach, let us use a sentiment dictionary to score our initially extracted tweets. We are going to leverage the `sentimentr` R package to learn the sentiments of the tweets we have collected.

Let us see how to score using the `sentiment` function from the `sentimentr` package:

```
> library(sentimentr, quietly = TRUE)
> sentiment.score <- sentiment(tweet.df$text)
> head(sentiment.score)
   element_id sentence_id word_count  sentiment
```

1:	1	1	8	0.0000000
2:	2	1	8	0.3535534
3:	3	1	3	0.0000000
4:	3	2	4	0.0000000
5:	3	3	7	0.0000000
6:	4	1	14	−0.8418729

The `sentiment` function in `sentimentr` calculates a score between −1 and 1 for each of the tweets. In fact, if a tweet has multiple sentences, it will calculate the score for each sentence. A score of −1 indicates that the sentence has very negative polarity. A score of 1 means that the sentence is very positive. A score of 0 refers to the neutral nature of the sentence.

 Refer to `https://cran.r-project.org/web/packages/sentimentr/index.html` for more details about the `sentimentr` package.

However, we need the score to beat the tweet level and not at the sentence level. We can take the average value of the score across all the sentences in a tweet.

Calculate the average value of `sentiment.scores` for each tweet:

```
> library(dplyr, quietly = TRUE)
> sentiment.score <- sentiment.score %>% group_by(element_id) %>%
summarise(sentiment = mean(sentiment))
> head(sentiment.score)
# A tibble: 6 x 2
  element_id  sentiment
       <int>      <dbl>
1          1  0.0000000
2          2  0.3535534
3          3  0.0000000
4          4 -0.4209365
5          5  0.0000000
6          6  0.0000000
```

Here, the `element_id` refers to the individual tweet. By grouping by `element_id` and calculating the average, we can get the sentiment score at the tweet level.

We now have the scores for each tweet.

Let us now add the sentiment to our original `tweet.df.` data frame. Going forward, we only need the text and its sentiment; let us subset those columns from `tweet.df`:

```
> tweet.df$polarity <- sentiment.score$sentiment
> tweet.final <- tweet.df[,c('text','polarity')]
```

We have our dataset prepared now, with the tweet text and the sentiment score.

Our sentiment is still a real value. Let us convert it to a categorical variable.

We remove all records with a polarity value of 0. These are records with neutral sentiments. If our polarity is less than zero, we mark the tweet as negative, otherwise, it is positive:

```
> tweet.final <- tweet.final[tweet.final$polarity != 0, ]
> tweet.final$sentiment <- ifelse(tweet.final$polarity < 0,
"Negative","Positive")
> tweet.final$sentiment <- as.factor(tweet.final$sentiment)
> table(tweet.final$sentiment)

Negative Positive
    200      168
```

Using `ifelse`, we have discretized the real-valued sentiment score into a binary variable. We added an identifier column. With that, we have the training data ready. Finally, the `table` command shows us the class distribution. Our class distribution is imbalanced.

Let us say we are building a discriminative model such as logistic regression or SVM, where the model is trying to learn a boundary between the classes. It expects an equal number of positive classes and negative classes. If the number of positive classes is greater than or less than the number of negative classes in the dataset, we have a class imbalance problem.

There are several techniques to balance the dataset. Some of them are downsampling, upsampling, SMOTE, and so on. We will leverage the function `upSample` in the `caret` package to create more records in the minority class. This should produce better results in the classification models.

Manage the class distribution:

```
> library(caret, quietly = TRUE)
> tweet.balanced <- upSample(x = tweet.final$text, y =
tweet.final$sentiment)
> names(tweet.balanced) <- c('text', 'sentiment')
> table(tweet.balanced$sentiment)

Negative Positive
    200      200
```

The `upSample` function looks at the class distribution and repeatedly samples from the Positive class to balance. The final table command shows the new class distribution.

Refer to the caret R package for class imbalance problems: `https://topepo.github.io/caret/subsampling-for-class-imbalances.html`

In this chapter, we are going to learn the distribution of positive and negative classes independently and use them for our predictions. Hence, we don't need to do balance the classes.

Finally, we add an `ID` column to our dataset:

```
> tweet.final$id <- seq(1, nrow(tweet.final))
```

Before we move on to the next section, let us spend some time understanding the inner workings of our dictionary-based `sentiment` function. The `sentiment` function utilizes a sentiment lexicon (Jockers, 2017) from the `lexicon` package. It preprocesses the given text as follows:

- Paragraphs are split into sentences
- Sentences are split into words
- All punctuation is removed except commas, semicolons, and colons
- Finally, words are stored as tuples, for example, $w\_\{5,2,3\}$ means the third word in the second sentence of the fifth paragraph

Each word is looked up in the lexicon, and positive and negative words are tagged with $+1$ and -1 respectively. Let us call the words which have received a score as the polarized words. Not all words will receive a score. Only those found in the lexicons receive a score. We can pass a customer lexicon through the `polarity_dt` parameter to the `sentiment` function.

For each of the polarized words, n words before them and n words after them are considered, and together they are called **polarized context clusters**. The parameter n can be set by the user. The words in the polarized context cluster can be tagged as either of the following:

- Neutral
- Negator
- Amplifier
- De-amplifier
- Adversative conjunctions

A dictionary of these words can be passed through the `valence_shifter_dt` parameter. Looking up this dictionary, the neighboring words can be tagged. The weights for these are passed through the `amplifier.weight` and `adversative.weight` parameters.

Each polarized word is weighted now based on `polarity_dt`, and also weighted based on the number of valence shifters/words surrounding it, which are tagged either as amplifiers or adversative conjunctions. Neutrally tagged weights have no weights.

For more details about the weight and scoring, refer to R help for the `sentiment` function.

Text pre-processing

Before we build our model, we need to prepare our data so it can be provided to our model. We want a feature vector and a class label. In our case, the class label can take two values, positive or negative depending on if the sentence has a positive or a negative sentiment. Words are our features. We will use the bag-of-words model to represent our text as features. In a bag-words-model, the following steps are performed to transform a text into a feature vector:

1. Extract all unique individual words from the `text` dataset. We call a `text` dataset a corpus.
2. Process the words. Processing typically involves removing numbers and other characters, placing the words in lowercase, stemming the words, and removing unnecessary white spaces.
3. Each word is assigned a unique number and together they form the vocabulary. A word *uknown* is added to the vocabulary. This is for the unknown words we will be seeing in future datasets.
4. Finally, a document term matrix is created. The rows of this matrix are the document IDs, and the columns are formed by the words from the vocabulary.

Consider this simple example:

- **d1**: Cats hate dogs
- **d2**: Dogs chase cats

The binary document term matrix is now as follows:

chase	cats	hate	dogs
0	1	1	1
1	1	0	1

We need to pre-process our tweets in a similar manner. We will use the `tm` R package to pre-process our twitter text.

Let us proceed to use the `tm` package to create a document term matrix:

```
library(tm)
get.dtm <- function(text.col, id.col, input.df, weighting){

  title.reader <- readTabular(mapping=list(content=text.col, id=id.col))
  corpus <- Corpus(DataframeSource(input.df),
readerControl=list(reader=title.reader))
  corpus <- tm_map(corpus, removePunctuation)
  corpus <- tm_map(corpus, removeNumbers)
  corpus <- tm_map(corpus, stripWhitespace)
  corpus <- tm_map(corpus, removeWords, stopwords("english"))
  corpus <- tm_map(corpus, content_transformer(tolower))
  dtm <- DocumentTermMatrix(corpus, control = list(weighting = weighting))
  return(dtm)
}

> dtm <- get.dtm('text','id', tweet.final,"weightTfIdf")
> dtm.mat <- as.matrix(dtm)
```

The `get.dtm` function creates a document term matrix from the given data frame. It does text pre-processing/normalization before creating the actual document term matrix. Preprocessing involves removing any punctuation, removing numbers, stripping unwanted white space, removing English stop words, and finally converts the text into lowercase.

The following is a list of English stop words stored in the `tm` package:

```
> stopwords("english")
 [1] "i"          "me"         "my"         "myself"     "we"
"our"        "ours"
 [8] "ourselves"  "you"        "your"       "yours"      "yourself"
"yourselves" "he"
[15] "him"        "his"        "himself"    "she"        "her"
"hers"       "herself"
[22] "it"         "its"        "itself"     "they"       "them"
"their"      "theirs"
```

```
[29] "themselves" "what"        "which"        "who"         "whom"
"this"          "that"
......
```

The output is truncated, as we have not shown all the stop words. In text mining, stop words are considered those which do not contribute much to the context of the text. Let's say we have two documents--if we want to differentiate them, we cannot use stop words to find what those two documents are uniquely representing. Hence, we typically remove these words from our text as a pre-processing exercise.

Let us look at the document term matrix:

```
<<DocumentTermMatrix (documents: 62, terms: 246)>>
Non-/sparse entries: 677/14575
Sparsity            : 96%
Maximal term length: 17
>
```

We have around 62 documents and 246 words. Document term matrices are typically sparse, as all words don't appear in all the documents. This brings us to the weighting scheme. When we explained the document term matrix, we used a binary weightage scheme. A one was added the cell if a word was present in a document; if the word did not appear in the document, a zero was added. We can use a different weighting scheme called **term-frequency inverse document frequency**.

Term-frequeny inverse document frequency (TFIDF)

The **term frequency** (**tf**) for a given word w is the number of times the word occurs in document d. Conveniently, we can write it as `tf(w, d)`. In our case, this is how many times it appears in a tweet. Term frequencies are called local weights. They indicate the importance of a word in a document. Many times, they are normalized by dividing it by the number of words in a document, that is the length of the document. The higher the value of `tf` of a word in a document, the higher the importance.

The document frequency or *df* for a given word *w* is the number of documents in which the word has occurred. Document frequency is considered the global weight.

Inverse document frequency or `idf` is calculated as follows:

idf(w, d) = log (number of documents in the corpus / 1 + document frequency of the word)

Term-frequency inverse document frequency or TFIDF is the product of `tf` and `idf`. They define the importance of a word in our corpus. According to this scheme, the most frequently occurring words are not given high importance since they don't carry enough information to differentiate one tweet from another.

Let us peek at our document term matrix:

```
> dtm.mat[1:2,10:15]
   Terms
Docs android art artstationhq ashtonsummers attack away
   1        0   0            0             0      1    0
   2        0   0            0             0      1    0
```

You can see the TFIDF value for the word `fire` in document 2 is `0.27`.

Introduction to Information Retrieval, by Christopher Manning, is a good place to start to dig deeper into word weighting schemes. You can get it at `https://nlp.stanford.edu/IR-book/pdf/irbookonlinereading.pdf`.

TFIDF is a great weighting scheme. It has been successfully used in many text mining projects and information retrieval projects. We are going to use a modified version of TFIDF called **Delta TFIDF** for our feature generation.

Delta TFIDF

The problem with `TFIDF` is it fails to differentiate between words from the perspective of implicit sentiments. During the calculation of `TFIDF`, no knowledge of the document sentiment is added. Hence, it may not serve as a good differentiating feature for sentiment classification.

Delta TFIDF was proposed by Justin Martineau and Tim Finin in their paper *Delta TFIDF: An Improved Feature Space for Sentiment Analysis*: `http://ebiquity.umbc.edu/_file_directory_/papers/446.pdf`.

Delta TFIDF is calculated for each word and document combination as follows:

- Finds `Ctd`, the number of times the word occurs in the document, term frequency of the word.
- Finds `nt`, the number of negative documents in which the word has occurred.
- Finds `pt`, the number of positive documents in which the word has occurred.

Now, Delta TFIDF for a word w in a document *d* is:

```
Ctd * log ( nt / pt)
```

Let us calculate Delta TFIDF in R:

```
> dtm <- get.dtm('text','id', tweet.final, "weightTf")
> dtm
<<DocumentTermMatrix (documents: 368, terms: 1234)>>
Non-/sparse entries: 2804/451308
Sparsity           : 99%
Maximal term length: 19
```

We get the document term matrix for our whole corpus. The rows are our document and the columns are our vocabulary. We use term frequency for our weighting scheme. Our `dtm` is very sparse. There are a lot of cells with zero values. Let us throw away some terms and try to reduce the sparsity of our document term matrix.

```
> dtm <- removeSparseTerms(dtm, 0.98)
> dtm
<<DocumentTermMatrix (documents: 368, terms: 58)>>
Non-/sparse entries: 934/20410
Sparsity           : 96%
Maximal term length: 11

> dtm.mat <- as.matrix(dtm)
```

After reducing the sparseness, we convert our document term matrix to a matrix object.

Now let us split our data into a positive tweets dataset and a negative tweets dataset and get their respective document term matrices:

```
dtm.pos <- get.dtm('text','id', tweet.final[tweet.final$sentiment ==
'Positive',],"weightBin")
dtm.neg <- get.dtm('text','id', tweet.final[tweet.final$sentiment ==
'Negative',],"weightBin")

dtm.pos.mat <- as.matrix(dtm.pos)
dtm.neg.mat <- as.matrix(dtm.neg)
```

`dtm.post.mat` and `dtm.neg.mat` are the matrix representations of the positive and the negative tweet corpuses.

Let us find the document frequencies of words in both the corpuses:

```
pos.words.df <- colSums(dtm.pos.mat)
neg.words.df <- colSums(dtm.neg.mat)
```

By summing up the columns, we get the document frequencies. `pos.words.df` contains the words and their document frequencies in the positive corpus.

Similarly, `neg.words.df` contains the words and their document frequencies in the negative corpus.

Let us get all the unique words and the document IDs:

```
> tot.features <- colnames(dtm.mat)
> doc.ids <- rownames(dtm.mat)
```

We have all the information needed to calculate our final score.

Let us calculate the Delta TFIDF:

```
c.dtm.mat <- dtm.mat

for( i in 1:length(tot.features)){
  for ( j in 1:length(doc.ids)){
    # Number of times the term has occured in the document
    ctd <- dtm.mat[doc.ids[j], tot.features[i]]
    # Number for documents in pos data with the term
    pt <- pos.words.df[tot.features[i]]
    # Number for documents in pos data with the term
    nt <- neg.words.df[tot.features[i]]
    score <- ctd * log( nt / pt)
    if(is.na(score)){
      score <- 0
    }
    c.dtm.mat[doc.ids[j], tot.features[i]] <- score
  }
}
```

Our `dtm.mat` has the term frequency for each word and document. We use `pos.words.df` and `neg.words.df` to find the document frequency of a word in both positive and negative corpuses. Finally, we update `c.dtm.mat` with the new score.

We have calculated the Delta TFIDF. This brings us to the end of this section. We have prepared our data to be consumed by the model. Let us proceed to build our sentiment classification model.

Building a sentiment classifier

In the beginning of the chapter we devoted a section to understand kernel density estimation and how it can be leveraged to approximate the probability density function for the given samples from a random variable. We are going to use it in this section.

We have a set of tweets positively labeled. Another set of tweets negatively labeled. The idea is to learn the PDF of these two data sets independently using kernel density estimation.

From Bayes rule, we know that

$$P(Label \mid x) = P(x \mid label) * P(label) / P(x)$$

Here, $P(x \mid label)$ is the `likelihood`, $P(label)$ is prior, and $P(x)$ is the evidence. Here the label can be positive sentiment or negative sentiment.

Using the PDF learned from kernel density estimation, we can easily calculate the `likelihood`, $P(x \mid label)$

From our class distribution, we know the prior $P(label)$

For any new tweet, we can now calculate using the Bayes Rule,

```
P(Label = Positive | words and their delta tfidf weights)

P(Label = Negative | words and their delta tfidf weights)
```

Viola, we have our sentiment classifier assembled based on kernel density estimation.

Package `naivebayes`, provides a function `naive_bayes`, where we can use a kernel to build a classifier as we have proposed.

Before we jump into our use case, let us see quickly how KDE can be leveraged to classify the Iris data set. More information about this data set is available in `https://archive.ics.uci.edu/ml/datasets/iris`.

Iris dataset and KDE classifier:

```
library(naivebayes)
data(iris)

iris.model <- naive_bayes(x = iris[,1:4], y= iris$Species, usekernel =
TRUE)
plot(iris.model)
```

We pass the first 4 columns as our features, x and the last column species as our y variable. There are three classes in this dataset. There is a total of 150 records, 50 records per each class.

Let us look at the plot of our model:

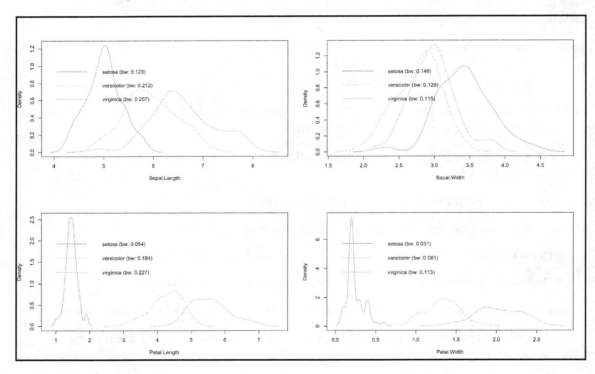

We have a plot for every column in `iris` dataset. Let us look at the `petal.width` column. There are three density plots each representing, P(Petal.width, setosa), P(Petal.width, versicolor), and finally P(Petal.width, virginica) one for each class variable. Each of them represents the underlying distribution of `Petal.width` for each one of the classes.

Other plots can be interpreted similarly. Using this PDF we can now classify the data into one of the three classes. Hopefully, this gives an idea of how the underlying distribution discovered by KDE can be used to separate the records into their respective class instance.

We are going to apply the same principle to our tweets.

Let us proceed to build our classifier:

```
model <- naive_bayes(x = dtm.mat, y = tweet.final$sentiment, usekernel =
TRUE)
```

We use the **naivebayes** R package. The function `naive_bayes` is used to build the model. You can see that we have set the `useKernel` parameter to `TRUE`. This informs the function to use KDE for calculating the `likelihood`.

To understand the model constructed, you can run the following:

```
str(model)
```

This will help you view the various properties of this model.

Having built the model, we can use the standard `predict` function to predict the label for unknown tweets.

The prediction using our model is as follows:

```
preds <- predict(model, newdata = dtm.mat, type = "class")

library(caret)
confusionMatrix(preds, tweet.final$sentiment)
```

Let us look at the confusion matrix output:

```
Confusion Matrix and Statistics

          Reference
Prediction Negative Positive
  Negative      128       58
  Positive       72      110
                Accuracy : 0.6467
                  95% CI : (0.5955, 0.6956)
     No Information Rate : 0.5435
     P-Value [Acc > NIR] : 3.744e-05
                   Kappa : 0.2928
 Mcnemar's Test P-Value : 0.2542
             Sensitivity : 0.6400
             Specificity : 0.6548
```

```
        Pos Pred Value : 0.6882
        Neg Pred Value : 0.6044
           Prevalence : 0.5435
       Detection Rate : 0.3478
 Detection Prevalence : 0.5054
    Balanced Accuracy : 0.6474
      'Positive' Class : Negative
```

We have an accuracy of 64%. Can we understand why we reached this number? A good way to investigate this is to look at the features fed to this model. In this case, the words we have fed as features. Looking at the PDF of words for both positive and negative sentiment, we should be able to throw some light on our model performance.

Let us look at some of the variables and their PDF for positive and negative sentiments:

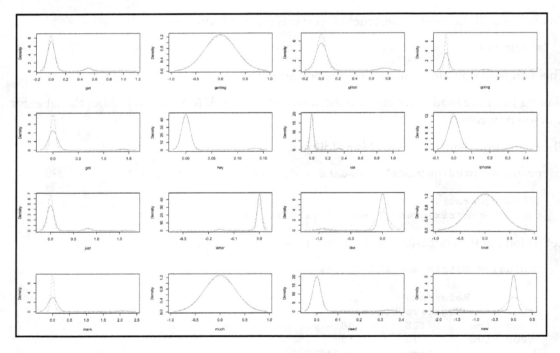

The graph represents a subset of words used for classification. It is evident that underlying PDF estimated by kernel density estimate is not much different for the positive and the negative classes. PDF for positive and negative are represented by the red and green line. In most of the cases both the PDF are overlapping each other. Compare these plots to the plot we generated for the `Iris` dataset, where the PDFs were distinctly separate. Hence the model does not have enough classification power.

What can we do to improve the model?

1. Collect more data.
2. To create our training set, we did an unsupervised approach of using a dictionary to get the sentiment. Users can try using other lexicons.
3. Once the dictionary based approach returns the result, we can then manually curate it and make it more robust.

That brings us to the end of the section. We have shown you a simple Naive Bayes classifier using KDE estimates for calculating the `likelihood`. You can go ahead and use other classification methods and try to compare the results. Another good exercise would be to compare the normal TFIDF features to the Delta TFIDF features.

Assembling an RShiny application

Our `RShiny` application will be able to do the following:

- Search Twitter for a keyword/hashtag
- Display the top 100 results
- Show the sentiment for the top 100 tweets

Let us first load all the necessary libraries and authenticate into our Twitter account:

```
library(shiny)
library(twitteR, quietly = TRUE)
library(stringr)
library(sentimentr, quietly = TRUE)
library(dplyr, quietly = TRUE)


consumer.key <- ""
consumer.secret <- ""
access.token <- ""
token.secret <- ""

setup_twitter_oauth(consumer.key, consumer.secret, access.token,
token.secret)
```

Fill in your `consumer.keys`, `secret`, `access.token`, and `token.secret`.

Let us build the user interface part:

```
ui <- fluidPage(
  navbarPage("TweetSenti",
             tabPanel("Search Tweets"
                      , textInput("search","search",value="#bladerunner")
                      , dataTableOutput("results")
                      ),
             tabPanel("Tag Sentiment"
                      ,dataTableOutput("sentiment"))
  )
)
```

We have a navigation panel at the top. The first navigation panel has a textbox in which we can enter our search string. A default value is provided, so when you open the application, you will have the search results available for that string. We have a data table output following the textbox. This is where we display the tweet results.

In the second navigation panel, we have the data table output, where we want to show the tweets and their sentiments.

Now let us write the server side of the code:

```
server <- function(input, output) {
  tweet.df <- reactive({
    tweet.results <- searchTwitter(input$search, n=100,lang = "en")
    tweet.df <- twListToDF(tweet.results)
    # Remove retweets
    tweet.df <- tweet.df[tweet.df$isRetweet == FALSE, ]
    # Cleanup tweets
    tweet.df <- data.frame(tweet.df['text'])
    tweet.df$text =str_replace_all(tweet.df$text,"[\\.\\,\\;]+", " ")
    tweet.df$text =str_replace_all(tweet.df$text,"http\\w+", "")
    tweet.df$text =str_replace_all(tweet.df$text,"@\\w+", " ")
    tweet.df$text =str_replace_all(tweet.df$text,"[[:punct:]]", " ")
    tweet.df$text =str_replace_all(tweet.df$text,"[[:digit:]]", " ")
    tweet.df$text =str_replace_all(tweet.df$text,"^ ", " ")
    tweet.df$text =str_replace_all(tweet.df$text," $", " ")
    tweet.df$text =str_replace_all(tweet.df$text,"[<].*[>]", " ")
    # Get sentiment
    sentiment.score <- sentiment(tweet.df$text)
    sentiment.score <- sentiment.score %>% group_by(element_id) %>%
summarise(sentiment = mean(sentiment))
    tweet.df$polarity <- sentiment.score$sentiment
    tweet.df$sentiment <- ifelse(tweet.df$polarity <0,
"Negative","Positive")
    return(tweet.df)
  })
```

```
output$results <- renderDataTable({
  tweet.df()['text']
})
output$sentiment <- renderDataTable({
  tweet.df()
})
}
```

`tweet.df` is declared as a reactive expression. It will change if the text in our search box changes. Here, we search Twitter for the search string provided. Capture the returned tweets, clean them up, calculate their polarity scores, and keep them ready.

It's simple from now on. `output$results` return a data frame. It takes the data frame from our `tweet.df` reactive expression. This one only returns the text column.

`output$sentiment` behaves the same way as `output$results`, except that it returns the whole data frame.

 Reactive expressions are expressions that can read reactive values and call other reactive expressions. Whenever reactive value changes, any reactive expressions that depended on it are marked as invalidated and will automatically re-execute if necessary. - RShiny web page.

Finally, let us declare the complete application:

```
shinyApp(ui = ui, server = server)
```

When we run this application, we see the following screen:

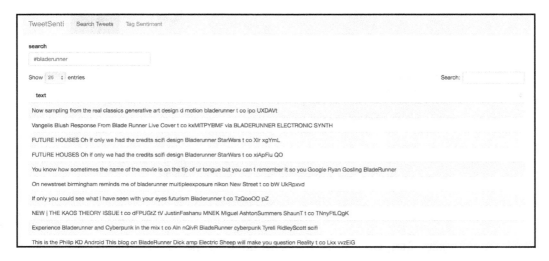

You can see the cleaned up tweets for `#BladeRunner`.

We can change the search string and have the new results shown:

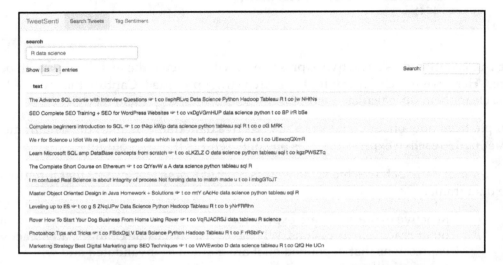

You can see that we have changed the query to `R data science`.

Let us look at the next tab:

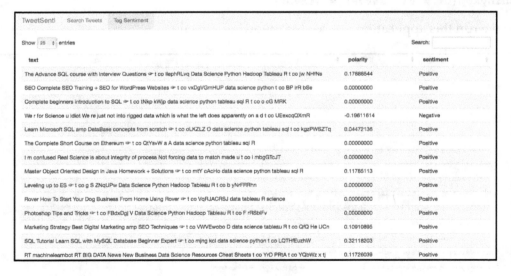

In the preceding screenshot, we can see the sentiment for the tweets.

Complete R code

The following is the complete R code used for this project:

```
# Generate data
data <- rnorm(1000, mean=25, sd=5)
data.1 <- rnorm(1000, mean=10, sd=2)
data <- c(data, data.1)

# Plot histogram
hist(data)
# View the bins
hist(data, plot = FALSE)

# Histogram with modified bins
hist(data, breaks = seq(0,50,2))



# Kernel Density estimation
kde = density(data)
plot(kde)



library(pdfCluster)
kde.1  <- kepdf(data)
plot(kde.1)
kde.1@kernel
kde.1@par



# Twitter Text
library(twitteR, quietly = TRUE)

consumer.key <- ""
consumer.secret <- ""
access.token <- ""
token.secret <- ""

setup_twitter_oauth(consumer.key, consumer.secret, access.token,
token.secret)
```

```r
blade_runner <- searchTwitter("#bladeRunner", n=100,lang = "en")
tweet.df <- twListToDF(blade_runner)
head(tweet.df)

head(tweet.df[tweet.df$isRetweet == FALSE, ]$text)


# Data gold set prepration
library(sentimentr, quietly = TRUE)
sentiment.score <- sentiment(tweet.df$text)
head(sentiment.score)

library(dplyr, quietly = TRUE)
sentiment.score <- sentiment.score %>% group_by(element_id) %>%
summarise(sentiment = mean(sentiment))
head(sentiment.score)


tweet.df$polarity <- sentiment.score$sentiment
tweet.final <- tweet.df[,c('text','polarity')]
head(tweet.final)

tweet.final$sentiment <- ifelse(tweet.final$polarity <0,
"Negative","Positive")
head(tweet.final)
table(tweet.final$sentiment)

library(caret, quietly = TRUE)
tweet.final$sentiment <- as.factor(tweet.final$sentiment)
tweet.final <- upSample(x = tweet.final$text, y = tweet.final$sentiment)
names(tweet.final) <- c('text', 'sentiment')
head(tweet.final)
table(tweet.final$sentiment)
tweet.final$id <- seq(1, nrow(tweet.final))


# Remove non graphical characters
library(stringr)
tweet.final$text =str_replace_all(tweet.final$text,"[^[:graph:]]", " ")

# KDE Classifier
library(tm)
get.dtm <- function(text.col, id.col, input.df, weighting){

  title.reader <- readTabular(mapping=list(content=text.col, id=id.col))
  corpus <- Corpus(DataframeSource(input.df),
readerControl=list(reader=title.reader))
  corpus <- tm_map(corpus, removePunctuation)
```

```
  corpus <- tm_map(corpus, removeNumbers)
  corpus <- tm_map(corpus, stripWhitespace)
  corpus <- tm_map(corpus, removeWords, stopwords("english"))
  corpus <- tm_map(corpus, content_transformer(tolower))
  dtm <- DocumentTermMatrix(corpus, control = list(weighting = weighting))
  return(dtm)
}

stopwords("english")

dtm <- get.dtm('text','id', tweet.final, "weightTf")
dtm.mat <- as.matrix(dtm)

# delta tf-idf
dtm.pos <- get.dtm('text','id', tweet.final[tweet.final$sentiment ==
'Positive',],"weightBin")
dtm.neg <- get.dtm('text','id', tweet.final[tweet.final$sentiment ==
'Negative',],"weightBin")

dtm.pos.mat <- as.matrix(dtm.pos)
dtm.neg.mat <- as.matrix(dtm.neg)

pos.words.df <- colSums(dtm.pos.mat)
neg.words.df <- colSums(dtm.neg.mat)

pos.features <- colnames(dtm.pos.mat)
neg.features <- colnames(dtm.neg.mat)
tot.features <- unique(c(pos.features, neg.features))
doc.ids <- rownames(dtm.mat)

for( i in 1:length(tot.features)){
  for ( j in 1:length(doc.ids)){
    # Number of times the term has occured in the document
    ctd <- dtm.mat[doc.ids[j], tot.features[i]]
    # Number for documents in pos data with the term
    pt <- pos.words.df[tot.features[i]]
    # Number for documents in pos data with the term
    nt <- neg.words.df[tot.features[i]]
    score <- ctd * log( nt / pt)
    if(is.na(score)){
      score <- 0
    }
    dtm.mat[doc.ids[j], tot.features[i]] <- score
  }
}


library(naivebayes)
```

```
model <- naive_bayes(x = dtm.mat, y = tweet.final$sentiment, usekernel =
TRUE)
model$prior
predict(model, newdata = dtm.mat[1:2, ], type = "prob")
```

The following is the `RShiny` application's complete source code:

```
library(shiny)
library(twitteR, quietly = TRUE)
library(stringr)
library(sentimentr, quietly = TRUE)
library(dplyr, quietly = TRUE)




consumer.key <-
consumer.secret <-
access.token <-
token.secret <-

setup_twitter_oauth(consumer.key, consumer.secret, access.token,
token.secret)
>


server <- function(input, output) {
  tweet.df <- reactive({
    tweet.results <- searchTwitter(input$search, n=100,lang = "en")
    tweet.df <- twListToDF(tweet.results)
    # Remove retweets
    tweet.df <- tweet.df[tweet.df$isRetweet == FALSE, ]
    # Cleanup tweets
    tweet.df <- data.frame(tweet.df['text'])
    tweet.df$text =str_replace_all(tweet.df$text,"[\\.\\,\\;]+", " ")
    tweet.df$text =str_replace_all(tweet.df$text,"http\\w+", "")
    tweet.df$text =str_replace_all(tweet.df$text,"@\\w+", " ")
    tweet.df$text =str_replace_all(tweet.df$text,"[[:punct:]]", " ")
    tweet.df$text =str_replace_all(tweet.df$text,"[[:digit:]]", " ")
    tweet.df$text =str_replace_all(tweet.df$text,"^ ", " ")
    tweet.df$text =str_replace_all(tweet.df$text," $", " ")
    tweet.df$text =str_replace_all(tweet.df$text,"[<].*[>]", " ")
    # Get sentiment
    sentiment.score <- sentiment(tweet.df$text)
    sentiment.score <- sentiment.score %>% group_by(element_id) %>%
summarise(sentiment = mean(sentiment))
    tweet.df$polarity <- sentiment.score$sentiment
```

```
      tweet.df$sentiment <- ifelse(tweet.df$polarity <0,
"Negative","Positive")
      return(tweet.df)
   })

   output$results <- renderDataTable({
      tweet.df()['text']
   })
   output$sentiment <- renderDataTable({
      tweet.df()
   })
}

ui <- fluidPage(
   navbarPage("TweetSenti",
               tabPanel("Search Tweets"
                        , textInput("search","search",value="#bladerunner")
                        , dataTableOutput("results")
                        ),
               tabPanel("Tag Sentiment"
                        ,dataTableOutput("sentiment"))
   )
)

shinyApp(ui = ui, server = server)
```

Summary

We started this chapter with a discussion about the KDE and its usefulness in understanding the underlying distribution of data. We proceeded by explaining how to extract tweets from Twitter for a given search string in R. Then, we proceeded to explain the sentiment ming, dictionary, and machine learning approaches. Using a dictionary approach, we calculated the sentiment scores for the tweets. We further explained text pre-processing routines required to prepare the text data. We covered weighting schemes for creating document term matrixes. We discussed the classic tfidf and the new Delta TFIDF schemes. We created our training set using the Delta TFIDF scheme. Using this training set, we finally built a Naive Bayes KDE classifier to classify tweets based on the sentiment the text carried.

In the next chapter, we will be working on Record Linakage. A master data management technique to do data dedpulication.

6
Record Linkage - Stochastic and Machine Learning Approaches

In a large database of records, synonymous records pose a great problem. Two records referring to the same entity are considered to be synonymous. In the absence of a common identifier, such as a primary key or foreign key, joining such records based on the entities is a tough task. Let's illustrate this with a quick example. Consider the following two records:

Sno	First name	Middle name	Last name	Address	City	State	Zip
1	John	NULL	NULL	312 Delray Ave	Deer Field	FL	33433
2	John	NULL	Sanders	312 Delray Beach Ave	Deer Field	FL	33433

Both the records refer to the same entity, one Mr. John. Record linkage refers to an umbrella of algorithms that are designed to solve the exact same problem. Record linkage plays a key role today in various applications such as CRM, Loyalty to name a few. They are an integral part of today's sophisticated business intelligence systems and master data management systems.

Disabled Airplane Pilots – a successful application of record linkage: A database consisting of records of 40,000 airplane pilots licensed by the U.S. **Federal Aviation Administration (FAA)** and residing in Northern California was matched to a database consisting of individuals receiving disability payments from the social security administration. Forty pilots whose records turned up on both databases were arrested (`https://www.soa.org/library/newsletters/the-actuary-magazine/2007/february/link2007feb.aspx`).

In this chapter, we will cover the following topics:

- Introducing a use case that can be solved by record linkage algorithms
- Demonstrating the use of the R package, `RecordLinkage`
- Covering stochastic record linkage algorithms
- Implementing machine learning-based record linkage algorithms
- Building an `RShiny` application

The code for this chapter was written in RStudio Version 0.99.491. It uses R version 3.3.1. As we work through our example we will introduce the R packages `RecordLinkage` we will be using. During our code description, we will be using some of the output printed in the console. We have included what will be printed in the console immediately following the statement which prints the information to the console, so as to not disturb the flow of the code.

Introducing our use case

Our customer owns and operates water theme parks. Last year, he had induced a couple of small-time firms to solicit customers to purchase theme park tickets. The problem at hand now is with one of the small-time firms--let's call it Solit. Solit claims that in the last quarter, it was able to channel close to 15,000 customers to buy tickets at the various theme parks. Neither our customer nor Solit has an exact list of the customers. Both of them have their own database of customers. The problem at hand is how many exact customers were channeled by Solit? The data contains the first name, middle name, last name, and date of birth of the customers. Keep in mind the data fields can differ slightly, for example, two records referring to the same entity, say John, may have a small change in the last name or a slightly different date of birth:

fname_c1	fname_c2	lname_c1	lname_c2	by	bm	bd
CARSTEN	NA	MEIER	NA	1949	7	22
GERD	NA	BAUER	NA	1968	7	27
ROBERT	NA	HARTMANN	NA	1930	4	30
STEFAN	NA	WOLFF	NA	1957	9	2
RALF	NA	KRUEGER	NA	1966	1	13
JUERGEN	NA	FRANKE	NA	1929	7	4
GERD	NA	SCHAEFER	NA	1967	8	1
UWE	NA	MEIER	NA	1942	9	20
DANIEL	NA	SCHMIDT	NA	1978	3	4
MICHAEL	NA	HAHN	NA	1971	2	27

The preceding data is **RLdata500** from the `RecordLinkage` package. We are using this data to demonstrate our use case.

The preceding image is a snapshot of the data from our customer and Solit. Assume that we have merged the database records from both the parties. The record number indicates the source of the record, that is whether they came from our customer or Solit. If we can find duplicates in this dataset, that should serve as the first step in identifying the customers channeled by Solit.

Demonstrating the use of RecordLinkage package

We will leverage the `RecordLinkage` package in R. The data shown in the previous section is available with the package:

`RecordLinkage`: Record linkage in R provides functions to link and deduplicate datasets. Methods based on a stochastic approach are implemented, as well as classification algorithms from the machine learning domain. Authors: Andreas Borg and Murat Sariyar.

```
> library(RecordLinkage, quietly = TRUE)
> data(RLdata500)
> str(RLdata500)
'data.frame':   500 obs. of  7 variables:
```

```
    $ fname_c1: Factor w/ 146 levels "ALEXANDER","ANDRE",..: 19 42 114 128 112
77 42 139 26 99 ...
    $ fname_c2: Factor w/ 23 levels "ALEXANDER","ANDREAS",..: NA NA NA NA NA
NA NA NA NA NA ...
    $ lname_c1: Factor w/ 108 levels "ALBRECHT","BAUER",..: 61 2 31 106 50 23
76 61 77 30 ...
    $ lname_c2: Factor w/ 8 levels "ENGEL","FISCHER",..: NA NA NA NA NA NA NA
NA NA NA ...
    $ by       : int  1949 1968 1930 1957 1966 1929 1967 1942 1978 1971 ...
    $ bm       : int  7 7 4 9 1 7 8 9 3 2 ...
    $ bd       : int  22 27 30 2 13 4 1 20 4 27 ...
> head(RLdata500)
    fname_c1 fname_c2 lname_c1 lname_c2   by bm bd
1   CARSTEN     <NA>    MEIER     <NA> 1949  7 22
2      GERD     <NA>    BAUER     <NA> 1968  7 27
3    ROBERT     <NA> HARTMANN     <NA> 1930  4 30
4    STEFAN     <NA>    WOLFF     <NA> 1957  9  2
5      RALF     <NA>  KRUEGER     <NA> 1966  1 13
6   JUERGEN     <NA>   FRANKE     <NA> 1929  7  4
```

Our data, RLdata500, has 500 records and 7 variables, which includes first name, last name, and date of birth details. The first and last names are separated into two components denoted by the suffixes, _c1 and _c2. The date of birth is split into year, day, and month. Let's look at the steps that we are going to follow to implement record linkage:

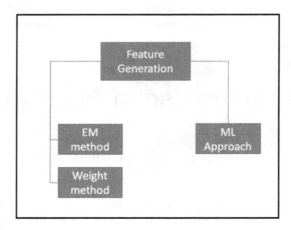

Feature generation is the first step in record linkage. Once we have the desired features, we can solve the record linkage problem either using a stochastic approach or by fitting a machine learning model to the generated features.

Feature generation

We will use `compare.dedup` to generate the features:

```
> rec.pairs <- compare.dedup(RLdata500
+                           ,blockfld = list(1, 5:7)
+                           ,strcmp =   c(2,3,4)
+                           ,strcmpfun = levenshteinSim)
> summary(rec.pairs)

Deduplication Data Set

500 records
1221 record pairs

0 matches
0 non-matches
1221 pairs with unknown status

> matches <- rec.pairs$pairs
> matches[c(1:3, 1203:1204), ]
      id1 id2 fname_c1 fname_c2   lname_c1 lname_c2 by bm bd is_match
1       1 174        1       NA 0.1428571       NA  0  0  0       NA
2       1 204        1       NA 0.0000000       NA  0  0  0       NA
3       2   7        1       NA 0.3750000       NA  0  0  0       NA
1203  448 497        1       NA 0.0000000       NA  0  0  0       NA
1204  450 477        1       NA 0.0000000       NA  0  0  0       NA
```

We have 500 records; we should generate *500*(500-1)/ 2* pairs to do the comparisons--in general, for *n* records it will be *n(n-1)/2* pairs. In a large dataset, this may be tedious. The `blockfld` parameter helps us alleviate this problem. It helps reduce the number of pairs by focusing on certain constraints while generating the pairs:

```
blockfld = list(1, 5:7)
```

Our constraints are represented in a list. We say we need either to match the first column or columns 5 up to 7 for two records to qualify to become a pair. You can see in the results that we are finally left with only 1,221 pairs:

```
Deduplication Data Set

500 records
1221 record pairs

0 matches
0 non-matches
1221 pairs with unknown status
```

The `dedup` function returns a list:

```
> str(rec.pairs)
List of 4
 $ data        :'data.frame':    500 obs. of  7 variables:
  ..$ fname_c1: Factor w/ 146 levels "ALEXANDER","ANDRE",..: 19 42 114 128
112 77 42 139 26 99 ...
  ..$ fname_c2: Factor w/ 23 levels "ALEXANDER","ANDREAS",..: NA NA NA NA
NA NA NA NA NA NA ...
  ..$ lname_c1: Factor w/ 108 levels "ALBRECHT","BAUER",..: 61 2 31 106 50
23 76 61 77 30 ...
  ..$ lname_c2: Factor w/ 8 levels "ENGEL","FISCHER",..: NA NA NA NA NA NA
NA NA NA NA ...
  ..$ by      : int [1:500] 1949 1968 1930 1957 1966 1929 1967 1942 1978
1971 ...
  ..$ bm      : int [1:500] 7 7 4 9 1 7 8 9 3 2 ...
  ..$ bd      : int [1:500] 22 27 30 2 13 4 1 20 4 27 ...
 $ pairs       :'data.frame':    1221 obs. of  10 variables:
  ..$ id1     : num [1:1221] 1 1 2 2 2 4 4 4 4 4 ...
  ..$ id2     : num [1:1221] 174 204 7 43 169 19 50 78 83 133 ...
  ..$ fname_c1: num [1:1221] 1 1 1 1 1 1 1 1 1 1 ...
  ..$ fname_c2: num [1:1221] NA NA NA NA NA NA NA NA NA NA ...
  ..$ lname_c1: num [1:1221] 0.143 0 0.375 0.833 0 ...
  ..$ lname_c2: num [1:1221] NA NA NA NA NA NA NA NA NA NA ...
  ..$ by      : num [1:1221] 0 0 0 1 0 0 1 0 0 0 ...
  ..$ bm      : num [1:1221] 0 0 0 1 0 0 0 0 1 0 ...
  ..$ bd      : num [1:1221] 0 0 0 1 0 0 0 0 0 0 ...
  ..$ is_match: num [1:1221] NA NA NA NA NA NA NA NA NA NA ...
 $ frequencies: Named num [1:7] 0.00685 0.04167 0.00926 0.11111 0.01163 ...
  ..- attr(*, "names")= chr [1:7] "fname_c1" "fname_c2" "lname_c1"
"lname_c2" ...
 $ type        : chr "deduplication"
 - attr(*, "class")= chr "RecLinkData"
```

The entry pairs in the list form a data frame that has all the generated features. We capture this data frame under the name matches:

```
matches <- rec.pairs$pairs
```

Let's look at the first two rows of this data frame. Each row compares two records:

	id1	id2	fname_c1	fname_c2	lname_c1	lname_c2	by	bm	bd	is_match
1	1	174	1	NA	0.1428571	NA	0	0	0	NA
2	1	204	1	NA	0.0000000	NA	0	0	0	NA

The first instance compares records 1 and 174. There is a perfect match in the first component of the first name. Both the entities do not have a second component for the first name. We see a float number in the first component of the last name. This number is the output of a string comparison. There is no match in the date of birth fields. The final column is a `is_match` indicating if we have a match. We will get to the last column later. Let's start with the string comparison.

String features

Let's look at the `dedup` function invocation once again:

```
> rec.pairs <- compare.dedup(RLdata500
+                           ,blockfld = list(1, 5:7)
+                           ,strcmp =    c(2,3,4)
+                           ,strcmpfun = levenshteinSim).
```

The `strcmp` and `strcmpfun` parameters dictate on which fields we need to do string comparison and what kind of string comparison we need to apply. We pass a vector indicating the column IDs to `strcmp`. We need to do string comparisons in columns 2, 3, and 4. We want to use the `Levenshtein` distance to find the similarity between two strings.

 Levenshtein distance (LD) is a measure of similarity between two strings, which we will refer to as the source string (*s*) and the target string (*t*). The distance is the number of deletions, insertions, or substitutions required to transform *s* into *t* (https://en.wikipedia.org/wiki/Levenshtein_distance).

Let's look at the records 1 and 174; we see the first name matching, but no match with the rest of the fields. The Levenshtein distance of 0.142857 also states how far the last names are from each other:

```
> RLdata500[1,]
   fname_c1 fname_c2 lname_c1 lname_c2   by bm bd
1  CARSTEN     <NA>    MEIER     <NA> 1949  7 22
> RLdata500[174,]
     fname_c1 fname_c2 lname_c1 lname_c2   by bm bd
174  CARSTEN     <NA>  SCHMITT     <NA> 2001  6 27
```

We need to state the exact columns where string comparisons should be applied. Not specifying this may lead to unexpected results:

```
> rec.pairs.matches <- compare.dedup(RLdata500
+                                   ,blockfld = list(1, 5:7)
+                                   ,strcmp =    TRUE
+                                   ,strcmpfun = levenshteinSim)
> head(rec.pairs.matches$pairs)
  id1 id2 fname_c1 fname_c2 lname_c1 lname_c2   by   bm   bd is_match
1   1 174        1       NA 0.1428571       NA 0.00  0.5  0.5       NA
2   1 204        1       NA 0.0000000       NA 0.50  0.5  0.0       NA
3   2   7        1       NA 0.3750000       NA 0.75  0.5  0.0       NA
4   2  43        1       NA 0.8333333       NA 1.00  1.0  1.0       NA
5   2 169        1       NA 0.0000000       NA 0.50  0.0  0.5       NA
6   4  19        1       NA 0.1428571       NA 0.50  0.5  0.0       NA
```

You can see that the function has also calculated the string comparisons for the date of birth fields!

We had excluded the first column from string comparison. It was used as a blocking field. However, we can use string comparison for the first column. In that case, the string comparison is performed before the blocking.

Phonetic features

The RecordLinkage package includes Soundex and Pho_h algorithms to compare string columns. In our example, we want to use columns 2, 3, and 4 for string comparison, specified by the list we pass to the phonetic parameter, and use the Pho_h function by passing it to the phonfun parameter:

Soundex is a phonetic algorithm for indexing names by sound, as pronounced in English. The goal is for homophones to be encoded to the same representation so that they can be matched despite minor differences in spelling. https://en.wikipedia.org/wiki/Soundex

Let us generate some phoenetic-based features:

```
> rec.pairs.matches <- compare.dedup(RLdata500
+                                    ,blockfld = list(1, 5:7)
+                                    ,phonetic =    c(2,3,4)
+                                    ,phonfun   = pho_h)
> head(rec.pairs.matches$pairs)
  id1 id2 fname_c1 fname_c2 lname_c1 lname_c2 by bm bd is_match
1   1 174        1      NA        0       NA  0  0  0       NA
2   1 204        1      NA        0       NA  0  0  0       NA
3   2   7        1      NA        0       NA  0  0  0       NA
4   2  43        1      NA        1       NA  1  1  1       NA
5   2 169        1      NA        0       NA  0  0  0       NA
6   4  19        1      NA        0       NA  0  0  0       NA
> RLdata500[2,]
  fname_c1 fname_c2 lname_c1 lname_c2   by bm bd
2     GERD     <NA>    BAUER     <NA> 1968  7 27
> RLdata500[43,]
   fname_c1 fname_c2 lname_c1 lname_c2   by bm bd
43     GERD     <NA>   BAUERH     <NA> 1968  7 27
```

If we compare the results with the string matching output, we see that we find no match between record IDs 1 and 174. Let's look at instance 4, where records id1, 2 and id2, 43 are compared:

```
> RLdata500[2,]
  fname_c1 fname_c2 lname_c1 lname_c2   by bm bd
2     GERD     <NA>    BAUER     <NA> 1968  7 27
> RLdata500[43,]
   fname_c1 fname_c2 lname_c1 lname_c2   by bm bd
43     GERD     <NA>   BAUERH     <NA> 1968  7 27
```

The last name in those cases sound similar, hence the algorithm has captured them as similar records.

 The string and phonetic comparisons cannot be used simultaneously for the same column.

Stochastic record linkage

Given the features of two records/entities, the job of stochastic record linkage is to give a measure of the closeness of the two entities. The final job is to find if the two records refer to the same entity. This can be accomplished by building a threshold-based classifier based on the weights.

We will show how to leverage two methods, emWeights and epiWeights, implemented in the RecordLinkage package.

Expectation maximization method

The method, emWeights, is based on the expectation maximization algorithm to derive from the weights, a measure of the closeness of two entities. According to this method, two conditional probabilities, one for match and an other for no match, has to be derived.

P (features | match = 0) and P (features | match = 1) are estimated using the expectation maximization algorithm. The weights are calculated as the ratio of these two probabilities. This approach is called the **Fellegi-Sunter model**.

```
> library(RecordLinkage)
> data("RLdata500")
> rec.pairs <- compare.dedup(RLdata500
+                           ,blockfld = list(1, 5:7)
+                           ,strcmp =   c(2,3,4)
+                           ,strcmpfun = levenshteinSim)
> pairs.weights <- emWeights(rec.pairs)

> hist(pairs.weights$Wdata)
>
```

 Using the EM Algorithm for weight computation in the Fellegi-Sunter model of record linkage - William E. Winkler.

As seen in the feature generation section, we use the `dedup` function to generate string comparison features. With the features, we invoke the `emWeights` function to get the Fellegi-Sunter weights. The output of `emWeights` is a list:

```
> str(pairs.weights)
List of 8
 $ data        :'data.frame':    500 obs. of  7 variables:
  ..$ fname_c1: Factor w/ 146 levels "ALEXANDER","ANDRE",..: 19 42 114 128
112 77 42 139 26 99 ...
  ..$ fname_c2: Factor w/ 23 levels "ALEXANDER","ANDREAS",..: NA NA NA NA
NA NA NA NA NA NA ...
  ..$ lname_c1: Factor w/ 108 levels "ALBRECHT","BAUER",..: 61 2 31 106 50
23 76 61 77 30 ...
  ..$ lname_c2: Factor w/ 8 levels "ENGEL","FISCHER",..: NA NA NA NA NA NA
NA NA NA NA ...
  ..$ by      : int [1:500] 1949 1968 1930 1957 1966 1929 1967 1942 1978
1971 ...
  ..$ bm      : int [1:500] 7 7 4 9 1 7 8 9 3 2 ...
  ..$ bd      : int [1:500] 22 27 30 2 13 4 1 20 4 27 ...
 $ pairs       :'data.frame':    1221 obs. of  10 variables:
  ..$ id1     : num [1:1221] 1 1 2 2 2 4 4 4 4 4 ...
  ..$ id2     : num [1:1221] 174 204 7 43 169 19 50 78 83 133 ...
  ..$ fname_c1: num [1:1221] 1 1 1 1 1 1 1 1 1 1 ...
  ..$ fname_c2: num [1:1221] NA NA NA NA NA NA NA NA NA NA ...
  ..$ lname_c1: num [1:1221] 0.143 0 0.375 0.833 0 ...
  ..$ lname_c2: num [1:1221] NA NA NA NA NA NA NA NA NA NA ...
  ..$ by      : num [1:1221] 0 0 0 1 0 0 1 0 0 0 ...
  ..$ bm      : num [1:1221] 0 0 0 1 0 0 0 0 1 0 ...
  ..$ bd      : num [1:1221] 0 0 0 1 0 0 0 0 0 0 ...
  ..$ is_match: num [1:1221] NA NA NA NA NA NA NA NA NA NA ...
 $ frequencies: Named num [1:7] 0.00685 0.04167 0.00926 0.11111 0.01163 ...
  ..- attr(*, "names")= chr [1:7] "fname_c1" "fname_c2" "lname_c1"
"lname_c2" ...
 $ type        : chr "deduplication"
 $ M           : num [1:128] 0.000355 0.001427 0.004512 0.01815 0.001504 ...
 $ U           : num [1:128] 2.84e-04 8.01e-06 2.52e-05 7.10e-07 2.83e-06
...
 $ W           : num [1:128] 0.322 7.477 7.486 14.641 9.053 ...
 $ Wdata       : num [1:1221] -10.3 -10.3 -10.3 12.8 -10.3 ...
 - attr(*, "class")= chr "RecLinkData"
>
```

The `Wdata` vector stores the weights for Record Linkage based on an EM algorithm, higher values indicate better matches. Let's plot this data as a histogram to look at the weights distribution:

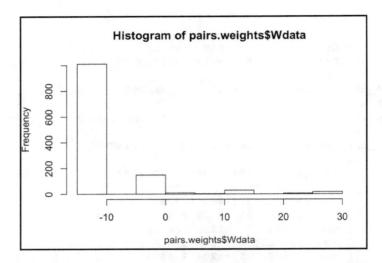

The histogram is skewed with a lot of negative weights and very few positive weights. This gives us a hint that we have very few matches in our dataset. Alternatively, we can view the weight distribution as follows:

```
> summary(pairs.weights)

Deduplication Data Set

500 records
1221 record pairs

0 matches
0 non-matches
1221 pairs with unknown status


Weight distribution:

[-15,-10]  (-10,-5]    (-5,0]     (0,5]     (5,10]    (10,15]    (15,20]
(20,25]    (25,30]
     1011          0       148         9          2         29          0
5          17
>
```

The `getPairs` function conveniently gives the weights for the pair:

```
> weights.df<-getPairs(pairs.weights)
> head(weights.df)
    id fname_c1 fname_c2 lname_c1 lname_c2   by bm bd      Weight
1   48   WERNER     <NA>  KOERTIG     <NA> 1965 11 28
2  238  WERNIER     <NA>  KOERTIG     <NA> 1965 11 28  29.628078
3
4   68   PETEVR     <NA>    FUCHS     <NA> 1972  9 12
5  190    PETER     <NA>    FUCHS     <NA> 1972  9 12  29.628078
6
```

For record IDs `48` and `238`, the weight is `29.62`. The higher the weight is, the more probability there is of a match. With the weights, now we can use a threshold-based classification model. We can derive the thresholds from either the histogram or the weight distribution. We are going to choose the upper threshold, that is, for a match, we need a weight of 10 or more. For a no match, we set the lower threshold as `5`, and any entity pairs with less than `5` will be tagged as a no match. The `emClassify` function is used to classify the entities as match and no match:

```
> pairs.classify <- emClassify(pairs.weights, threshold.upper = 10,
threshold.lower = 5)
> summary(pairs.classify)

Deduplication Data Set

500 records
1221 record pairs

0 matches
0 non-matches
1221 pairs with unknown status


Weight distribution:

[-15,-10]   (-10,-5]    (-5,0]     (0,5]    (5,10]   (10,15]   (15,20]
(20,25]    (25,30]
     1011          0       148         9         2        29         0
5          17

51 links detected
2 possible links detected
1168 non-links detected

Classification table:
```

```
              classification
true status      N    P    L
       <NA>    1168    2   51
```

The label N stands for no match or no links found. Label P stands for possible matches and label L for matches aka links founds. We see that with our given threshold, 51 matches were found. Let's make a single data frame to collate all our results:

```
> final.results <- pairs.classify$pairs
> final.results$weight <- pairs.classify$Wdata
> final.results$links <- pairs.classify$prediction
> head(final.results)
  id1 id2 fname_c1 fname_c2 lname_c1 lname_c2 by bm bd is_match   weight
links
1   1 174        1       NA 0.1428571       NA  0  0  0       NA -10.28161
N
2   1 204        1       NA 0.0000000       NA  0  0  0       NA -10.28161
N
3   2   7        1       NA 0.3750000       NA  0  0  0       NA -10.28161
N
4   2  43        1       NA 0.8333333       NA  1  1  1       NA  12.76895
L
5   2 169        1       NA 0.0000000       NA  0  0  0       NA -10.28161
N
6   4  19        1       NA 0.1428571       NA  0  0  0       NA -10.28161
N
>
```

Let us use the data frame `final.results` to plot a histogram:

```
counts <- table(final.results$links)
barplot(counts, main="Link Distribution",
        xlab="Link Types")
```

A bar graph of links columns to look at our prediction distribution is as follows:

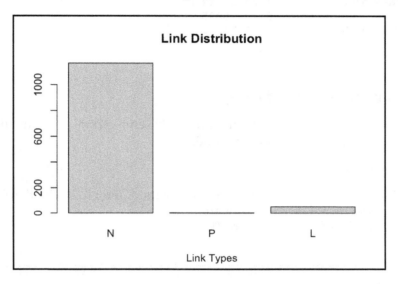

Finally, we can give the list of matches to our customer:

```
> weights.df.srow <-getPairs( pairs.weights, single.rows = TRUE)
> final.matches <- final.results[final.results$links == 'L',]
>
> final <- merge(final.matches, weights.df.srow)
> final <- subset(final, select = -c(fname_c1.2, fname_c2.2, lname_c1.2,
lname_c2.2, by.2, bm.2, bd.2, weight))
> head(final)
   id1 id2 fname_c1 fname_c2  lname_c1 lname_c2 by bm bd is_match links
fname_c1.1 fname_c2.1 lname_c1.1
1 106 175        1       NA 1.0000000       NA  1  0  1       NA     L
ANDRE        <NA>    MUELLER
2 108 203        1       NA 1.0000000       NA  0  1  1       NA     L
GERHARD      <NA>    FRIEDRICH
3 112 116        1       NA 0.8000000       NA  1  1  1       NA     L
GERHARD      <NA>    ERNSR
4 119 131        0       NA 0.1111111       NA  1  1  1       NA     L
ALEXANDER    <NA>    FRIEDRICH
5 120 165        1       NA 0.8750000       NA  1  1  1       NA     L
FRANK        <NA>    BERGMANN
6 125 193        1       NA 0.8750000       NA  1  1  1       NA     L
CHRISTIAN    <NA>    MUELLEPR
   lname_c2.1 by.1 bm.1 bd.1   Weight
1       <NA> 1976    2   25 11.86047
2       <NA> 1987    2   10 10.29360
```

```
3      <NA> 1980    12    16 12.76895
4      <NA> 1968     8    14 23.37222
5      <NA> 1998    11     8 12.76895
6      <NA> 1974     8     9 12.76895
>
```

Weights-based method

The epiWeights function implements the weights-based method. R documentation has a nice introduction to the weights-based method:

```
> help("epiWeights")
```

 For more details about the weights method, refer to P. Contiero et al. The Epilink record linkage software.
Methods Inf Med., 44(1):66–71, 2005.

The mechanism of invoking and finally generating the results is very similar to how we did it using emWeights:

```
library(RecordLinkage)
data("RLdata500")

# weight calculation
rec.pairs <- compare.dedup(RLdata500
                        ,blockfld = list(1, 5:7)
                        ,strcmp =    c(2,3,4)
                        ,strcmpfun = levenshteinSim)

pairs.weights <- epiWeights(rec.pairs)
hist(pairs.weights$Wdata)
```

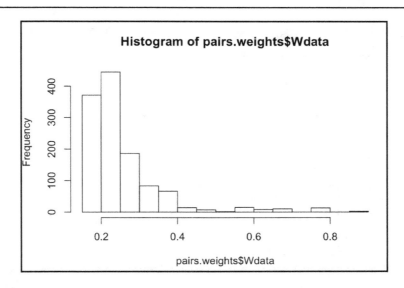

One again, the distribution is similar to our histogram from the emWeights method. Let's see an alternate view of the weights distribution:

```
> summary(pairs.weights)

Deduplication Data Set

500 records
1221 record pairs

0 matches
0 non-matches
1221 pairs with unknown status


Weight distribution:

[0.15,0.2] (0.2,0.25] (0.25,0.3] (0.3,0.35] (0.35,0.4] (0.4,0.45]
(0.45,0.5] (0.5,0.55] (0.55,0.6]
       371        445        186         83         66         14
7          1         15
(0.6,0.65] (0.65,0.7] (0.7,0.75] (0.75,0.8] (0.8,0.85] (0.85,0.9]
         8         10          0         13          0          2
>
```

Once again we will use `getPairs` and `emClassify` as we did in `emWeights`:

```
weights.df<-getPairs(pairs.weights)
head(weights.df)

# Classification
pairs.classify <- emClassify(pairs.weights, threshold.upper = 0.5,
threshold.lower = 0.3)

# View the matches
final.results <- pairs.classify$pairs
final.results$weight <- pairs.classify$Wdata
final.results$links <- pairs.classify$prediction
head(final.results)

counts <- table(final.results$links)
barplot(counts, main="Link Distribution",
        xlab="Link Types")
```

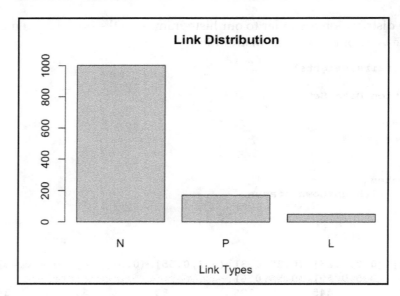

Generate our final list for our customer:

```
> weights.df.srow <-getPairs( pairs.weights, single.rows = TRUE)
> final.matches <- final.results[final.results$links == 'L',]
>
> final <- merge(final.matches, weights.df.srow)
> final <- subset(final, select = -c(fname_c1.2, fname_c2.2, lname_c1.2,
lname_c2.2, by.2, bm.2, bd.2, weight))
```

```
> head(final)
   id1 id2 fname_c1 fname_c2  lname_c1 lname_c2 by bm bd is_match links
fname_c1.1 fname_c2.1 lname_c1.1
1 106 175        1       NA 1.0000000      NA  1  0  1       NA     L
ANDRE         <NA>     MUELLER
2 108 203        1       NA 1.0000000      NA  0  1  1       NA     L
GERHARD       <NA>    FRIEDRICH
3 112 116        1       NA 0.8000000      NA  1  1  1       NA     L
GERHARD       <NA>      ERNSR
4 120 165        1       NA 0.8750000      NA  1  1  1       NA     L
FRANK         <NA>    BERGMANN
5 125 193        1       NA 0.8750000      NA  1  1  1       NA     L
CHRISTIAN       <NA>    MUELLEPR
6 127 142        1       NA 0.8333333      NA  1  1  0       NA     L
KARL          <NA>      KLEIN
   lname_c2.1 by.1 bm.1 bd.1   Weight
1      <NA> 1976    2   25 0.6910486
2      <NA> 1987    2   10 0.6133400
3      <NA> 1980   12   16 0.7518301
4      <NA> 1998   11    8 0.7656562
5      <NA> 1974    8    9 0.7656562
6      <NA> 2002    6   20 0.6228760
>
```

Machine learning-based record linkage

The record linkage problem is modeled as a machine learning problem. It is solved in both unsupervised and supervised manners. In cases where we only have the features of the tuples we want to de-dupe and don't have ground truth information, an unsupervised learning method such as K-means is employed.

Let us look at the unsupervised learning.

Unsupervised learning

Let's start with an unsupervised machine learning technique, K-means clustering. K-means is a well-known and popular clustering algorithm and works based on the principles of expectation maximization. It belongs to the class of iterative descent clustering methods. Internally, it assumes the variables are of quantitative type and uses Euclidean distance as a similarity measure to arrive at the clusters.

The K is a parameter to the algorithm. K stands for the number of clusters we need. Users need to provide this parameter.

 Refer to *The Elements of Statistical Learning,* Chapter 14 for a more in-depth introduction to the K-means algorithm.

Unsupervised techniques are appealing as they don't require us to build a training set. For us to use a supervised technique, we need to create a training set, a tuple consisting of our features, and a label to say if that record pair is a match or no-match. Till now in our case, we haven't had a training dataset. Hence, let's start with an unsupervised technique:

```
> library(RecordLinkage, quietly = TRUE)
> data("RLdata500")
> rec.pairs <- compare.dedup(RLdata500
+                            ,blockfld = list(1, 5:7)
+                            ,strcmp =   c(2,3,4)
+                            ,strcmpfun = levenshteinSim)
> kmeans.model <- classifyUnsup(rec.pairs, method = "kmeans")
> summary(kmeans.model)

Deduplication Data Set

500 records
1221 record pairs

0 matches
0 non-matches
1221 pairs with unknown status


150 links detected
0 possible links detected
1071 non-links detected

Classification table:

          classification
true status    N     P     L
      <NA> 1071     0   150
```

We generate our features using the `compare.dedup` method. This time we are sticking to string-based features. The `classifyUnSup` method invokes K-means from the package, `e1071`. A K value of 2 is supplied to the algorithm. As we see the output of the algorithm, we see that K-means has created two groups, one for no link represented by `N` and has around 1,071 records assigned to that cluster. Around 150 are assigned to the `L` cluster:

```
> final.results <- kmeans.model$pairs
> final.results$prediction <- kmeans.model$prediction
> head(final.results)
  id1 id2 fname_c1 fname_c2   lname_c1 lname_c2 by bm bd is_match prediction
1   1 174        1       NA 0.1428571       NA  0  0  0       NA          N
2   1 204        1       NA 0.0000000       NA  0  0  0       NA          N
3   2   7        1       NA 0.3750000       NA  0  0  0       NA          N
4   2  43        1       NA 0.8333333       NA  1  1  1       NA          L
5   2 169        1       NA 0.0000000       NA  0  0  0       NA          N
6   4  19        1       NA 0.1428571       NA  0  0  0       NA          N
>
```

We extract the input pairs and the prediction, where `L` stands for link available aka match and `N` stands for no link available aka no match.

In cases where we have the ground truth, that is features for the tuples and also the ground truth saying if the tuples are representing the same entity, then we can leverage classification modes in supervised settings. Let us look at the supervised learning

Supervised learning

In a supervised learning scenario, we need to provide the algorithm with a set of training tuples. Each tuple has our features from record pairs and a label classifying the tuple as either a match or no match. In our case, we don't have any labeled data.

The `RecordLinkage` package provides a numeric vector called `identity.RLdata500`, which stores the matching record number for every record number. We can pass this using an identity parameter to `compare.dedup`:

```
> str(identity.RLdata500)
 num [1:500] 34 51 115 189 72 142 162 48 133 190 ...
> str(identity.RLdata500)
 num [1:500] 34 51 115 189 72 142 162 48 133 190 ...
> rec.pairs <- compare.dedup(RLdata500
+                            ,identity = identity.RLdata500
+                            ,blockfld = list(1, 5:7)
+ )
> head(rec.pairs$pairs)
```

	id1	id2	fname_c1	fname_c2	lname_c1	lname_c2	by	bm	bd	is_match
1	1	174	1	NA	0	NA	0	0	0	0
2	1	204	1	NA	0	NA	0	0	0	0
3	2	7	1	NA	0	NA	0	0	0	0
4	2	43	1	NA	0	NA	1	1	1	1
5	2	169	1	NA	0	NA	0	0	0	0
6	4	19	1	NA	0	NA	0	0	0	0

If you see the output of `rec.pairs$pairs`, you will notice that now the `is_match` column says if the record pair is a match or no match. Previously, when we did not provide the identity parameter, it was initialized to NA. We are going to leverage this output to train our classification model:

```
> train <- getMinimalTrain(rec.pairs)
> model <- trainSupv(train, method ="bagging")
> train.pred <- classifySupv(model, newdata = train)
> test.pred  <- classifySupv(model, newdata = rec.pairs)
>
> summary(train.pred)

Deduplication Data Set

500 records
17 record pairs

9 matches
8 non-matches
0 pairs with unknown status


9 links detected
0 possible links detected
8 non-links detected

alpha error: 0.000000
beta error: 0.000000
accuracy: 1.000000


Classification table:

          classification
true status N P L
     FALSE 8 0 0
      TRUE 0 0 9
> summary(test.pred)

Deduplication Data Set
```

```
500 records
1221 record pairs

49 matches
1172 non-matches
0 pairs with unknown status


52 links detected
0 possible links detected
1169 non-links detected

alpha error: 0.020408
beta error: 0.003413
accuracy: 0.995905


Classification table:

            classification
true status     N     P     L
      FALSE  1168     0     4
       TRUE     1     0    48
>
```

Using the `getMinimalTrain` function, we get a small set of records from our `rec.pairs` as our training data. We initialize and train a `bagging` model using this data with the `trainSupv` function. Finally, using the `classifySupv` function, we run our model on our training data and test data, which is the whole `rec.pairs` in this case to get the predictions. Finally, using the `summary` function, we can look at the accuracy of our model. We have a 100% accurate model in our training set. `RecordLinkage` supports a lot of classification models, including `neural networks`, `svm`, `bagging`, and `trees`. As we have a very small training set, it is advisable to use `bagging` or `svm`. Finally, we have around 99% accuracy on our whole dataset.

Alternatively, we can leverage our unsupervised clustering output. Use that as an initial training set to build our first supervised learning model:

```
> rec.pairs <- compare.dedup(RLdata500
+                            ,blockfld = list(1, 5:7)
+                            ,strcmp =    c(2,3,4)
+                            ,strcmpfun = levenshteinSim)
>
> # Run K-Means Model
> kmeans.model <- classifyUnsup(rec.pairs, method = "kmeans")
>
```

```
> # Change the original rec.pairs with rec.pairs from K-Means
> pairs <- kmeans.model$pairs
> pairs$prediction <- kmeans.model$prediction
> head(pairs)
  id1 id2 fname_c1 fname_c2  lname_c1 lname_c2 by bm bd is_match prediction
1   1 174        1       NA 0.1428571       NA  0  0  0       NA          N
2   1 204        1       NA 0.0000000       NA  0  0  0       NA          N
3   2   7        1       NA 0.3750000       NA  0  0  0       NA          N
4   2  43        1       NA 0.8333333       NA  1  1  1       NA          L
5   2 169        1       NA 0.0000000       NA  0  0  0       NA          N
6   4  19        1       NA 0.1428571       NA  0  0  0       NA          N
>
```

We pass our `rec.pairs` to the clustering method and extract the pairs with their predictions. We want to replace the `is_match` column with our predictions. However, the values should be 0 or 1 in the `is_match` column instead of N or L:

```
> pairs$is_match <- NULL
> pairs$is_match <- ifelse(pairs$prediction == 'N', 0,1)
> pairs$prediction <- NULL
> pairs[is.na(pairs)] <- 0
> head(pairs)
  id1 id2 fname_c1 fname_c2  lname_c1 lname_c2 by bm bd is_match
1   1 174        1        0 0.1428571        0  0  0  0        0
2   1 204        1        0 0.0000000        0  0  0  0        0
3   2   7        1        0 0.3750000        0  0  0  0        0
4   2  43        1        0 0.8333333        0  1  1  1        1
5   2 169        1        0 0.0000000        0  0  0  0        0
6   4  19        1        0 0.1428571        0  0  0  0        0
>
> rec.pairs$pairs <- pairs
> head(rec.pairs$pairs)
  id1 id2 fname_c1 fname_c2  lname_c1 lname_c2 by bm bd is_match
1   1 174        1        0 0.1428571        0  0  0  0        0
2   1 204        1        0 0.0000000        0  0  0  0        0
3   2   7        1        0 0.3750000        0  0  0  0        0
4   2  43        1        0 0.8333333        0  1  1  1        1
5   2 169        1        0 0.0000000        0  0  0  0        0
6   4  19        1        0 0.1428571        0  0  0  0        0
>
>
```

Now, having changed our `is_match` column to binary, we replace the original pairs data frame in `rec.pairs` with our modified data frame pairs. With this achieved, we can follow the process of generating a small train test, building a model, and verifying the accuracy of the model as we did in the previous section:

```
train <- getMinimalTrain(rec.pairs)
Warning message:
In getMinimalTrain(rec.pairs) :
  Comparison patterns in rpairs contain string comparison values!
> model <- trainSupv(train, method ="bagging")
> train.pred <- classifySupv(model, newdata = train)
> test.pred  <- classifySupv(model, newdata = rec.pairs)
>
> summary(train.pred)

Deduplication Data Set

500 records
82 record pairs

38 matches
44 non-matches
0 pairs with unknown status


38 links detected
0 possible links detected
44 non-links detected </strong>

alpha error: 0.000000
beta error: 0.000000
accuracy: 1.000000


Classification table:

          classification
true status  N  P  L
     FALSE 44  0  0
      TRUE  0  0 38
> summary(test.pred)

Deduplication Data Set

500 records
1221 record pairs
```

```
150 matches
1071 non-matches
0 pairs with unknown status


150 links detected
0 possible links detected
1071 non-links detected

alpha error: 0.000000
beta error: 0.000000
accuracy: 1.000000


Classification table:

            classification
true status    N    P    L
      FALSE 1071    0    0
       TRUE    0    0  150
```

We have achieved a 100% accuracy in both our training and whole datasets.

Building an RShiny application

Our `RShiny` application will have the following features,

- Load the `RLdata500` from the `RecordLinkage` package and display to the user
- Implement the weights algorithm and display the weight range as a histogram
- Allow the user to select the lower and upper thresholds of weights for classification
- Based on the user-selected threshold, do a record matching and display the duplicate entities discovered.

Let us see the code for the user interface:

```
ui <- fluidPage(
  navbarPage("Record Linkage",
    tabPanel("Load"
      , dataTableOutput("records")
    ),
    tabPanel("Weights Method"
      ,plotOutput("weightplot")
      ,sliderInput("lowerthreshold", "Weight Lower threshold:",
```

```
        min = 0.0, max = 1.0,
        value =0.2)
    ,sliderInput("upperthreshold", "Weight Upper threshold:",
        min = 0.0, max = 1.0,
        value =0.5)
    ,dataTableOutput("weights")
    )
  )
)
```

There are two panels, one to show the RLdata500 and an other one to show the results of the weights algorithm.

Let us look at the server side code:

```
server <- function(input, output) {
  output$records <- renderDataTable({
    RLdata500
  })

  output$weights <- renderDataTable({
    rec.pairs <- compare.dedup(RLdata500
                              ,blockfld = list(1, 5:7)
                              ,strcmp =   c(2,3,4)
                              ,strcmpfun = levenshteinSim)
    pairs.weights <- emWeights(rec.pairs)
    pairs.classify <- emClassify(pairs.weights, threshold.upper =
input$upperthreshold, threshold.lower = input$lowerthreshold)
    final.results <- pairs.classify$pairs
    final.results$weight <- pairs.classify$Wdata
    final.results$links <- pairs.classify$prediction
    final.results
  })
  output$weightplot <- renderPlot({
    rec.pairs <- compare.dedup(RLdata500
                              ,blockfld = list(1, 5:7)
                              ,strcmp =   c(2,3,4)
                              ,strcmpfun = levenshteinSim)
    pairs.weights <- epiWeights(rec.pairs)
    hist(pairs.weights$Wdata)
  })
}
```

`output$records`, renders the `RLdata500` as a data frame.

`outptu$weights` runs the `emweights` algorithm and displays the histogram. The user interface provides a slider for threshold selection. The user can choose the necessary threshold based on the histogram displayed. Using these thresholds, a classification is made and the results are shown to the user.

Let us see the first tab:

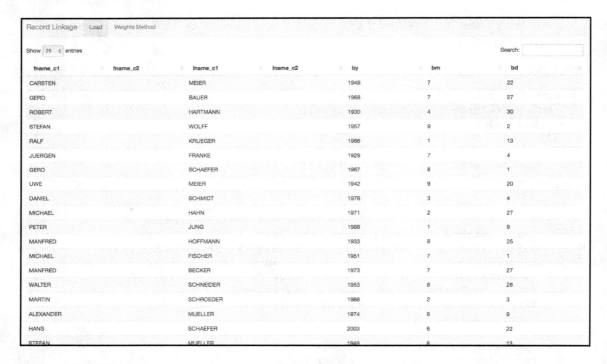

This page displays the `RLdata500` dataset.

Let us see the next tab:

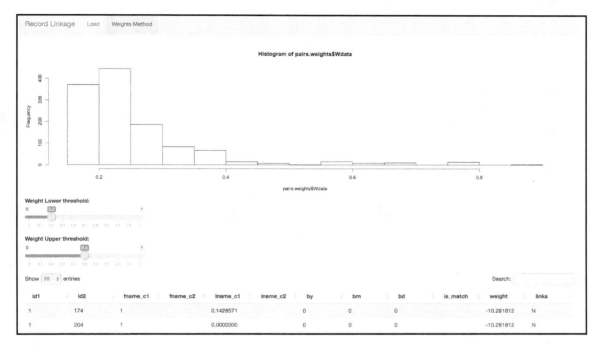

The results of the `emWeight` algorithm is shown are a histogram. The histogram shows the range of weights thrown by the `emWeight` algorithm. In order to find duplicates, users can select a lower and upper threshold for weights and pass them to `emClassify` method.

Complete R code

The complete R code for this chapter is given as follows. We have split the different algorithms used for record linkage into different sections, for ease of reading.

Feature generation

Let us begin with the feature generation R code:

```
library(RecordLinkage, quietly = TRUE)


###### Quick look at our data #########
data(RLdata500)
str(RLdata500)
head(RLdata500)


#### Feature generation #############

rec.pairs <- compare.dedup(RLdata500
                        ,blockfld = list(1, 5:7)
                        ,strcmp =   c(2,3,4)
                        ,strcmpfun = levenshteinSim)

summary(rec.pairs)

matches <- rec.pairs$pairs
matches[c(1:3, 1203:1204), ]

RLdata500[1,]
RLdata500[174,]

# String features
rec.pairs.matches <- compare.dedup(RLdata500
                            ,blockfld = list(1, 5:7)
                            ,strcmp =   c(2,3,4)
                            ,strcmpfun = levenshteinSim)

# Not specifying the fields for string comparision
rec.pairs.matches <- compare.dedup(RLdata500
                            ,blockfld = list(1, 5:7)
                            ,strcmp =   TRUE
                            ,strcmpfun = levenshteinSim)

head(rec.pairs.matches$pairs)

# String comparision before blocking
rec.pairs.matches <- compare.dedup(RLdata500
                            ,blockfld = list(1, 5:7)
                            ,strcmp =   c(1,2,3,4)
                            ,strcmpfun = levenshteinSim)
head(rec.pairs.matches$pairs)
```

```
# Phoenotic features
rec.pairs.matches <- compare.dedup(RLdata500
                                ,blockfld = list(1, 5:7)
                                ,phonetic =   c(2,3,4)
                                ,phonfun  = pho_h)

head(rec.pairs.matches$pairs)

RLdata500[2,]
RLdata500[43,]
```

After feature generation, let us look at the code for the expectation maximization method.

Expectation maximization method

The expectation maximization algorithm for record linkage:

```
>
library(RecordLinkage)
data("RLdata500")

# Em weight calculation
rec.pairs <- compare.dedup(RLdata500
                        ,blockfld = list(1, 5:7)
                        ,strcmp =    c(2,3,4)
                        ,strcmpfun = levenshteinSim)
pairs.weights <- emWeights(rec.pairs)
hist(pairs.weights$Wdata)

summary(pairs.weights)

weights.df<-getPairs(pairs.weights)
head(weights.df)

# Classification
pairs.classify <- emClassify(pairs.weights, threshold.upper = 10,
threshold.lower = 5)

# View the matches
final.results <- pairs.classify$pairs
final.results$weight <- pairs.classify$Wdata
final.results$links <- pairs.classify$prediction
head(final.results)

counts <- table(final.results$links)
barplot(counts, main="Link Distribution",
```

```
          xlab="Link Types")

# Final output to our customer
weights.df.srow <-getPairs( pairs.weights, single.rows = TRUE)
final.matches <- final.results[final.results$links == 'L',]

final <- merge(final.matches, weights.df.srow)
final <- subset(final, select = -c(fname_c1.2, fname_c2.2, lname_c1.2,
lname_c2.2, by.2, bm.2, bd.2, weight))
head(final)
```

This is the complete source code for the expectation maximization method. Let us now look at the weights method.

Weights-based method

The weights-based algorithm for record linkage:

```
library(RecordLinkage)
 data("RLdata500")

 # weight calculation
 rec.pairs <- compare.dedup(RLdata500
 ,blockfld = list(1, 5:7)
 ,strcmp = c(2,3,4)
 ,strcmpfun = levenshteinSim)

 pairs.weights <- epiWeights(rec.pairs)
 hist(pairs.weights$Wdata)

 summary(pairs.weights)

 weights.df<-getPairs(pairs.weights)
 head(weights.df)

 # Classification
 pairs.classify <- emClassify(pairs.weights, threshold.upper = 0.5,
threshold.lower = 0.3)

 # View the matches
 final.results <- pairs.classify$pairs
 final.results$weight <- pairs.classify$Wdata
 final.results$links <- pairs.classify$prediction
 head(final.results)

 counts <- table(final.results$links)
```

```
barplot(counts, main="Link Distribution",
xlab="Link Types")

# Final output to our customer
weights.df.srow <-getPairs( pairs.weights, single.rows = TRUE)
final.matches <- final.results[final.results$links == 'L',]

final <- merge(final.matches, weights.df.srow)
final <- subset(final, select = -c(fname_c1.2, fname_c2.2, lname_c1.2,
lname_c2.2, by.2, bm.2, bd.2, weight))
head(final)
```

This completes the weights-based method.

Machine learning method

Finally, there is the machine learning method for record linkage:

```
library(RecordLinkage, quietly = TRUE)
data("RLdata500")

# weight calculation
rec.pairs <- compare.dedup(RLdata500
                           ,blockfld = list(1, 5:7)
                           ,strcmp =   c(2,3,4)
                           ,strcmpfun = levenshteinSim)

# Unsupervised classification
kmeans.model <- classifyUnsup(rec.pairs, method = "kmeans")
summary(kmeans.model)

final.results <- kmeans.model$pairs
final.results$prediction <- kmeans.model$prediction
head(final.results)


# Supervised Learning 1
str(identity.RLdata500)
rec.pairs <- compare.dedup(RLdata500
                           ,identity = identity.RLdata500
                           ,blockfld = list(1, 5:7)
)
head(rec.pairs$pairs)

train <- getMinimalTrain(rec.pairs)
```

```
model <- trainSupv(train, method ="bagging")
train.pred <- classifySupv(model, newdata = train)
test.pred  <- classifySupv(model, newdata = rec.pairs)

summary(train.pred)
summary(test.pred)

# Supervised learning 2
rec.pairs <- compare.dedup(RLdata500
                          ,blockfld = list(1, 5:7)
                          ,strcmp =   c(2,3,4)
                          ,strcmpfun = levenshteinSim)

# Run K-Means Model
kmeans.model <- classifyUnsup(rec.pairs, method = "kmeans")

# Change the original rec.pairs with rec.pairs from K-Means
pairs <- kmeans.model$pairs
pairs$prediction <- kmeans.model$prediction
head(pairs)

pairs$is_match <- NULL
pairs$is_match <- ifelse(pairs$prediction == 'N', 0,1)
pairs$prediction <- NULL
pairs[is.na(pairs)] <- 0
head(pairs)

rec.pairs$pairs <- pairs
head(rec.pairs$pairs)

train <- getMinimalTrain(rec.pairs)
model <- trainSupv(train, method ="bagging")
train.pred <- classifySupv(model, newdata = train)
test.pred  <- classifySupv(model, newdata = rec.pairs)

summary(train.pred)
summary(test.pred)
```

Having seen the source code for all the different methods, let us now proceed to look at the complete source code for our RShiny application.

RShiny application

The RShiny application source code:

```r
library(shiny)
library(RecordLinkage)
data("RLdata500")


server <- function(input, output) {
  output$records <- renderDataTable({
    RLdata500
  })

  output$weights <- renderDataTable({
    rec.pairs <- compare.dedup(RLdata500
                               ,blockfld = list(1, 5:7)
                               ,strcmp =   c(2,3,4)
                               ,strcmpfun = levenshteinSim)
    pairs.weights <- emWeights(rec.pairs)
    pairs.classify <- emClassify(pairs.weights, threshold.upper =
input$upperthreshold, threshold.lower = input$lowerthreshold)
    final.results <- pairs.classify$pairs
    final.results$weight <- pairs.classify$Wdata
    final.results$links <- pairs.classify$prediction
    final.results
  })
  output$weightplot <- renderPlot({
    rec.pairs <- compare.dedup(RLdata500
                               ,blockfld = list(1, 5:7)
                               ,strcmp =   c(2,3,4)
                               ,strcmpfun = levenshteinSim)
    pairs.weights <- epiWeights(rec.pairs)
    hist(pairs.weights$Wdata)
  })
}

ui <- fluidPage(
  navbarPage("Record Linkage",
             tabPanel("Load"
                      , dataTableOutput("records")
             ),
             tabPanel("Weights Method"
                      ,plotOutput("weightplot")
                      ,sliderInput("lowerthreshold", "Weight Lower
threshold:",
                                   min = 0.0, max = 1.0,
```

```
                                        value =0.2)
                    ,sliderInput("upperthreshold", "Weight Upper
threshold:",
                                   min = 0.0, max = 1.0,
                                   value =0.5)
                    ,dataTableOutput("weights")
                    )
    )
)

shinyApp(ui = ui, server = server)
```

Summary

We introduced the problem of record linkage and emphasized its importance. We introduced the package, RecordLinkage, in R to solve record linkage problems. We started with generating features, string- and phonetic-based, for record pairs so that they can be processed further down the pipeline to dedup records. We covered expectation maximization and weights-based methods to perform a dedup task on our record pairs. Finally, we wrapped up the chapter by introducing machine learning methods for dedup tasks. Under unsupervised methods, K-means clustering was discussed. We further leveraged the output of the K-means algorithm to train a supervised model.

In the next chapter we go through streaming data and its challenges. We will build a stream clustering algorithm for a given streaming data.

7
Streaming Data Clustering Analysis in R

In all those instances where data is collected from various sources, brought to a centralized location, and stored for analysis, that data is called as data at rest. There is a huge time delay between the time the data was recorded and when the analysis was performed. Analyzing the last 6 months' inventory data is an example of data at rest. Today, majority of data analysis is performed using data at rest.

With the number of Internet of Things projects on the rise, there is a great demand today to perform analysis on data in motion, also called streaming data. Streaming data is becoming ubiquitous with the number of addressable sensors and devices being added to the internet. As an example from computer network monitoring: an intrusion detection system analysis, the network packets received in real time to quickly determine if the system is compromised and takes an appropriate action. Latency is key when analyzing data in motion.

A data stream is a continuous inflow of ordered points in a multi-dimensional space. The ordering can be done either explicitly through timestamps or by some other index. The major challenge in analysis is the unbounded nature of such streams. At any point in time, we don't see all the data. This poses a lot of restrictions on the algorithms that can process this data. The algorithm has to work on a limited set of data at any point in time. It has to make quick decisions in a single pass. The real-time nature of this process demands high throughput. Lastly, but most importantly, the algorithm has to deal with any drift present in the data streams. A future stream may have completely drifted in terms of the distribution or the properties of the data compared to the present stream.

In this chapter, we will cover the following topics:

- Introducing streaming data and the challenges it comes with
- Introducing stream clustering
- Introducing `stream` package in R to work on streaming data
- Adopting a stream clustering algorithm for a simulated sensor network

The code for this chapter was written in RStudio Version 0.99.491. It uses R version 3.3.1. As we work through our example, we will introduce the R `stream` packages we will be using. During our code description, we will be using some of the output printed in the console. We have included what will be printed in the console, immediately following the statement which prints the information to the console, so as to not disturb the flow of the code.

Streaming data and its challenges

Streaming data poses infrastructural and processing challenges. Major tech companies are inventing new data structures and server mechanisms to handle the huge volume and velocity of the streaming data. Software infrastructures such as Kafka, Storm, Bolt, and other similar technologies are being invented to handle this from an infrastructure perspective. We will not go into the details here. Our concern is primarily with the processing challenges.

The processing challenges in stream data are shown in the following figure:

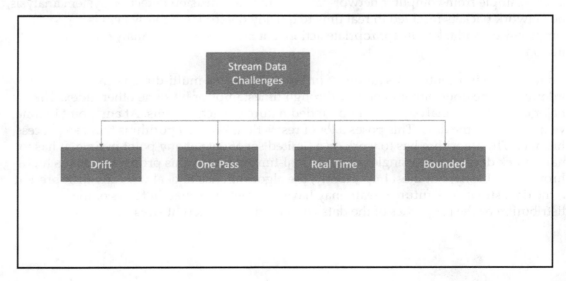

Bounded problems

The first challenge is deciding on a window, and what size window we need to accommodate to make sense of the incoming data. By window, we mean storing the last *n* data points. For streaming data, it is rare to actually process records one at a time. One of the most common ways to process streaming data is to process them in a window. This can either bundle data points into a group and process them as a unit or it can be a changing group of n data points (or x time) where older records are discarded and newer records added.

Drift

The second challenge is the non-stationary aspect of the streaming data. Data is considered stationary if its statistical attributes such as mean, standard deviation, and others do not vary over time. However, we cannot make this assumption for streaming data. This non-stationary behavior is also called drift. Our algorithms should be able to spot and handle drifts efficiently.

The paper, *Open Challenges for Data Stream Mining Research*, by Georg Kremp et. al (http://www.kdd.org/exploration_files/16-1-2014.pdf), clearly classifies the various issues with processing the stream data.

They explain drift in terms of volatility:

- Volatility corresponds to a dynamic environment with ever-changing patterns. Here, old data is of limited use, even if it could be saved and processed again later. This is due to changes, that can affect the induced data mining models in multiple ways: change of the target variable, change in the available feature information, and drift.
- Drift is a phenomenon that occurs when the distributions of features x and target variables y change in time.
- In supervised learning, drift can affect the posterior $P(y|x)$, the conditional feature $P(x|y)$, the feature $P(x)$, and the class prior $P(y)$ distribution.

Single pass

Further, the incoming stream has to be processed in a single pass. Any delay may lead to the loss of data or loss of a window of opportunity.

Real time

Finally, the algorithm has to be fast enough; it has to process the data at the same speed at which the data arrives.

Now that we have elicited the processing issues associated with stream processing, let us move on to the next section.

Introducing stream clustering

Clustering can be defined as the task of separating a set of observations/tuples into groups/clusters so that the intra-cluster records are similar and the inter-cluster records are dissimilar. There are several approaches to clustering when we are dealing with data at rest. In streaming data, data continues to arrive at a particular rate. We don't have the luxury of accessing the data randomly or making multiple passes on the data. Among the data stream clustering methods, a large number of algorithms use a two-phase scheme which consists of an online component that processes data stream points and produces summary statistics, and an offline component that uses the summary data to generate the clusters.

The online/offline two-stage processing is the most common framework adopted by many of the stream clustering algorithms.

Before we go on to explain the online/offline two-stage process, let us quickly look at `micro-clusters`.

`Micro-clusters` are created by a single pass to the data. As each data point arrives, it is assigned to the closest `micro-cluster`. You can think of a `micro-cluster` as a summary of similar data points. The summary is typically stored in the form of a cluster center, the local density of the point, and may include more statistics, such as variance. In the stream, if we are not able to allocate a new incoming data point to any of the existing `micro-clusters`, a new micro-cluster is formed with that data point.

The online step deals with `micro-cluster` formation. As the data arrives, either new `micro-clusters` are created or points are assigned to existing `micro-clusters`.

Macro-cluster

When a more robust clustering is either demanded by the user or by the application, the offline stage kicks off. Here the `micro-clusters` generated in the online steps are used as initial centers. A more rigorous clustering is performed in the background to generate the final list of clusters, called a **macro-cluster**. Since this is not time-critical, it can be executed the same way we work on data at rest.

 For more on online/offline processing, refer to *A Framework for Clustering Evolving Data Streams,* by Aggarwal CC, Han J, Wang J, Yu PS (2003)." In Proceedings of the International Conference on Very Large Data Bases (VLDB '03), pp. 81- 92.

For a more rigorous treatment of the various stream data clustering algorithm, please refer to *State-of-the-art on clustering data streams Mohammed Ghesmoune,* by Mustapha Lebbah and Hanene Azzag: `https://bdataanalytics.biomedcentral.com/track/pdf/10.1186/s41044-016-0011-3?site=bdataanalytics.biomedcentral.com`

Introducing the stream package

Package stream is based on two major components:

1. **Data stream data** is used to connect to data streams.
2. **Data stream task** is to used to perform a data mining task on the data stream.

It's an extensible framework to work on data in motion.

Let us quickly look at the major components inside this framework:

Let us look at the individual boxes in the subsequent sections.

Data stream data

Data stream data (**DSD**) is an abstraction layer which connects to any streaming data source (of course, with some small hacks, which we will see as we progress). The stream package provides several DSD implementations.

Let us look at them:

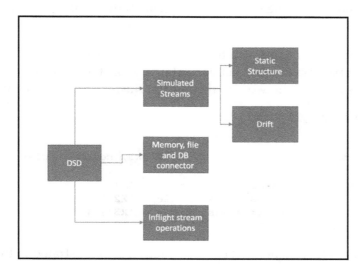

DSD as a static simulator

As a simulator DSD can simulate static streams as well as streams with drift. In cases where we are developing algorithms to work on streaming data, we can use this simulator feature effectively.

Let us see how DSD can be leveraged as a data simulator:

```
> library(stream, quietly = TRUE)
> set.seed(100)
> gaussian.stream <- DSD_Gaussians(k = 3, d = 3, noise = .01)
> gaussian.stream
Mixture of Gaussians
Class: DSD_Gaussians, DSD_R, DSD_data.frame, DSD
With 3 clusters in 3 dimensions
>
> data <- get_points(gaussian.stream, n = 100, class = TRUE)
> head(data)
          X1        X2        X3 class
1 0.3431437 0.4621701 0.4151013     2
2 0.6684551 0.4715456 0.4162625     3
3 0.2367551 0.3512569 0.7573724     1
4 0.4465450 0.5563404 0.4582585     2
5 0.3563359 0.5492573 0.4994724     2
6 0.2147759 0.3112417 0.7310448     1
```

The `DSD_Guassian` function is a data generator. We want it to generate three-dimensional data points, specified by parameter `d`. We want them in three different clusters, specified by parameter `k`.

Calling the `get_points` function with this stream and specifying the number of tuples to be generated, using parameter `n`, we get our dataframe of 100 points in a three-dimensional space. With the class parameter, we also request the cluster group the point it belongs to.

Let us plot these points:

```
library(plotly)
p <- plot_ly(data, x = ~X1, y = ~X2, z = ~X3, color = ~class) %>%
    add_markers() %>%
    layout(scene = list(xaxis = list(title = 'X1'),
                        yaxis = list(title = 'X2'),
                        zaxis = list(title = 'X3')))
p
```

A 3D plot of the data points generated by `DSD_Gaussian` is illustrated in the following figure:

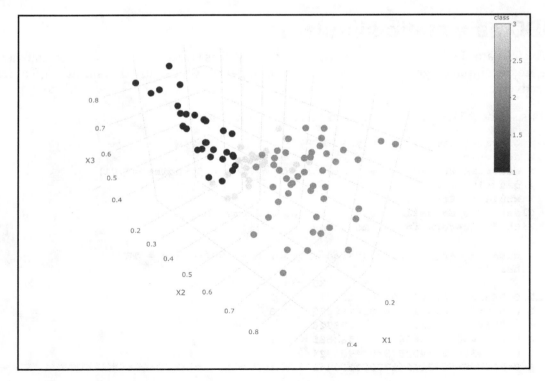

If we want to have a simulation function mimicking a live IoT system, where data is generated every *n* seconds/minutes, we can place the DSD function inside a while loop with a timer. Calling this while loop would continuously generate data every *n* seconds/minutes as per the timer configuration.

There are a lot of data generators available within the stream package. Refer to the stream documentation to learn more about other data generators: `https://cran.r-project.org/web/packages/stream/vignettes/stream.pdf`

DSD as a simulator with drift

Drift is a key component in streaming data. As we start receiving the data, there may be a change in the nature of the data, say in terms of variance or other statistical properties. Let us say initially the stream throws data points with a particular mean and a standard deviation. Over time, the mean and the standard deviation of the data is changed. This constitutes a drift.

The streaming algorithm should be able to accommodate these drifts.

 Refer to the following for more information about drifts: `https://en.wikipedia.org/wiki/Concept_drift`

DSD has some generators that can incorporate the drift:

```
> drift.stream <- DSD_MG(dim = 2)
> cluster.1 <- MGC_Linear(dim = 2)
> add_keyframe(cluster.1, time=1,  dens=50, par=5, center=c(0,0))
> add_keyframe(cluster.1, time=20, dens=50, par=5, center=c(50,50))
> add_keyframe(cluster.1, time=40,dens=50, par=5, center=c(50,100))
> add_cluster(drift.stream,cluster.1)


>
```

`DSD_MG` stands for moving generator. It's a drift generator consisting of several MGCs. In this example, we have used a linear MGC. The `add_key` function frame allows us to specify the drift happening over time. Inside the function, we define the centers of the cluster for a particular time period denoted by the parameter time. We have defined three frames where the center is changed.

Let us call the drift.stream for the first time:

```
> drift.stream
Moving Data Generator
Class: DSD_MG, DSD_R, DSD_data.frame, DSD
With 1 clusters in 2 dimensions. Time is 1
> data <- get_points(drift.stream, n = 1000)
> plot_ly(data, x = ~X1, y= ~X2) %>% add_markers() %>% layout(title =
'time around 1')
```

Look at the time, it says 1. Let us get the data at this time and plot the same.

Look at the clusters formed at time around 1:

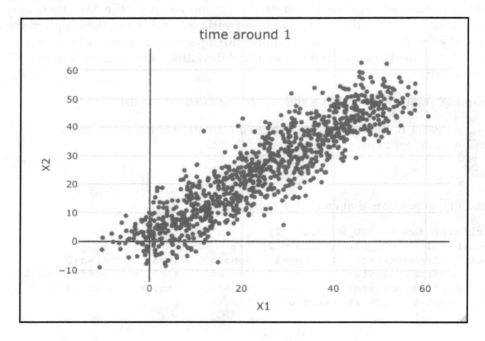

Let us now invoke drift.stream again:

```
> drift.stream
Moving Data Generator
Class: DSD_MG, DSD_R, DSD_data.frame, DSD
With 1 clusters in 2 dimensions. Time is 21.02
> data <- get_points(drift.stream, n = 1000)
> plot_ly(data, x = ~X1, y= ~X2) %>% add_markers() %>% layout(title =
'time around 20')
```

Now we see that time is around 20. Let u get another 1,000 points and plot them.

The plot of points gathered around time 20 is shown in the following figure:

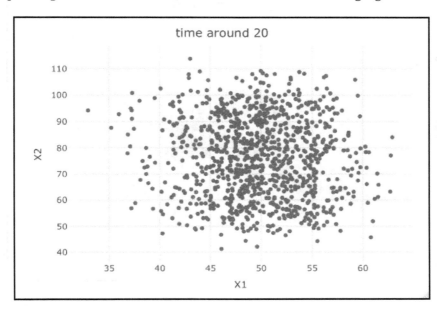

Clearly, the center has changed compared to the last time frame.

Let us invoke drift.stream again:

```
> drift.stream
Moving Data Generator
Class: DSD_MG, DSD_R, DSD_data.frame, DSD
With 1 clusters in 2 dimensions. Time is 41.02
> data <- get_points(drift.stream, n = 1000)
> plot_ly(data, x = ~X1, y= ~X2) %>%  add_markers() %>% layout(title =
'time around 40')
```

We see that time is now around 40. Let us take another 1000 data points.

Plot the data points extracted **time around 40**:

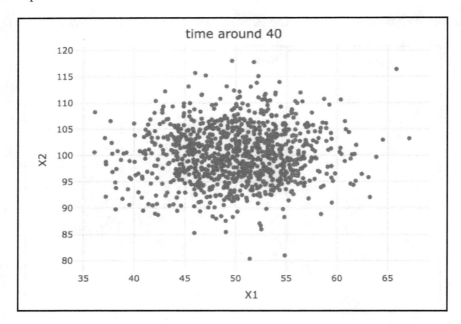

The three graphs convey the drift clearly. We can see the centers of the clusters shifting over time.

There are several other useful functions, such as writing and reading streams to disk, playing back the stream, and many others. We strongly urge you to go through the package documentation.

A curious reader may be wondering, in both examples we showed, we sampled the data at a particular time stamp. We never used the stream of data in real time. Please bear with us until we discuss our use case. We will show how the stream can be fed into clustering algorithm, so the algorithms can now work on the incoming stream of data and not on sampled data at different time stamps. Though stream package does not provide a direct mechanism to do this, we achieve this with an external time and matching the number of records sampled to the window size we need to process.

DSD connecting to memory, file, or database

DSD_Memory provides a streaming interface to a matrix or a dataframe in memory. One of the interesting ways to use DSD_Memory is to make it replay an old stream data.

Let us look at a small R example:

```
> random.stream <- DSD_Gaussians(k = 2, d = 4, mu =
rbind(c(200,77,20,750),c(196,80,16,790)))
> data.un <- get_points(random.stream, n =2000)
> head(data.un)
        X1       X2       X3       X4
1 199.9456 77.09095 19.98670 750.1129
2 195.9696 80.10380 16.01115 789.9727
3 196.0109 79.95394 16.08678 790.1042
4 199.9882 77.03385 20.00825 750.0069
5 200.0485 76.84687 19.94311 750.0130
6 200.0462 76.94537 20.00657 750.0701
>
```

We used DSD_Gaussian to create some random four-dimensional records, and have stored them in a dataframe called data.un.

Let us create a DSD_Memory object:

```
> replayer <- DSD_Memory(data.un, k = NA)
> replayer
Memory Stream Interface
Class: DSD_Memory, DSD_R, DSD_data.frame, DSD
With NA clusters in 4 dimensions
Contains 2000 data points - currently at position 1 - loop is FALSE
>
```

We have created a memory stream interface to our dataframe: data.un. Now, we can play this dataframe as we like:

```
> get_points(replayer, n=5)
        X1       X2       X3       X4
1 199.9456 77.09095 19.98670 750.1129
2 195.9696 80.10380 16.01115 789.9727
3 196.0109 79.95394 16.08678 790.1042
4 199.9882 77.03385 20.00825 750.0069
5 200.0485 76.84687 19.94311 750.0130
> replayer
Memory Stream Interface
Class: DSD_Memory, DSD_R, DSD_data.frame, DSD
With NA clusters in 4 dimensions
```

```
Contains 2000 data points - currently at position 6 - loop is FALSE
>
```

Using `get_points`, we have extracted five points. We can now see that our interface is in position 6.

Let us go ahead and rewind it:

```
> reset_stream(replayer, pos = 2)
> replayer
Memory Stream Interface
Class: DSD_Memory, DSD_R, DSD_data.frame, DSD
With NA clusters in 4 dimensions
Contains 2000 data points - currently at position 2 - loop is FALSE
```

We can see that it has now gone back to position 2.

`DSD_ReadCSV` can help to read a very large CSV file line by line, if it cannot be loaded into memory completely.

`DSD_ReadDB` can be used with an open query to a database.

Inflight operation

`DSD_ScaleStream` can be used to standardize (centering and scaling) data in a data stream in-flight.

We saw various types of DSD in this section. DSD acting as a simulator is primarily used for experimentation. It comes in handy when we need to try new data analysis algorithms. The DSD to read a CSV file or read a database can come in very handy in real-world applications.

Can we connect this DSD to an actual data stream?

There are several ways to achieve this; some of them include:

1. We can write our own DSD derived from the abstract DSD class.
2. An actual stream can be made to be written to a CSV file or a database. In this case, we can leverage `DSD_Memory` to read the stream.

Data stream task

Data stream task is responsible for the data analysis task which can be performed using streaming data. Clustering, Classification and Pattern Matching algorithm are implemented as data stream task classes. Our focus for this chapter is only clustering algorithms.

Data stream clustering is implemented as a part of the **data stream task** (**DST**) in the stream package. It is called a **DSC class**. DSC_R is a native R implementation of the clustering algorithms. DSC_MOA provides an interface to algorithms implemented in the MOA Java framework. In this chapter, we will be only looking at DSC_R, the native R algorithms.

 Refer to https://moa.cms.waikato.ac.nz/ for more information about the stream MOA algorithms in Java.

The DSC classes provide two functions to perform the online and the offline steps.

The update() function accepts a DSD and a DSC object, and creates the micro-clusters. At any point, we can query this class for the number of micro-clusters formed.

The recluster function performs the offline step. The macro-clusters are formed from the micro-clusters inside this function.

Let us look at how to code up a data stream clustering method using the stream package. Let us do the online part to begin with, where we want to form micro-clusters:

```
> stream <- DSD_Gaussians(k = 3, d = 2, noise = .05)
> stream
Mixture of Gaussians
Class: DSD_Gaussians, DSD_R, DSD_data.frame, DSD
With 3 clusters in 2 dimensions
```

We have used a Gaussian data generator, generating a two-dimensional data formed into three clusters.

Now that we have created our data generator, let us move on to our clustering algorithm:

```
> clus.alg <- DSC_DBSTREAM(r = 0.03)
> clus.alg
DBSTREAM
Class: DSC_DBSTREAM, DSC_Micro, DSC_R, DSC
Number of micro-clusters: 0
Number of macro-clusters: 0
>
```

We use the `DBStream` algorithm, a density-based stream clustering algorithm. Once we initialize this algorithm, we see 0 micro and macro- clusters.

Refer to R Help for more information about `DBStream`:

```
> help("DSC_DBSTREAM")
```

`DBStream` is a density-based stream clustering algorithm. It is based on a clustering scheme called leader based clustering.

Internally, the `DBStream` algorithm stores, for each micro-cluster, a data point that defines its center. This data point is called as the leader. It also stores the density of the cluster in an area defined by the radius threshold. This threshold is provided by the user. While initializing `DBStream`, we provided as the radius an `r` parameter.

An incoming new data point is assigned to an existing `micro-cluster` if it is within a fixed radius of its center. The assigned point increases the density estimate of the chosen cluster and the `micro-cluster` center is updated to move towards the new data point.

If the data point falls into the assignment area of several micro-clusters, then all of them are updated.

If a data point cannot be assigned to any existing micro-cluster, a new `micro-cluster` is created for the point.

Refer to the paper, *Clustering Data Streams Based on Shared Density Between Micro-Clusters*, by Michael Hahsler and Matthew Bolan˜os, for more information about `DBStream`.

With this understanding, let's call the `update` function to create `micro-clusters`:

```
> update(clus.alg, stream, n =100)
> clus.alg
DBSTREAM
Class: DSC_DBSTREAM, DSC_Micro, DSC_R, DSC
Number of micro-clusters: 5
Number of macro-clusters: 2
```

As you can see, we call the `update` function every time with both our DSD object `stream` and DSC object `clus.alg`. During each call, we pull around 100 records, `n =100`

Let us call `update` a couple of more times:

```
> update(clus.alg, stream, n =100)
> clus.alg
DBSTREAM
Class: DSC_DBSTREAM, DSC_Micro, DSC_R, DSC
```

```
Number of micro-clusters: 5
Number of macro-clusters: 2
> update(clus.alg, stream, n =100)
> clus.alg
DBSTREAM
Class: DSC_DBSTREAM, DSC_Micro, DSC_R, DSC
Number of micro-clusters: 26
Number of macro-clusters: 9
>
```

The update function creates the micro-clusters. We can see the number of micro-clusters from the shell output.

Finally, we plot our data points and the micro-clusters using plot(clus.alg, stream)

We can see the data points and the micro-clusters in the following graph:

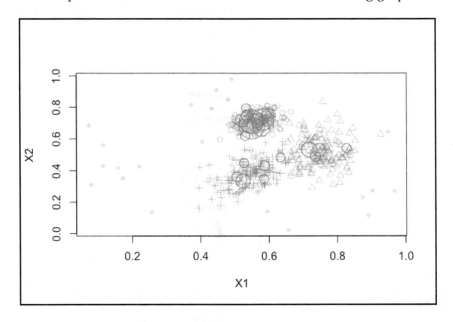

 The DSC_DBSTREAM has inbuilt reclustering, hence you can see the macro-clusters in the output. There is no need to run a separate offline process.

Now that we have our clusters, both micro and macro, we need a good way to evaluate the quality of these clusters. A good clustering algorithm should produce the output in such a way that the inter-cluster distance is large and the intra-cluster distance is small. The `stream` package provides a function called `evaluate` to find the quality of the clustering algorithm's output:

```
> evaluate(clus.alg, stream)
Evaluation results for micro-clusters.
Points were assigned to micro-clusters.

        numMicroClusters       numMacroClusters            numClasses
noisePredicted
             19.00000000             9.00000000            4.00000000
59.00000000
             noiseActual         noisePrecision                   SSQ
silhouette
              4.00000000             0.06779661            0.37199376
-0.24233735
               precision                 recall                    F1
purity
              0.36732394             0.43524700            0.39841124
0.96610169
               Euclidean              Manhattan                  Rand
cRand
              0.22540333             0.40000000            0.60222222
0.10446136
                     NMI                     KP                 angle
diag
              0.37345360             0.12308440            0.40000000
0.40000000
                      FM                Jaccard                    PS
average.between
              0.39984577             0.24876002            0.12500000
0.25608681
          average.within           max.diameter         min.separation
ave.within.cluster.ss
              0.26016421             0.69081358            0.01146022
0.02673695
                      g2           pearsongamma                  dunn
dunn2
             -0.01003498            -0.01443557            0.01658946
0.11266664
                 entropy               wb.ratio                    vi
              1.68978117             1.01592196            1.74616537
>
```

It gives a lot of different evaluation metrics. We can choose one among them based on our criteria.

 For more information about cluster evaluation, refer to Aggarwal C (ed.) (2007). *Data Streams-Models and Algorithms*, {Springer-Verlag}.

Further, we can explore some of the properties of the cluster.

Let us look at the centers:

```
> get_centers(clus.alg)
            X1          X2
1    0.24035102  0.4769484
2    0.61903877  0.7785408
3    0.09048444  0.6077917
4    0.45838678  0.4750770
5    0.65574421  0.7321404
6    0.42560108  0.4119006
7    0.66837103  0.8586109
8    0.27094119  0.4815417
9    0.20066268  0.5062597
10   0.71940633  0.8555310
11   0.69742484  0.7534610
12   0.54654100  0.7193082
13   0.33136166  0.4365419
14   0.67962076  0.8084548
15   0.50300757  0.4063990
16   0.31194759  0.4616342
17   0.51461571  0.3636863
18   0.40740645  0.4830899
19   0.24665434  0.5142459
20   0.38753463  0.3952418
21   0.62428589  0.7322719
22   0.56448909  0.6729860
23   0.60190595  0.6677850
24   0.43539255  0.4932142
25   0.37732500  0.5350057
26   0.54251405  0.3728828
>
```

We can see here the centers of 26 `micro-clusters`.

Let us look at the weights:

```
> get_weights(clus.alg)
 [1] 9.501785 4.621436 3.635122 4.680784 7.485784 4.578379 5.600460
7.496766 7.532477 3.828183 3.703409
[12] 3.700424 8.310565 4.692228 7.538048 7.520924 4.729492 6.511032
3.795303 8.584987 4.732915 4.741074
[23] 3.775582 4.749276 3.868962 3.947070
```

The preceding code gives the weights of different clusters.

There are many more clustering algorithms implemented in the stream. Refer to the documentation for other algorithms.

 The chapter, *Experimental Comparision of different algorithms*, in *Introduction to Stream: An Extensible Framework for Data Stream Clustering Research with R*, by Michael Hahsler is a good place to understand different algorithms.

Hopefully, by now we are equipped with enough information to solve our use case using `stream` package.

Use case and data

We have four artificial sensors installed in the field and our digital control system collects the information from these sensors. We need to put a real-time analysis system in place. We need a feature in that system to cluster the incoming data and display those clusters in real time in a digital dashboard. The idea is users watching those dashboards will be alerted immediately for some anomaly or malfunction if they see unusual cluster patterns.

This example is inspired by the sensor network example given in pubnub at: `https://www.pubnub.com/developers/realtime-data-streams/sensor-network/`.

The following diagram should sufficiently visualize our use case:

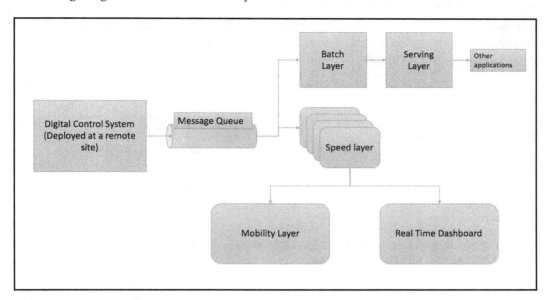

What we have here is a lambda architecture (http://lambda-architecture.net/).

Our digital control system is generating data at a particular rate. It has the following sensors installed:

- Radiation sensor (millrads/hour)--the range of data is between 195 and 202
- Humidity (%)--the range of data is between 74 and 82
- Temperature (c)--the range of data is between 15 and 28
- Lightlevel (w/m2)--the range of data is between 700 and 800

These data from the sensors are pumped to a message queue. We have two systems consuming the data from our message queue.

Speed layer

This is where the real-time analysis of the incoming data is performed. Our R code will be running here. If this layer was realized by say apache storm and bolt (http://storm.apache.org/), the bolts would be running our cluster creation code.

The speed layer talks to the real-time dashboard and the mobility layer. The micro-clusters discovered as pushed to the dashboard and to the mobility layer.

Batch layer

We are not concerned about the batch layer for this exercise. The batch layer is responsible for keeping the master data intact. Since it has a very low latency, we have the speed layer to process the continuous stream of data.

Now that we have a good idea of the overall architecture of our system, let us proceed to develop the stream clustering algorithm. For the cluster algorithm development purpose, we are going to leverage the DSD simulators in the `stream` package to act as our sensors in the digital control system.

DSD data generation:

```
> sensor.stream <- DSD_Gaussians(k = 2, d = 4, mu =
rbind(c(200,77,20,750),c(196,80,16,790)))
> sensor.stream
Mixture of Gaussians
Class: DSD_Gaussians, DSD_R, DSD_data.frame, DSD
With 2 clusters in 4 dimensions
>
```

As you can see, we want `DSD_Gaussian` to generate a four-dimensional dataset, one for each sensor. We expect two clusters to be formed out of this dataset. The centers for the clusters are provided as a matrix to the `mu` parameter.

Let us look at the data which is generated and plot it:

```
> par(mfrow = c(2,2))
> data.un <- get_points(sensor.stream, n =100)
> head(data.un)
          X1       X2       X3        X4
1 200.1312 77.03498 19.99829 750.0906
2 200.0020 76.98179 19.96151 750.0078
3 200.0311 77.02906 19.92746 750.0481
4 199.9046 77.04594 20.00315 749.8901
5 196.0912 79.90257 15.95177 790.0594
6 196.0099 80.05955 15.98539 790.0288
> plot(density(data.un$X1), main = "Raw")
> plot(density(data.un$X2), main = "Raw")
> plot(density(data.un$X3), main = "Raw")
> plot(density(data.un$X4), main = "Raw")
```

The cluster centers are clearly visible in the following graphs:

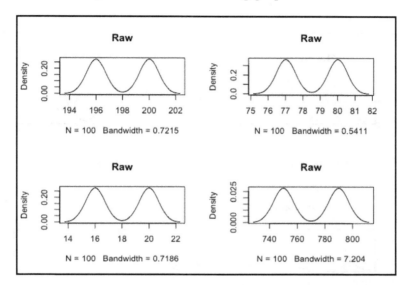

It's a good practice to scale the incoming data before we proceed to do any analysis. Luckily we have DSD_ScaleStream to apply scaling on the incoming stream data.

Let us see how to create and test our scaling procedure:

```
> stream.norm    <- DSD_ScaleStream(sensor.stream)
> stream.norm
Mixture of Gaussians (scaled)
Class: DSD_ScaleStream, DSD_R, DSD_data.frame, DSD
With 2 clusters in 4 dimensions
> data <- get_points(stream.norm, n = 100)
> head(data)
          X1          X2          X3          X4
1 -1.0369551   1.0456349  -1.0567690   1.0037279
2  0.9667943  -0.9731955   0.9932870  -0.9876052
3  0.9852470  -0.9199492   1.0301836  -0.9983958
4  0.9206461  -0.9828932   0.9730271  -0.9898524
5 -1.0389785   1.0077318  -1.0219917   1.0049668
6 -0.9604014   0.9818454  -1.0055215   1.0098879
> plot(density(data$X1), main = "Normalized")
> plot(density(data$X2), main = "Normalized")
> plot(density(data$X3), main = "Normalized")
> plot(density(data$X4), main = "Normalized")
> par(mfrow = c(1,1))
```

The `DSD_ScaleStream` class is used to scale the incoming data from our `Gaussian` stream. Let us plot this data:

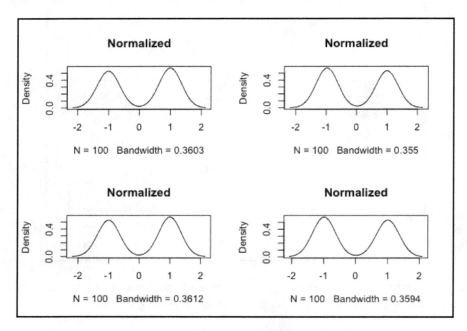

We have normalized our data and are ready to apply the clustering.

We are going to follow the online/offline approach.

Inside the `stream` package, we have a class, `DSC_TwoStage`, which will help us pipeline our online and offline algorithms. Let us see how we can use this class:

```
> micro.alg <- DSC_Sample(k = 10)
> macro.alg <- DSC_Kmeans(k = 2)
```

We begin with defining the online clustering algorithm for creating `micro-clusters`. We use the `DSC_Sample` class. It's one of the simplest online clustering algorithms. It extracts samples from a data stream using reservoir sampling. The extracted sample is stored as a set of `micro-clusters`. Before we proceed further, let us quickly look at the reservoir sampling.

Reservoir sampling

Given *n* items, where *n* is very large or not known in advance, the reservoir sampling algorithm helps us select *k* samples from *n* items. The algorithm to begin with initializes an array of size *k*. It then copies the first k items from the stream into the array. Now, it proceeds to evaluate each item in the array. A random number, *j*, between 0 and *i*, is generated, where *i* is the index of the item we are currently evaluating. If, *j* is in range of *0* to *k-1*, we replace the *j* element in the array with *i* th element in the stream.

 For more information about reservoir sampling, refer to: `https://en.wikipedia.org/wiki/Reservoir_sampling`

The parameter k, to `DSC_Sample`, is used to set the k value for the reservoir sampling, and eventually sets the number of micro-clusters we expect from the algorithm. In our case, we have set *k* to 10. Further down the code, we see that 10 `micro-clusters` are generated.

Next, we define the clustering algorithm for the offline step. In this case, we use a simple k-means algorithm:

"k-means clustering aims to partition n observations into k clusters in which each observation belongs to the cluster with the nearest mean, serving as a prototype of the cluster."- Wikipedia

We will not indulge in the details of the k-means algorithm here. More information about R k means can be found at `https://stat.ethz.ch/R-manual/R-devel/library/stats/html/kmeans.html`

Let us pipe these two algorithms together:

```
> pipe <- DSC_TwoStage(micro = micro.alg, macro = macro.alg)
> update(pipe, stream.norm, n = 1000)
> pipe
Reservoir sampling + k-Means (weighted)
Class: DSC_TwoStage, DSC_Macro, DSC
Number of micro-clusters: 10
Number of macro-clusters: 2
>

> evaluate(pipe, stream.norm,measure = c("numMicroClusters", "purity"),type
= "micro",n = 500)
Evaluation results for micro-clusters.
Points were assigned to micro-clusters.
```

```
numMicroClusters purity
   10 1
```

Using `DSC_TwoStage`, we pipe our online and offline algorithms together. By calling the `update` function, we are invoking our offline and online algorithm. We run our algorithm on our normalized data stream, `stream.norm`.

We see that we have two `macro-clusters` and 10 `micro-clusters`. Our clustering algorithm has done a good job in clustering the incoming data, since we knew that the stream had two clusters in it. Finally, we run the evaluation step. Purity is going to be our most critical evaluation measure.

Purity is one of the simplest measures to assess the quality of clusters. Purity is derived by summing up the number of majority elements in each cluster and dividing it by the total number of clusters. Look at the following example:

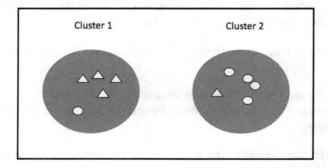

In cluster 1, the triangle is the majority class and the count is 4. In cluster 2, the circle is the majority class and the count is again 4. The purity is then *(4 + 4)/10*, so 0.8 is the purity of this cluster.

In our data case, we have achieved a purity of 1. Our clusters are therefore a very good fit to the incoming streaming data.

To summarize, what we did:

1. We used the DSD simulator to act as our data provider
2. We decided on our `micro-cluster` and macro cluster algorithms
3. We leveraged the `DSC_TwoStage` class to combine them and produce the cluster output
4. As shown in the previous sections, we can use the `get_centeres` to get the centroids

Now, we need to move this set up to our streaming infrastructure. It is beyond the scope of this book to show how to setup the streaming infrastructure shown above. However, we will give some pointers here to deploy our stream clustering algorithm:

1. We need to run R and install the necessary packages including `stream` package into our speed layer.
2. Assuming that the speed layer is some kind of set up similar to Apache storm and bolts, we can have the following setup:
   1. A storm bolt combination, reads the data from the message queue and populates a in-memory database. This can be a small `sqldb` in memory or other key value databases.
   2. Another storm bolt combination acts as follows:
      1. Use `DSD_ReadDB` to connect to the database using R DBI and extract the data.
      2. Micro/Macro Cluster twin, set up using `DSC_TwoStage` can now query the `DSD_ReadDB` at fixed intervals as defined by the overall application. When using function `update`, the window size can be passed as parameter n. The results of the clustering can now be pushed to the dashboard (or pull mechanism, from the dashboard can be setup). Function `get_points` and `get_centers` can provide the cluster details.

Hopefully, this gave an overview of how stream package can be used in a real-time data processing framework.

Complete R code

```
install.packages("stream")

library(stream, quietly = TRUE)
set.seed(100)
gaussian.stream <- DSD_Gaussians(k = 3, d = 3, noise = .01)
gaussian.stream

data <- get_points(gaussian.stream, n = 100, class = TRUE)
head(data)

library(plotly)
p <- plot_ly(data, x = ~X1, y = ~X2, z = ~X3, color = ~class) %>%
  add_markers() %>%
```

```
    layout(scene = list(xaxis = list(title = 'X1'),
                         yaxis = list(title = 'X2'),
                         zaxis = list(title = 'X3'))))
p


# Drift generators
drift.stream <- DSD_MG(dim = 2)
cluster.1 <- MGC_Linear(dim = 2)

add_keyframe(cluster.1, time=1,  dens=50, par=5, center=c(0,0))
add_keyframe(cluster.1, time=20, dens=50, par=5, center=c(50,50))
add_keyframe(cluster.1, time=40,dens=50, par=5, center=c(50,100))
add_cluster(drift.stream,cluster.1)

drift.stream
data <- get_points(drift.stream, n = 1000)
plot_ly(data, x = ~X1, y= ~X2) %>%  add_markers() %>% layout(title = 'time
around 1')

drift.stream
data <- get_points(drift.stream, n = 1000)
plot_ly(data, x = ~X1, y= ~X2) %>%  add_markers() %>% layout(title = 'time
around 20')

drift.stream
data <- get_points(drift.stream, n = 1000)
plot_ly(data, x = ~X1, y= ~X2) %>%  add_markers() %>% layout(title = 'time
around 40')


# Sample Data Stream Clustering

stream <- DSD_Gaussians(k = 3, d = 2, noise = .05)
stream
clus.alg <- DSC_DBSTREAM(r = 0.03)
clus.alg
update(clus.alg, stream, n =100)
clus.alg
update(clus.alg, stream, n =100)
clus.alg
head(get_centers(clus.alg))

# plot the data
plot(clus.alg, stream)

evaluate(clus.alg, stream)
```

```
# Simulate the data from a sensor network
sensor.stream <- DSD_Gaussians(k = 2, d = 4, mu =
rbind(c(200,77,20,750),c(196,80,16,790)))
sensor.stream

par(mfrow = c(2,2))
data.un <- get_points(sensor.stream, n =100)
head(data.un)

plot(density(data.un$X1), main = "Raw")
plot(density(data.un$X2), main = "Raw")
plot(density(data.un$X3), main = "Raw")
plot(density(data.un$X4), main = "Raw")


stream.norm   <- DSD_ScaleStream(sensor.stream)
stream.norm

data <- get_points(stream.norm, n = 100)
head(data)
plot(density(data$X1), main = "Normalized")
plot(density(data$X2), main = "Normalized")
plot(density(data$X3), main = "Normalized")
plot(density(data$X4), main = "Normalized")

par(mfrow = c(1,1))

# Perform Clustering
micro.alg <- DSC_Sample(k = 10)
macro.alg <- DSC_Kmeans(k = 2)
pipe <- DSC_TwoStage(micro = micro.alg, macro = macro.alg)

update(pipe, stream.norm, n = 1000)
pipe

evaluate(pipe, stream.norm,measure = c("numMicroClusters", "purity"),type =
"micro",n = 500)
```

Summary

The chapter started with an overview of data at motion and data at rest, also called as the streaming data. We further dwelled into the properties of streaming data and the challenges it poses while processing it. We introduced the stream clustering algorithm. The famous offline/online approach to stream clustering was discussed. Later on, we introduced various classes in `stream` package and how to use them. During that process, we discussed ideas about several data generators, DBSTREAM algorithms to find micro and macro clusters and several metrics to assess the quality of clusters. We then introduced our use case. We went ahead to design a clustering algorithm, with the online part based on reservoir sampling and the offline part was handled by k-means algorithm. Finally, we described the steps needed to take this whole setup in a real streaming environment.

In the next chapter, we will explore graph mining algorithms. We will show you how to use the package `igraph` to create and manipulate graphs. We will discuss Product Network Analysis and show how graph algorithms can assist in generating micro categories.

8
Analyze and Understand Networks Using R

Network analysis is the study of graphs. Graphs are defined by a set of nodes or vertices connected by edges. Both the nodes and vertices can have attributes describing them. Most importantly, the edges can carry weight, indicating the importance of the connection. When the directions of the edges are preserved, the graph is called a **directed graph**; when not preserved, it's called an **undirected graph**. Network analysis, or network theory, or graph theory provides a rich set of algorithms to analyze and understand graphs. The famous Koenigsberg problem (http://mathworld.wolfram.com/KoenigsbergBridgeProblem.html) introduced by Euler is one of the first graph theory problems to be studied. Koenigsberg is an old city in Prussia (modern day Russia). The river Pregal separates the city. There are two other islands. There are seven bridges connecting the islands and the cities. The Koenigsberg problem was to devise a walk through the city that would cross each of those bridges once and only once.

One graph structure that we all know today and is easy to relate to is the social network structure formed by various social media applications such as Facebook and LinkedIn. In these networks, people form the vertices and, when two of them are connected to each other, an edge is drawn between those vertices. The whole internet is a graph of connected machines. Other examples from biology include protein-protein interaction networks, genetic interaction networks, and so on.

When we represent a problem as a graph, it may give us a different point of view to solve that problem. Sometimes it can make the problem simpler to solve. One such problem that we are going to see in this chapter is assigning categories to items. More importantly, we will understand the micro-categorization of items in a retail setting. Though our example is from a retail setting, this technique is not limited to the retail domain. We will show how we can leverage graphs to assign categories to items. This technique is called the **Product Network Analysis**.

This chapter is loosely based on the following two papers: *Product Network Analysis – The Next Big Thing in Retail Data Mining*--a white paper by Forte Consultancy and *Extending Market Basket Analysis with Graph Mining Techniques: A Real Case,* by Ivan F. Videla-Cavieres , Sebastián A. Ríos, University of Chile, Department of Industrial Engineering, Business Intelligence Research Center (CEINE), Santiago, Chile.

Category management is very important for retailers. Having products grouped into the right category is the first step for retailers to manage their products. Downstream applications such as up-selling, cross-selling, and loyalty systems can benefit tremendously with the right category assignment. In the absence of a sophisticated product network analysis system, product categorization is done manually and is heavily dependent on the product features entered either by the suppliers or the procurement teams. This categorization may not be accurate and will be heavily biased by human judgment. It's impossible to expect concordance between two people in a task such as this one.

In this chapter, we will cover the following topics:

- Introducing the `igraph` package to create and manipulate graphs in R
- Going over our use case and data
- Preparing our data for consumption by the `igraph` package
- Applying graph clustering algorithms to identify product categories
- Building a `RShiny` application.

The code for this chapter was written in **RStudio Version 0.99.491**. It uses **R version 3.3.1**. As we work through our example, we will introduce the R packages, `igraph`, and `arules` that we will be using. During our code description, we will be using some of the output printed in the console. We have included what will be printed in the console immediately following the statement that prints the information to the console, so as not to disturb the flow of the code.

Graphs in R

We will use the R package, igraph, for our graph analysis needs. We will leverage the arules package to manipulate our data. If you don't have them installed, proceed to install them as follows:

```
>   install.packages("arules")
>   install.packages("igraph")
```

You can use the sessionInfo function from the utils package to look at the packages available for you in the current session.

Let's get started; create a simple graph, and plot it:

```
> library(igraph, quietly = TRUE)
> simple.graph <- graph_from_literal(A-B, B-C, C-D, E-F, A-E, E-C)
> plot.igraph(simple.graph)
```

This produces the following graph plot:

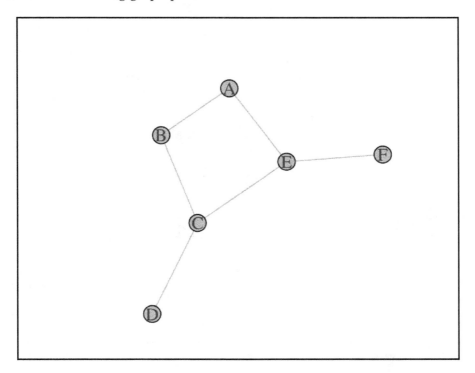

After including the igraph library, we used the graph_from_literal function to create a simple undirected graph with six nodes. The igraph package provides the plot.igraph function to visualize the graphs. There are several ways in which we can create a graph. For a complete list of the different methods available to create graphs, refer to http://igraph.org/r/#docs.

Alternatively, you can type the following to invoke the R help:

```
> help("igraph")
```

Let us see how to create a directed graph:

```
directed.graph <- graph_from_literal(A-+B, B-+C, C+-D, E-+F, A+-E, E-+C)
plot.igraph(directed.graph)
```

By adding the + sign while defining the edges, we define the direction of the graph.

The following plot shows the directed graph that we created:

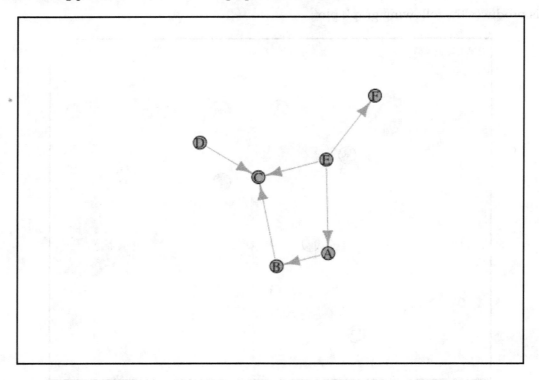

You can see the arrows now showing the direction of the edges.

Let's look at the following code snippet to show the vertices and edges of the graph:

```
> E(simple.graph) # Edges

+ 6/6 edges from 7432b4a (vertex names):
[1] A--B A--E B--C C--D C--E E--F
> V(simple.graph) # Vertices
+ 6/6 vertices, named, from 7432b4a:
[1] A B C D E F
> E(directed.graph) # Edges
+ 6/6 edges from 1bcc1e2 (vertex names):
[1] A->B B->C D->C E->A E->C E->F
> V(directed.graph) # Vertices
+ 6/6 vertices, named, from 1bcc1e2:
[1] A B C D E F
>
```

The `E()` and `V()` functions give the edges and vertices of our graph.

Let us change the properties of the graph:

```
> V(simple.graph)$name <- c('alice', 'bob','charlie','david',
'eli','francis')
> simple.graph <- set_vertex_attr(simple.graph ,"age", value = c('11',
'11','15','9', '8','11'))
> plot.igraph(simple.graph)
```

By calling the `name` property on all the vertices, we change the names of our vertices. Alternatively, we can also use the `set_vertex_attr` function to add/modify an attribute; in this example, we added a new attribute called **age**.

The following is the output from our graph plot:

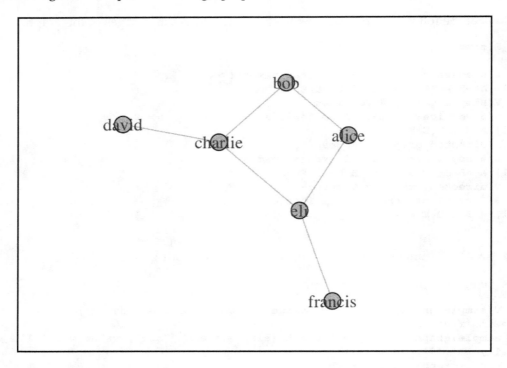

Further, based on the age property, we change the color of the vertex:

```
>V(simple.graph)$color <- ifelse(V(simple.graph)$age == '11',
"blue","green")
>plot.igraph(simple.graph)
```

Using the color slot, we have changed the color of the vertex based on the age property.

The graph now shows the vertex with different colors:

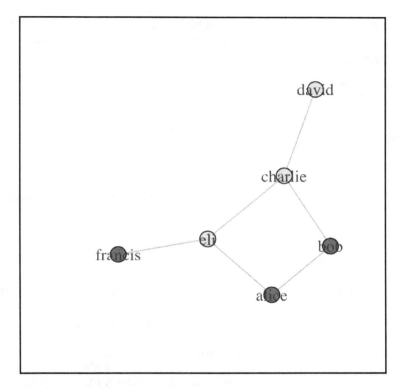

The preceding plot vertices are green where the age attribute is 11, otherwise they are blue.

Structural properties such as degree and strength help us understand the underlying structure of the graph. Many graph-based algorithms use these properties.

Degree of a vertex

The number of edges adjacent, that is, either entering or exiting a vertex, is the degree of a vertex. The degree function gives the degree of all the vertices in our graph.

We further use the E() function to refer to our graph's edges and add weights to the edges.

Strength of a vertex

The strength of a vertex is the sum of the weights of the edges adjacent on that node. The `strength` function gives us the strength of vertices in our graph. Let's look at a small code snippet to find the degree and strength of a graph:

```
> degree(simple.graph)
   alice     bob charlie   david     eli
       1       1       3       1       2
> E(simple.graph)$weight <- c(10,20,35,15,25,35)
> strength(simple.graph)
   alice     bob charlie   david     eli
      10      20      70      35      25
```

The functions `degree` and `strength` in `igraph` package can be invoked to get degree and strength.

Adjacency Matrix

Any graph can be represented as a matrix, called the **adjacency matrix**, where the rows and columns are the vertices of the graph. The presence of a value in a particular cell indicates an edge between the vertices. The cells can be populated with the edge weights too.

The `get.adjacency` function returns the incident or the adjacency matrix of our graph.

Let's look at a small code snippet to find the adjacency matrix for a graph:

```
> get.adjacency(simple.graph)
5 x 5 sparse Matrix of class "dgCMatrix"
        alice bob charlie david eli
alice     .   .     .       .    1
bob       .   .     1       .    .
charlie   .   1     .       1    1
david     .   .     1       .    .
eli       1   .     1       .    .
>
```

Function `get.adjacency` extracts the adjacency matrix from a given graph.

Finally, the following code snippet shows operations to delete nodes/edges:

```
simple.graph <- delete.edges(simple.graph, "alice|bob" )
simple.graph <- delete.vertices(simple.graph, 'francis')
```

With this we have covered some basic operations with a network.

More networks in R

In this section, let us see some more structural properties of a graph. Till now we created some simple graphs. It will be better to have some larger graphs to study the structural properties.

The R code for a lot of different networks built from a diverse source of input is available at `https://github.com/igraph/igraph/tree/master/nexus/download`.

Let's use the US airport network from the repository to show some structural properties of a graph:

```
url <-
"http://sites.google.com/site/cxnets/US_largest500_airportnetwork.txt"
tmp <- tempdir()
dest <- paste(sep="", tmp, "/", "usairport.txt")
download.file(url, dest)

usairport <- read_graph(dest, format="ncol")
```

We first download the file from an internet URL and use `read_graph` function to successfully create a graph. Let us now start looking at some structural properties.

Centrality of a vertex

The centrality of a vertex in a graph defines the *importance of that vertex* in the graph. Centrality can be calculated in a multitude of ways. Degree centrality is calculated based on the in-degree--the number of incoming edges--and the out-degree--the number of outgoing edges of the graph.

Let's look at the code to find the degree centrality:

```
> degrees <- degree(usairport, loops = FALSE)
> head(sort(degrees, decreasing = TRUE),10)
  0   1   2   6   5  17   7  20  10   9
145 136 132 130 122 114 114 110 109  98
```

In the preceding case, we use the `degree` function to find the degree centrality score. We have sorted it in descending order. Airport 0 has the highest centrality score. In this case, we have used both the in-degree and the out-degree. According to this analysis, airport 0 must be some important node in this network.

Nodes with a large out-degree are considered central, as they act as a source for a lot of nodes. A node with a large in-degree is considered prestigious.

Farness and Closeness of a node

The farness of a node is defined as the total distance of this node from all the other nodes.

Closeness is the inverse of farness. Another way of looking at it is that closeness is how long will it take to pass a message from a node to all other nodes.

The following snippet shows the closeness calculation using the `igraph` package:

```
> head(sort(closeness(usairport), decreasing = TRUE),10)
          253          124          287          243           22
6           406           35
7.974528e-08 7.948313e-08 7.921478e-08 7.921051e-08 7.918423e-08
7.917715e-08 7.912412e-08 7.897597e-08
          158           34
7.889165e-08 7.886183e-08
```

We have nested multiple functions, let us untangle them. First, we use the function `closeness` to get the closeness property for each vertex. We pass that output to `sort` function, and sort the results by decreasing order of closeness. Finally, we use the `head` function to pick the top 10 results from the sort output.

Having explored some of the properties of the graph, let us see an overview of some of the graph algorithms available in the `igraph` package.

Finding the shortest path between nodes

The shortest distance between two pairs of nodes is the path with the least amount of nodes in it. Let us see the shortest path between two nodes in our simple graph:

```
> shortest.paths(simple.graph, "alice")
      alice bob charlie david eli francis
alice     0   1       2     3   1       2
>
```

The `shortest.paths` method gives the shortest paths between our node `alice` and all the other nodes. The node `david` is far way from `alice`.

Random walk on a graph

Starting with a vertex, the algorithm takes the specified number of steps by selecting another vertex at random. Let us see a random walk:

```
> random_walk(simple.graph, start = "alice", steps = 3)

+ 3/6 vertices, named, from 7432b4a:
[1] alice eli   alice
```

We see that the algorithm moved to `eli` and came back to `alice`.

We hope this gives you an overview of how to use the `igraph` package. Let's now move to our use case and see how we can leverage the `igraph` package to solve our problem.

Use case and data

Category management is analyzing a discrete set of similar or related items sold by a retailer, grouped together, as a strategic business unit. This allows the retailer to then evaluate these units by their turnover and profitability. Brain F. Harris is the inventor of the study of category management. His eight-step process, famously called the **Brain Harris model**, is used widely today. For more information about category management, refer to http://www.nielsen.com/tw/en/insights/reports/2014/category-management-the-win-win-platform-for-manufacturers-and-retailers.html.

The Nielsen definition of a category is based on product features. Products that exhibit the following features are put under the same category:

- They should meet similar end-consumer needs
- Products should be interrelated, for example, substitutable
- We should be able to place the products together on a retailer shelf

When analyzing purchasing behavior, several patterns emerge; some products are sold together at the same time, some products are sold in a time sequential pattern, the sale of one product affects the sale of another and several others. These types of product interactions and patterns can either occur in the same category or across different categories. This leads to formation of micro-categories. Unfortunately, there are no simple ways to identify these micro-categories. Based on the products, market conditions, price points, consumer preference, and many other factors, several such micro-categories may emerge as more retail transactions aggregate.

A certain retailer has approached us with the problem of micro-categorization. Historically, using the product properties, the categories were created by the procurement team. Over a period of time, this manual process has introduced several inconsistencies in creating/assigning products to categories. Further, he believes that there exists several micro-categories for his products, which can be unearthed only by analyzing the transaction data. Evaluating profitability and turnover using the existing categories is of less use to him. All his supplementary systems including the loyalty system and the online selling platform can be made more effective with these new micro-categories. He has provided us with his historical transaction data. The data includes his past transactions, where each transaction is uniquely identified by an integer called `order_id` and the list of products present in the transaction called `product_id`.

This data and source can be downloaded from the Packt website.

```
> data <- read.csv('data.csv')
> head(data)
  order_id                         product_id
1   837080         Unsweetened Almondmilk
2   837080                   Fat Free Milk
3   837080                          Turkey
4   837080        Caramel Corn Rice Cakes
5   837080               Guacamole Singles
6   837080 HUMMUS 10OZ  WHITE BEAN EAT WELL
```

The given data is in a tabular format. Every row is a tuple of `order_id`, representing the transaction and `product_id`, the item included in that transaction. We need to transform this data so that we have all the pairs of products and the number of transactions in which they have occurred together. We will leverage the `arules` package to achieve this. This package provides the necessary infrastructure to store, manipulate, and analyze the retail transaction data. We have already covered the `arules` package in Chapter 1, *Association Rule Mining*. For more information about `arules` package, refer to https://cran.r-project.org/web/packages/arules/index.html.

Transaction data used in this chapter is from Instacart's public point of sale data
at https://tech.instacart.com/3-million-instacart-orders-open-sourced-d40d29eadj6f2.

Data preparation

Our data preparation task involves taking the transactions data and converting it to a form where we have product pairs and their transaction frequency. Transaction frequency is the number of transactions in which both the products have appeared. We will use these product pairs to build our graph. The vertices of our graph are the products. For every product pair, an edge is drawn in the graph between the corresponding product vertices. The weight of the edge is the transaction frequency.

We will use the `arules` package version 1.5-0 to help us perform this data preparation task:

```
> library(arules)
> transactions.obj <- read.transactions(file = 'data.csv', format =
"single",
+                                       sep = ",",
+                                       cols = c("order_id", "product_id"),
+                                       rm.duplicates = FALSE,
+                                       quote = "", skip = 0,
+                                       encoding = "unknown")
Warning message:
In asMethod(object) : removing duplicated items in transactions
> transactions.obj
transactions in sparse format with
 6988 transactions (rows) and
 16793 items (columns)
```

We begin with reading our transactions stored in the text file and create an `arules` data structure called **transactions**. Let's look at the parameters of `read.transactions`, the function used to create the transactions object. The first parameter, `file`, we pass to our text file where we have the transactions from the retailer. The second parameter, `format`, can take any of two values, single or basket, depending on how the input data is organized. In our case, we have a tabular format with two columns--one column representing the unique identifier for our transaction and the other column for a unique identifier representing the products present in our transaction. This format is named as single by `arules`. Refer to the `arules` documentation for a detailed description of all the parameters. On inspecting the newly created transactions object `transaction.obj`, we see that there are 6,988 transactions and 16,793 products.

Now that we have loaded the transaction data, let's proceed to find the product pairs:

```
> support      <- 0.015
>
> # Frequent item sets
> parameters = list(
+   support = support,
+   minlen  = 2,  # Minimal number of items per item set
+   maxlen  = 2, # Maximal number of items per item set
+   target  = "frequent itemsets"
+ )
>
> freq.items <- apriori(transactions.obj, parameter = parameters)
Apriori

Parameter specification:
 confidence minval smax arem  aval originalSupport maxtime support minlen
maxlen               target    ext
         NA    0.1    1 none FALSE            TRUE       5   0.015      2
2 frequent itemsets FALSE

Algorithmic control:
 filter tree heap memopt load sort verbose
    0.1 TRUE TRUE  FALSE TRUE    2    TRUE

Absolute minimum support count: 104

set item appearances ...[0 item(s)] done [0.00s].
set transactions ...[16793 item(s), 6988 transaction(s)] done [0.02s].
sorting and recoding items ... [109 item(s)] done [0.00s].
creating transaction tree ... done [0.00s].
checking subsets of size 1 2 done [0.00s].
writing ... [25 set(s)] done [0.00s].
creating S4 object  ... done [0.00s].
Warning message:
In apriori(transactions.obj, parameter = parameters) :
  Mining stopped (maxlen reached). Only patterns up to a length of 2
returned!
>
```

"Apriori is an algorithm for frequent itemset mining and association over transaction databases. It proceeds by identifying the frequent individual items in the database and extending them to larger and larger item sets as long as those itemsets appear sufficiently often in the database." -- Wikipedia

Generating frequent itemsets is the first phase of the apriori algorithm. We conveniently leverage this phase of the algorithm to generate our product pairs and the number of transactions in which they are present.

 To understand more about apriori, refer to `Chapter 1`, *Association Rule Mining*, of this book.

Let us do a quick recap from `Chapter 1`, *Association Rule Mining*.

The `apriori` algorithm works in two phases. Finding the frequent item sets is the first phase of the association rule mining algorithm. A group of product IDs is called an **item set**. The algorithm makes multiple passes to the database; in the first pass, it finds out the transaction frequency of all the individual items. These are item sets of `order 1`. Let's introduce the first interest measure `Support` here:

- `Support`: As said before, support is a parameter that we pass to this algorithm--a value between 0 and 1. Let's say we set the value to 0.1. We now say an item set is considered frequent and it should be used in the subsequent phases if and only if it appears in at least 10% of the transactions.

Now in the first pass, the algorithm calculates the transaction frequency for each product. At this stage, we have order 1 item sets. We will discard all those item sets that fall below our support threshold. The assumption here is that items with high transaction frequency are more interesting than the ones with very low frequency. Items with very low support are not going to make interesting rules further down in the pipeline. Using the most frequent items, we construct item sets with two products and find their transaction frequency, that is, the number of transactions in which both the items are present. Once again, we discard all the two-product item sets, also known also item sets of `order 2` that are below the given support threshold. We continue this way, until we finish. Let's look at a quick illustration:

Pass 1:

```
Support = 0.1
Product, transaction frequency
{item5}, 0.4
{item6}, 0.3
{item9}, 0.2
{item11}, 0.1
```

`item11` will be discarded in this phase as its transaction frequency is below the support threshold.

Pass 2:

```
{item5, item6}
{item5, item9}
{item6, item9}
```

As you can see, we have constructed item sets of order 2 using the filtered items from pass 1. We proceed to find their transaction frequency, discard item sets falling below our minimum support threshold, and step in to pass 3, where once again, we create item sets of `order 3`, calculate the transaction frequency, and perform filtering and move to pass 4. In one of the subsequent passes, we will reach a stage where we cannot create higher order item sets. That is when we stop.

The `apriori` method is used in `arules` packages to get the frequent items. This method takes two parameters, one transaction object, and the second parameter is a named list. We create a named list called **parameters**. Inside the named list, we have an entry for our support threshold. We have set our support threshold to 0.015. The `minlen` and `maxlen` parameters set a lower and upper cutoff on how many items we expect in our item sets. By setting our `minlen` and `maxlen` to 2, we say that we need only product pairs.

The `apriori` method returns an `itemset` object. Let's now extract the product pairs and their transaction frequency from the `itemset` object, `freq.items`:

```
> freq.items.df <- data.frame(item_set = labels(freq.items)
+                              , support = freq.items@quality)
> freq.items.df$item_set <- as.character(freq.items.df$item_set)
> head(freq.items.df)
                                       item_set support.support support.count
1                     {Banana,Honeycrisp Apple}      0.01617058           113
2                   {Banana,Organic Fuji Apple}      0.01817401           127
3                       {Banana,Cucumber Kirby}      0.01788781           125
4                         {Banana,Strawberries}      0.01931883           135
5 {Bag of Organic Bananas,Organic Zucchini}          0.01659989           116
6 {Organic Strawberries,Organic Whole Milk}          0.01617058           113
```

From the `itemset` object, `freq.items`, returned by `apriori`, we extract our product pairs and their transaction frequency count. The `item_set` column in our dataframe, `freq.items.df` refers to the product pair, the `support.count` column is the actual number of transactions in which both the products were present, and the `support.support` column gives the `support.count` value as a percentage. Notice that we have our product pairs enclosed weirdly in a curly brace. We need them in two different columns.

Let's write some cleaning code to remove those braces and also separate our product pairs into two different columns:

```
> library(tidyr)
> freq.items.df <- separate(data = freq.items.df, col = item_set, into =
c("item.1", "item.2"), sep = ",")
> freq.items.df[] <- lapply(freq.items.df, gsub, pattern='\\{',
replacement='')
> freq.items.df[] <- lapply(freq.items.df, gsub, pattern='\\}',
replacement='')
> head(freq.items.df)
                       item.1              item.2     support.support
support.count
1                      Banana    Honeycrisp Apple 0.0161705781339439
113
2                      Banana  Organic Fuji Apple 0.0181740125930166
127
3                      Banana      Cucumber Kirby 0.0178878076702919
125
4                      Banana        Strawberries 0.0193188322839153
135
5 Bag of Organic Bananas     Organic Zucchini 0.0165998855180309
116
6    Organic Strawberries Organic Whole Milk 0.0161705781339439
113
```

We leverage the `separate` function from the `tidyr` package to split the `item_set` column into two columns. As the products are separated by a comma, we specify the comma as the separator to a `separate` function. Once separated, we run a regular expression on those columns to remove the curly braces.

Let us now to create a new data frame with product pairs and weights:

```
> network.data <- freq.items.df[,c('item.1','item.2','support.count')]
> names(network.data) <- c("from","to","weight")
> head(network.data)
                     from                  to weight
1                    Banana    Honeycrisp Apple    113
2                    Banana  Organic Fuji Apple    127
3                    Banana      Cucumber Kirby    125
4                    Banana        Strawberries    135
5 Bag of Organic Bananas     Organic Zucchini    116
6    Organic Strawberries Organic Whole Milk    113
```

We retain only the `item.1`, `item.2`, and `support.count` columns. Next, we rename these columns to `from`, `to`, and `weight`. The `igraph` package expects this naming convention to create a graph object seamlessly. Finally, you can see that we have modified the data suit `igraph` package's graph manipulation functions.

We leveraged the `apriori` function in `arules` to prepare our dataset. Equipped with our dataset, let's proceed to perform product network analysis to discover micro-categories.

Product network analysis

There are two steps in product network analysis. The first step is to transform the point-of-sale data into product pairs and their transaction frequency. The second step is to create a graph using data from the first step and run a clustering algorithm on the graph. The subgraphs or the clusters formed are presented as the micro-categories. Also, some products in the graph play key roles. Clustering and visualizing these product subgraphs will also help us identify those key products. According to the white paper by Corte Consultancy, a product fitting any of the following definitions is considered as key to the network:

- **The core product**: In a subgraph or a cluster group, the product that is most commonly purchased in the group is termed as the core product of that group.
- **The connectors**: These are products that connect two subgraphs or clusters together. They are the ones that are typically bought first, if a customer starts shopping for products in that subgraph. Promoting this product as a part of cross-selling can influence customers who have never bought any products from this subgraph of products to start purchasing products present in this subgraph.

With our `network.data` data frame prepared in the exact manner we need, let's proceed to build a graph of products:

```
> set.seed(29)
> my.graph <- graph_from_data_frame(network.data)
> plot.igraph(my.graph,
+             layout=layout.fruchterman.reingold,
+             vertex.label.cex=.5,
+             edge.arrow.size=.1)
>
```

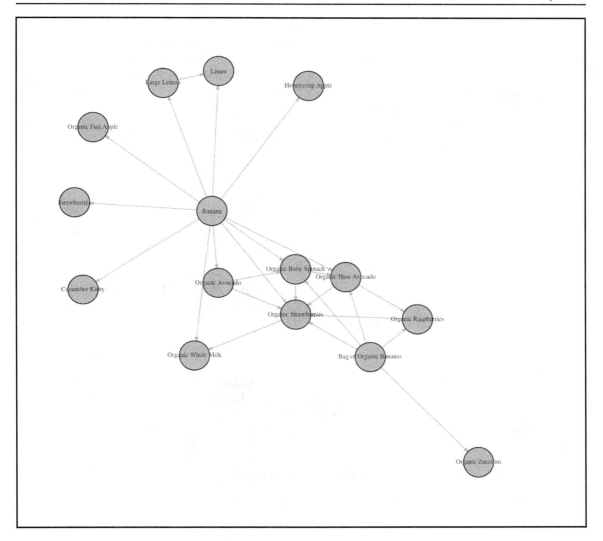

The preceding plot visualizes our graph.

Having built the graph, let's proceed to perform the clustering exercise, the second step in product network analysis. The clustering of graphs is performed by community detection algorithms. Communities discovered by the graphs are considered as clusters. Though there are some small nuances in equating communities to clusters, in this chapter, we will stick to the simple principle that the communities we discover in our graphs are going to be the clusters we want to consider for our product network analysis.

 Refer to the paper, *Detecting Community Structure in Networks,* by M. E. J. Newman, for in-depth analysis of clusters and communities.

Community in a graph: In a graph, community is a subset of vertices that are completely connected to each other. The correct technical term for it is clique. It is, ideally, groups of vertices within which connections are dense, but between which connections are sparser. It sounds very similar to the cluster cohesiveness requirement.

Community detection algorithms: These are a group of algorithms that, when applied on a graph, produce the most likely communities present in the graph. Traditional algorithms, such as hierarchical clustering, use similarity-based approaches to arrive at the communities. The more recent algorithms leverage several structural properties of the graph.

Walktrap algorithm: This algorithm is based on the random walk principle. The fundamental assumption with the random walk algorithm is as follows. A community typically has very few edges leading outside of the community. So if we perform a random walk from a vertex, we are more likely to stay within the community. We will use this algorithm to detect communities for our use case.

Let's go ahead and use the **walktrap** algorithm to discover communities/clusters:

```
> random.cluster <- walktrap.community(my.graph)

> random.cluster
IGRAPH clustering walktrap, groups: 2, mod: 0.26
+ groups:
  $`1`
  [1] "Banana"            "Large Lemon"      "Organic Avocado"
"Honeycrisp Apple"
  [5] "Organic Fuji Apple" "Cucumber Kirby"   "Strawberries"
"Organic Whole Milk"
  [9] "Limes"
  $`2`
  [1] "Bag of Organic Bananas" "Organic Strawberries"   "Organic Hass
Avocado"   "Organic Raspberries"
```

```
   [5] "Organic Baby Spinach"    "Organic Zucchini"
> groupings.df <- data.frame(products = random.cluster$names, group =
random.cluster$membership)
> head(groupings.df)
                 products group
1                  Banana     1
2 Bag of Organic Bananas     2
3   Organic Strawberries     2
4    Organic Hass Avocado     2
5     Organic Raspberries     2
6            Large Lemon     1
> groupings.df[groupings.df$group == 2,]
                 products group
2  Bag of Organic Bananas    2
3    Organic Strawberries    2
4     Organic Hass Avocado    2
5      Organic Raspberries    2
8      Organic Baby Spinach    2
13         Organic Zucchini    2
> groupings.df[groupings.df$group == 1,]
                 products group
1                  Banana    1
6            Large Lemon    1
7        Organic Avocado    1
9       Honeycrisp Apple    1
10 Organic Fuji Apple    1
11       Cucumber Kirby    1
12           Strawberries    1
14 Organic Whole Milk    1
15                Limes    1
```

We pass our graph to the `walktrap.community` function. We then move the cluster membership and cluster members to a data frame, `groupings.df`. Our random walk algorithm produced two subgraphs or communities.

Let's proceed to plot these clusters:

```
> plot(random.cluster,my.graph,
+               layout=layout.fruchterman.reingold,
+               vertex.label.cex=.5,
+               edge.arrow.size=.1)
```

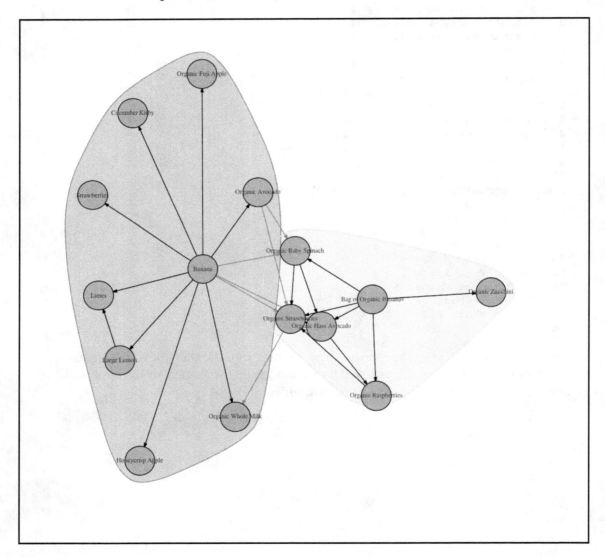

Let's start with the large cluster in the left side of the picture. It resembles a star schema, with **Banana** occupying the center. Let's confirm this by looking at some properties of the Banana vertex.

Let's look at the adjacency matrix of this graph:

```
> get.adjacency(my.graph)
15 x 15 sparse Matrix of class "dgCMatrix"
   [[ suppressing 15 column names 'Banana', 'Bag of Organic Bananas',
'Organic Strawberries' ... ]]
Banana                  . . 1 1 . 1 1 1 1 1 1 . 1 1
Bag of Organic Bananas . . 1 1 1 . . 1 . . . . 1 . .
Organic Strawberries    . . . . . . . . . . . . 1 .
Organic Hass Avocado   . . 1 . 1 . . . . . . . . . .
Organic Raspberries    . . 1 . . . . . . . . . . . .
Large Lemon             . . . . . . . . . . . . . 1
Organic Avocado        . . 1 . . . . 1 . . . . . . .
Organic Baby Spinach   . . 1 1 . . . . . . . . . . .
Honeycrisp Apple        . . . . . . . . . . . . . .
Organic Fuji Apple      . . . . . . . . . . . . . .
Cucumber Kirby          . . . . . . . . . . . . . .
Strawberries            . . . . . . . . . . . . . .
Organic Zucchini        . . . . . . . . . . . . . .
Organic Whole Milk      . . . . . . . . . . . . . .
Limes                   . . . . . . . . . . . . . .
>
```

If we quickly look at the adjacency matrix, it appears that Banana is the *Core Product* for this cluster. Banana is connected to most of the other products.

Let's look at the strength and degree for the Banana vertex:

```
> strength(my.graph)
                Banana Bag of Organic Bananas    Organic Strawberries
Organic Hass Avocado
                  1697                    941                    1191
789
    Organic Raspberries          Large Lemon        Organic Avocado
Organic Baby Spinach
                   414                    288                     422
845
       Honeycrisp Apple    Organic Fuji Apple         Cucumber Kirby
Strawberries
                   113                    127                     125
135
       Organic Zucchini    Organic Whole Milk                 Limes
                   116                    233                     270
> degree(my.graph)
```

```
                      Banana Bag of Organic Bananas    Organic Strawberries
Organic Hass Avocado
                   11                         5                        7
5
    Organic Raspberries             Large Lemon       Organic Avocado
Organic Baby Spinach
                    3                         2                        3
5
        Honeycrisp Apple    Organic Fuji Apple          Cucumber Kirby
Strawberries
                    1                         1                        1
1
        Organic Zucchini    Organic Whole Milk                  Limes
                    1                         2                        2
>
```

Banana has very high degree and strength, and thus there is more evidence to assign Banana as the *Core Product* for this cluster. Though it was evident that Banana is the most important product in the cluster from the graph plot, it gives us more confidence to look at some of the properties of the Banana vertex.

Having decided upon the *Core Product* as banana for the left cluster, let's do some random walking from the Banana vertex. We select an edge uniformly and randomly from all the out-degrees of Banana and do a specified number of steps. To find out more about random walk click `http://igraph.org/r/doc/random_walk.html`.

```
> for(var in seq(1,5)){
+   print (random_walk(my.graph, start = "Banana", steps = 2))
+ }
+ 2/15 vertices, named, from 16e82b7:
[1] Banana                  Organic Strawberries
+ 2/15 vertices, named, from 16e82b7:
[1] Banana            Organic Avocado
+ 2/15 vertices, named, from 16e82b7:
[1] Banana          Cucumber Kirby
+ 2/15 vertices, named, from 16e82b7:
[1] Banana Limes
+ 2/15 vertices, named, from 16e82b7:
[1] Banana          Strawberries
> random_walk(my.graph, start = "Banana", steps = 3)
+ 3/15 vertices, named, from 16e82b7:
[1] Banana                  Organic Baby Spinach Organic Hass Avocado
> random_walk(my.graph, start = "Banana", steps = 4)
+ 4/15 vertices, named, from 16e82b7:
[1] Banana                  Organic Avocado         Organic Baby Spinach Organic
Strawberries
> random_walk(my.graph, start = "Banana", steps = 5)
```

```
+ 4/15 vertices, named, from 16e82b7:
[1] Banana                Organic Avocado        Organic Strawberries Organic
Whole Milk
>
```

This random walk can expose some of the product affinities quickly without a lot of computation. Imagine working on large graphs with thousands of vertices; these random walks performed multiple times can quickly unearth product affinities.

> Another data source that can be used to experiment with the techniques described in this chapter is Amazon's online retail page which is available for download."
> #https://snap.stanford.edu/data/amazon0302.html

The Organic Avacado and Banana products in the left cluster can be termed as **The Connector**. They have a path into the right-side cluster. Promoting these products can induce the customers of the left cluster to start exploring or buying the products in the right cluster.

This brings us to the end of this section. Here, we were able to use the random walk principle-based community detection algorithm to find communities in our graph. These communities can be the new micro-categories. Further, we also identified our **core** and **connector** vertices.

Building a RShiny application

Our RShiny application will have the following features:

- Load a transaction file
- Calculate the product pairs and their transaction frequency, and display them
- Display the discovered communities from the product pairs dataset

Let us look at the user interface code:

```
ui <- fluidPage(
  navbarPage("Product Pairs",
             tabPanel("Transactions"
                      , fileInput("datafile", "select transactions csv
file",
                                  accept = c(
                                    "text/csv",
                                    "text/comma-separated-
values,text/plain",
```

```
                                    ".csv"
                                    )
                    )
                    , dataTableOutput("transactions")
            ),
            tabPanel("Product Pairs"
                    ,dataTableOutput("ppairs")),
            tabPanel("Community"
                    ,plotOutput("community"))
    )
)
```

We have three panels. In the first panel, we select a product transaction file and display it. In our second panel, we show the product pairs and their transaction counts. In the final panel, we display the communities we have discovered.

Let us look at the server-side code:

```
server <- function(input, output) {
  trans.obj <- reactive({
    data <- input$datafile
    transactions.obj <- read.transactions(file = data$datapath, format =
"single",
                                          sep = ",",
                                          cols = c("order_id",
"product_id"),

                                          rm.duplicates = FALSE,
                                          quote = "", skip = 0,
                                          encoding = "unknown")
    transactions.obj
  })
  trans.df <- reactive({
    data <- input$datafile
    if(is.null(data)){return(NULL)}
    trans.df <- read.csv(data$datapath)
    return(trans.df)
  })
  network.data <- reactive({
    transactions.obj <- trans.obj()
    support     <- 0.015
    # Frequent item sets
    parameters = list(
      support = support,
      minlen  = 2,  # Minimal number of items per item set
      maxlen  = 2, # Maximal number of items per item set
      target  = "frequent itemsets"
    )
    freq.items <- apriori(transactions.obj, parameter = parameters)
```

```
    # Let us examine our freq item sites
    freq.items.df <- data.frame(item_set = labels(freq.items)
                               , support = freq.items@quality)
    freq.items.df$item_set <- as.character(freq.items.df$item_set)
    # Clean up for item pairs
    library(tidyr)
    freq.items.df <- separate(data = freq.items.df, col = item_set, into =
c("item.1", "item.2"), sep = ",")
    freq.items.df[] <- lapply(freq.items.df, gsub, pattern='\\{',
replacement='')
    freq.items.df[] <- lapply(freq.items.df, gsub, pattern='\\}',
replacement='')
    # Prepare data for graph
    network.data <- freq.items.df[,c('item.1','item.2','support.count')]
    names(network.data) <- c("from","to","weight")
    return(network.data)
  })
  output$transactions <- renderDataTable({
    trans.df()
  })
  output$ppairs <- renderDataTable({
    network.data()
  })
  output$community <- renderPlot({
    network.data <- network.data()
    my.graph <- graph_from_data_frame(network.data)
    random.cluster <- walktrap.community(my.graph)
    plot(random.cluster,my.graph,
         layout=layout.fruchterman.reingold,
         vertex.label.cex=.5,
         edge.arrow.size=.1,height = 1200, width = 1200)
  })

}
```

Let us first look at the reactive expressions.

Let us look at `trans.df`:

```
trans.df <- reactive({
  data <- input$datafile
  if(is.null(data)){return(NULL)}
  trans.df <- read.csv(data$datapath)
  return(trans.df)
})
```

As soon as a file is uploaded, this file is read into a data frame, `trans.df`.

Let us look at `trans.obj`:

```
trans.obj <- reactive({
    data <- input$datafile
    transactions.obj <- read.transactions(file = data$datapath, format =
"single",
                                          sep = ",",
                                          cols = c("order_id",
"product_id"),
                                          rm.duplicates = FALSE,
                                          quote = "", skip = 0,
                                          encoding = "unknown")
    transactions.obj
})
```

The uploaded file is used to create a `transaction.object`.

Let us look at `network.data`:

```
network.data <- reactive({
    transactions.obj <- trans.obj()
    support      <- 0.015
    # Frequent item sets
    parameters = list(
      support = support,
      minlen  = 2,  # Minimal number of items per item set
      maxlen  = 2, # Maximal number of items per item set
      target  = "frequent itemsets"
    )
    freq.items <- apriori(transactions.obj, parameter = parameters)
    # Let us examine our freq item sites
    freq.items.df <- data.frame(item_set = labels(freq.items)
                                , support = freq.items@quality)
    freq.items.df$item_set <- as.character(freq.items.df$item_set)
    # Clean up for item pairs
    library(tidyr)
    freq.items.df <- separate(data = freq.items.df, col = item_set, into =
c("item.1", "item.2"), sep = ",")
    freq.items.df[] <- lapply(freq.items.df, gsub, pattern='\\{',
replacement='')
    freq.items.df[] <- lapply(freq.items.df, gsub, pattern='\\}',
replacement='')
    # Prepare data for graph
    network.data <- freq.items.df[,c('item.1','item.2','support.count')]
    names(network.data) <- c("from","to","weight")
    return(network.data)
})
```

Using the transaction object, the `apriori` function is invoked to get the product pairs. The output of the `apriori` is carefully formatted and a final data frame, `network.data`, is created.

The rest of the functions in the server renders these outputs to the respective slots in the UI.

Let us look at what the application looks like when started:

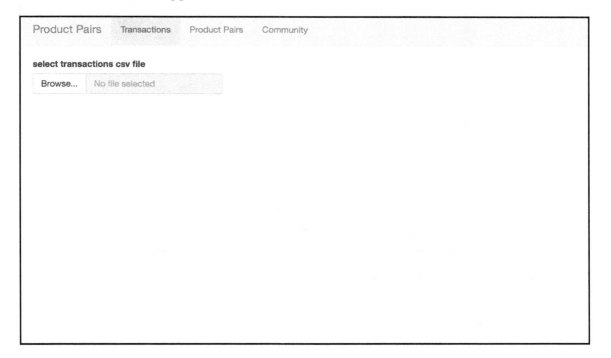

Using the file selector, we can select the transaction file. The transaction file should be a `.csv` file with two columns. One for the `order_id` and the other one for the `product_id`. In this version, we need to maintain the column names as `order_id` and `product_id`.

Once selected let us see how the screen changes:

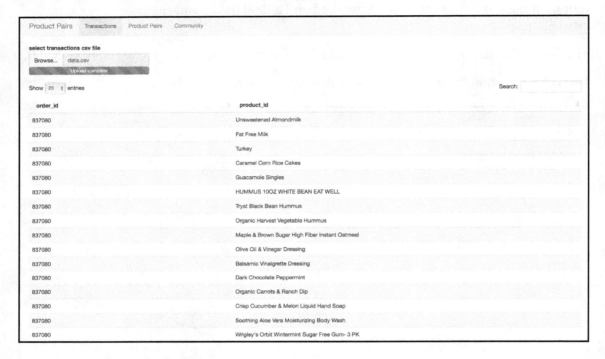

We see the orders and the products.

Let us move to the next tab product pairs:

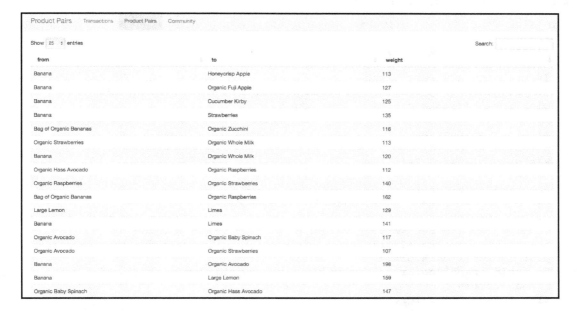

We see the product pairs and their transaction count.

Finally, let us look at the last tab, the community graph:

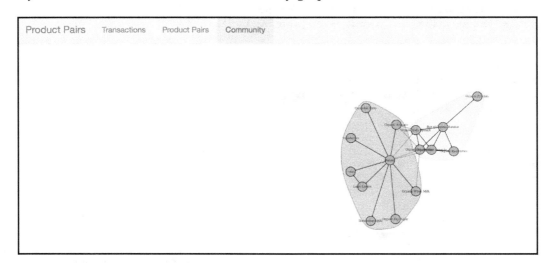

Our product community graph is displayed.

The complete R script

Here is the complete R script that we have used to demonstrate product network analysis:

```r
library(igraph, quietly = TRUE)

## Creating a simple graph
simple.graph <- graph_from_literal(A-B, B-C, C-D, E-F, A-E, E-C)
plot.igraph(simple.graph)

## Graph properties
E(simple.graph) # Edges
V(simple.graph) # Vertices

## Graph attributes
V(simple.graph)$name <- c('alice', 'bob','charlie','david',
'eli','francis')
simple.graph <- set_vertex_attr(simple.graph ,"age", value = c('11',
'11','15','9', '8','11'))
plot.igraph(simple.graph)
V(simple.graph)$color <- ifelse(V(simple.graph)$age == '11',
"blue","green")
plot.igraph(simple.graph)

# Structural properties
degree(simple.graph) # degree of nodes
E(simple.graph)$weight <- c(10,20,35,15,25,35)
strength(simple.graph) # strength of nodes
get.adjacency(simple.graph) # adjacency matrix


# Delete edges and nodes
simple.graph <- delete.edges(simple.graph, "alice|bob" )
simple.graph <- delete.vertices(simple.graph, 'francis')
plot(simple.graph)


# use case date
data <- read.csv('data.csv')
head(data)

## Prepare the data
library(arules)
transactions.obj <- read.transactions(file = 'data.csv', format = "single",
                                       sep = ",",
                                       cols = c("order_id", "product_id"),
                                       rm.duplicates = FALSE,
                                       quote = "", skip = 0,
```

```
                                         encoding = "unknown")
transactions.obj

# Interest Measures
support     <- 0.015

# Frequent item sets
parameters = list(
  support = support,
  minlen  = 2,   # Minimal number of items per item set
  maxlen  = 2,   # Maximal number of items per item set
  target  = "frequent itemsets"
)


freq.items <- apriori(transactions.obj, parameter = parameters)

# Let us examine our freq item sites
freq.items.df <- data.frame(item_set = labels(freq.items)
                            , support = freq.items@quality)
freq.items.df$item_set <- as.character(freq.items.df$item_set)
head(freq.items.df)

# Clean up for item pairs
library(tidyr)
freq.items.df <- separate(data = freq.items.df, col = item_set, into =
c("item.1", "item.2"), sep = ",")
freq.items.df[] <- lapply(freq.items.df, gsub, pattern='\\{',
replacement='')
freq.items.df[] <- lapply(freq.items.df, gsub, pattern='\\}',
replacement='')
head(freq.items.df)

# Prepare data for graph
network.data <- freq.items.df[,c('item.1','item.2','support.count')]
names(network.data) <- c("from","to","weight")
head(network.data)

## Build the graph
library(igraph, quietly = TRUE)
set.seed(29)
my.graph <- graph_from_data_frame(network.data)
plot.igraph(my.graph,
            layout=layout.fruchterman.reingold,
            vertex.label.cex=.5,
            edge.arrow.size=.1)


## Clustering
```

```
random.cluster <- walktrap.community(my.graph)
str(random.cluster)
random.cluster
groupings.df <- data.frame(products = random.cluster$names, group =
random.cluster$membership)
head(groupings.df)
groupings.df[groupings.df$group == 2,]
groupings.df[groupings.df$group == 1,]

plot(random.cluster,my.graph,
            layout=layout.fruchterman.reingold,
            vertex.label.cex=.5,
            edge.arrow.size=.1)

get.adjacency(my.graph)
strength(my.graph)
degree(my.graph)

## Random walks
for(var in seq(1,5)){
  print (random_walk(my.graph, start = "Banana", steps = 2))
}

random_walk(my.graph, start = "Banana", steps = 3)
random_walk(my.graph, start = "Banana", steps = 4)
random_walk(my.graph, start = "Banana", steps = 5)
```

RShiny app code:

```
library(shiny)
library(arules)
library(igraph, quietly = TRUE)


server <- function(input, output) {
  trans.obj <- reactive({
    data <- input$datafile
    transactions.obj <- read.transactions(file = data$datapath, format =
"single",
                                          sep = ",",
                                          cols = c("order_id",
"product_id"),

                                          rm.duplicates = FALSE,
                                          quote = "", skip = 0,
                                          encoding = "unknown")

    transactions.obj
  })
  trans.df <- reactive({
```

```
      data <- input$datafile
      if(is.null(data)){return(NULL)}
      trans.df <- read.csv(data$datapath)
      return(trans.df)
    })
  network.data <- reactive({
    transactions.obj <- trans.obj()
    support      <- 0.015
    # Frequent item sets
    parameters = list(
      support = support,
      minlen  = 2,   # Minimal number of items per item set
      maxlen  = 2, # Maximal number of items per item set
      target  = "frequent itemsets"
    )
    freq.items <- apriori(transactions.obj, parameter = parameters)
    # Let us examine our freq item sites
    freq.items.df <- data.frame(item_set = labels(freq.items)
                                  , support = freq.items@quality)
    freq.items.df$item_set <- as.character(freq.items.df$item_set)
    # Clean up for item pairs
    library(tidyr)
    freq.items.df <- separate(data = freq.items.df, col = item_set, into =
c("item.1", "item.2"), sep = ",")
    freq.items.df[] <- lapply(freq.items.df, gsub, pattern='\\{',
replacement='')
    freq.items.df[] <- lapply(freq.items.df, gsub, pattern='\\}',
replacement='')
    # Prepare data for graph
    network.data <- freq.items.df[,c('item.1','item.2','support.count')]
    names(network.data) <- c("from","to","weight")
    return(network.data)
  })
  output$transactions <- renderDataTable({
    trans.df()
  })
  output$ppairs <- renderDataTable({
    network.data()
  })
  output$community <- renderPlot({
    network.data <- network.data()
    my.graph <- graph_from_data_frame(network.data)
    random.cluster <- walktrap.community(my.graph)
    plot(random.cluster,my.graph,
         layout=layout.fruchterman.reingold,
         vertex.label.cex=.5,
         edge.arrow.size=.1,height = 1200, width = 1200)
  })
```

```
}

ui <- fluidPage(
  navbarPage("Product Pairs",
             tabPanel("Transactions"
                      , fileInput("datafile", "select transactions csv
file",
                                  accept = c(
                                    "text/csv",
                                    "text/comma-separated-
values,text/plain",
                                    ".csv"
                                  )
                      )
                      , dataTableOutput("transactions")
             ),
             tabPanel("Product Pairs"
                      ,dataTableOutput("ppairs")),
             tabPanel("Community"
                      ,plotOutput("community"))
  )
)

shinyApp(ui = ui, server = server)
```

Summary

We started this chapter by explaining our problem and dataset and conducted product categorization using network/graph theory. We introduced the R package, `igraph`, to create and manipulate graphs. We set out discovering some of the properties of the graph and also a little bit about the graphs and random walks. We used the `arules` package to find frequent pairs of items and finally applied the graph clustering algorithm to our data to discover product categories. We were also able to identify important vertices performing the role of the core and connectors.

Index

Z